Building and Distributing Agentic AI Solutions

A Comprehensive Guide to Productizing AI

Julian Soh
John Tidwell
Priyanshi Singh

Apress®

Building and Distributing Agentic AI Solutions: A Comprehensive Guide to Productizing AI

Julian Soh
Seattle, WA, USA

John Tidwell
Brandon, MS, USA

Priyanshi Singh
Danville, CA, USA

ISBN-13 (pbk): 979-8-8688-2585-9
ISBN-13 (electronic): 979-8-8688-2586-6
https://doi.org/10.1007/979-8-8688-2586-6

Managing Director, Apress Media LLC: Welmoed Spahr
Acquisitions Editor: Smriti Srivastava
Editorial Assistant: Marina Engler

Cover designed by eStudioCalamar

Cover image designed by kjpargeter on Magnific

Distributed to the book trade worldwide by Springer Science+Business Media New York, 1 New York Plaza, New York, NY 10004. Phone 1-800-SPRINGER, fax (201) 348-4505, e-mail orders-ny@springer-sbm.com, or visit www.springeronline.com. Apress Media, LLC is a Delaware LLC and the sole member (owner) is Springer Science + Business Media Finance Inc (SSBM Finance Inc). SSBM Finance Inc is a **Delaware** corporation.

For information on translations, please e-mail booktranslations@springernature.com; for reprint, paperback, or audio rights, please e-mail bookpermissions@springernature.com.

Apress titles may be purchased in bulk for academic, corporate, or promotional use. eBook versions and licenses are also available for most titles. For more information, reference our Print and eBook Bulk Sales web page at http://www.apress.com/bulk-sales.

Any source code or other supplementary material referenced by the author in this book is available to readers on GitHub. For more detailed information, please visit https://www.apress.com/gp/services/source-code.

If disposing of this product, please recycle the paper

This book would not have been possible without the support from family members, the technical community, esteemed colleagues, and customers who have welcomed us on their journey.

Special thanks to my co-authors, John Tidwell and Priyanshi Singh.

This book is dedicated to all the builders and creators.

Table of Contents

About the Authors

Julian Soh is a Forward Deployed software engineer with Microsoft and works with organizations to develop products that leverage emerging technologies on Microsoft and/or open-source platforms, specifically around applied/generative AI, and traditional ML like CNN and RNN for image and anomaly detection. With the rapid development in the field of embodied (physical) AI, Julian is leveraging his formal training as a mechanical engineer to help independent software vendors (ISVs) extend software design that could include wearables, embedded/real-time computing, and autonomous machines. His interest is in the intersection of software and the control of electromechanical systems, focusing on the areas of artificial intelligence and advanced analytics for independent software vendors (ISVs) who develop software solutions based on the Microsoft technology stack. Julian holds a BS in Mechanical Engineering and is pursuing his MS in Electrical and Computer Engineering at the University of Washington.

John Tidwell is Chief Technology Officer at YoungWilliams, where he leads a team responsible for the ongoing design, development, and deployment of Priya, an innovative AI-driven government service solution that leverages Microsoft Azure's AI platform. With expertise in Azure cloud technologies, generative AI, DevOps, and Agile software development, John has guided numerous projects from concept to production. His technical leadership includes architecting scalable systems, driving strategic cloud adoption, and mentoring development teams to achieve excellence. John holds multiple Azure certifications, including Azure AI, and is actively pursuing a Master of Science in Computer Science specializing in Artificial Intelligence and Machine Learning at Georgia Tech.

Priyanshi Singh is a senior artificial intelligence and machine learning technical specialist at Microsoft, specializing in designing end-to-end cloud solutions that leverage generative AI models and AI implementation best practices. She holds a master's degree in Data Science from New York University and has a robust background as a data scientist, focusing on machine learning techniques for predictive analytics, computer vision, and natural language processing. Priyanshi is dedicated to helping the public sector and independent software vendors (ISVs) transform citizen services through artificial intelligence. She has been recognized as Microsoft's FY24 State and Local Government Pinnacle Winner for her exceptional contributions to AI adoption and the growth of Azure business. Additionally, Priyanshi is a sports enthusiast, excelling in badminton and enjoying golf and billiards.

About the Technical Reviewer

Mittal Mehta is an accomplished technology leader with deep expertise in **AI-driven automation, DevOps automation, configuration management, and release engineering** for both on-premises and cloud-based enterprise applications. With more than two decades of hands-on experience, he has built scalable automation frameworks and end-to-end delivery pipelines that enhance reliability, speed, and governance across the software life cycle.

He is passionate about exploring and adopting emerging technologies, particularly in the areas of AI-driven automation, intelligent workflows, and application life cycle optimization. Mittal has extensive experience working with Microsoft technologies, including Azure DevOps, Power Automate, and PowerShell, and has architected numerous cloud automation solutions using Azure and modern DevOps toolchains.

Based in Bangalore, he currently serves as a Principal Consultant in AI automation where he leads automation strategy, cloud enablement, and AI-powered engineering initiatives for enterprise applications.

Introduction

This book is for the creators, builders, and entrepreneurs looking to incorporate AI in new or existing software (or maybe hardware) products. We hoped to capture the key aspects of product development, from ideation to the Go-To-Market (GTM) motion leveraging distribution channels like the Microsoft Marketplace.

One of the challenges when developing an AI product is the understanding of cost and what adoption could look like. We have attempted to provide a good foundation to determine cost and a proposed way to model adoption. Entrepreneurs, product and marketing executives, and financial officers are our target audience because there are chapters in this book that are focused on the economic aspects of AI productization.

Many new and trending AI technologies are also introduced and these form the platform on which products are being built. Technologies such as Azure Foundry, frontier models, agentic frameworks, and the Model Context Protocol are covered, along with sample codes and an accompanying GitHub repository. This portion of the book will provide our technical audience with actual hands-on exposure and insight to the learnings from our engagement with technical teams across various industries.

All the topics were carefully selected based on real-world experiences and while this is ever evolving, we hope this book will provide a strong foundation for any AI productization journey.

CHAPTER 1

AI Landscape and Productization Opportunities

At the time of writing, ChatGPT[1] is three years old. Prior to that, generative AI was an experimental technology for niche firms, AI engineers, and data scientists. Fast forward to late 2025, it has evolved into a core business capability worldwide. No other technology has experienced a higher adoption rate. A study[2] conducted by Vanderbilt University in August 2024 found that Generative AI reached a 39.5% adoption rate in just two years, compared to

- 20% for the Internet (after two years)
- 20% for personal computers (after three years)

AI has driven the stocks of major technology companies like Microsoft, Amazon, and Google to record highs on the promise of this AI revolution. In return, these companies have poured billions into infrastructure, particularly power and compute (GPUs), and R&D to meet demand.

[1] 1 OpenAI unveiled ChatGPT to the world on November 30, 2022.

[2] Vanderbilt Study: `https://news.harvard.edu/gazette/story/2024/10/generative-ai-embraced-faster-than-internet-pcs/`

J. Soh et al., *Building and Distributing Agentic AI Solutions*,
https://doi.org/10.1007/979-8-8688-2586-6_1

We, the authors, have worked in technology and written about Cloud Computing since the day it became mainstream, and to witness a global shortage of compute at the biggest cloud providers is something we never thought we would see.

But what is important, and therefore the focus of this book, is the need for builders, entrepreneurs, and engineers to build AI-enabled products and services or, at the very least, transform existing solutions by infusing AI capabilities. Companies are scrambling to hire skilled AI workers, and historically, we are seeing more startups by young entrepreneurs building businesses based on AI.[3]

This book is meant to help innovators, builders, and aspiring businessmen grasp an understanding on the foundational aspects of building an AI-enabled product or service. The topics we will cover in detail should touch on the entire life cycle of product development.

A Mainstream Revolution

Global adoption is extremely broad. Although the United States and China lead in AI development and patents, wrestling each other for talent and raw materials, the beneficiary is a worldwide audience. AI adoption is widespread: major hubs include the United States, India, the UK, Canada, and Germany, with cities like London, San Francisco, Bangalore, and Singapore emerging as vibrant AI centers.

Over 16,500 companies and 6,000 startups are active in generative AI worldwide, reflecting a vast ecosystem of solution providers and innovators. This explosion is backed by venture funding (nearly $4 billion in VC poured into GenAI in just one quarter of 2024) and rapid talent growth. And this is not slowing anytime soon.

[3] https://www.forbes.com/sites/sarahemerson/2024/12/03/30-under-30-ai-2025-the-young-entrepreneurs-coding-the-future/

In 2025, several key trends started to emerge:

- Multimodal AI (models that understand/generate text, images, audio, etc.) and conversational AI are major drivers of innovation.
- Organizations have moved beyond just experimenting – roughly 44% of companies were running pilot programs for generative AI and 10% had reached production scale by late 2024, and these numbers have only climbed in 2025.
- Early adopters report significant productivity gains and operational improvements, motivating others to follow. In fact, industry estimates suggest the question is no longer whether to adopt GenAI, but how to implement it effectively and responsibly.

With respect to the last trend cited above, we would argue that first-to-market innovators are way past discussing the ethical nature of AI, and have started to adopt and implement industry-backed standards. It may be an unpopular opinion, but we feel that existing discussions that continue to question the use of AI in lieu of adoption is a futile effort to resist change and is bound to fail. Remember, there were a lot of naysayers and doomsday predictions at every inflection point. For AI, we have entered the maturation phase.

This maturation that brings the adoption of standards includes

- Ensuring factual accuracy, security, and ethical use of AI
- Investing in governance and AI training programs as AI becomes central to products and workflows
- Helping regulators with AI laws and legislation – from EU AI Act efforts to sector-specific guidelines – to set guardrails for responsible AI deployment

Overall, late 2025's landscape is one of widespread enthusiasm tempered by pragmatic execution: generative AI is widely recognized as a game-changer (potentially $6–8 trillion in economic impact according to McKinsey). Furthermore, during the Q3 Calendar Year 2025 season of earnings reports, the "Magnificent 7" group of companies reported continued, but easing, global shortage of GPUs, which is an indicator of demand, and provided guidance on increased capital investment. While nothing is guaranteed, there are abundant signals that AI is not a passing fad, and that is why we should include it as a core feature in any product or service.

Who Are AI Customers?

Before we talk about AI-enabled products and services, the important question to ask is "who are the customers?" Just like how the PC became an indispensable tool spanning every industry and household, AI is doing the same, but more specifically, because of Generative AI.

Generative AI brought us the Large Language Model (LLM) and LLMs speak our language, and we mean this in the most literal sense. As a result, the answer is *everyone, every industry and every entity – private, public, education, consumer.*

We have always heard of the different inflection points in the history of technology – steam engines, electricity, personal computing, the Internet. We are now in the midst of another major inflection point with AI.

When PCs debuted, users needed to possess knowledge to interact with the technology. These are primarily text-based commands with cryptic syntax that were not standards-based. Apple, followed by Microsoft, penetrated the consumer and enterprise markets with the Graphical User Interface (GUI), which is what opened the floodgates for adoption. Yes, we can argue that Xerox was the inventor of the GUI, but that is not the point. The point is that the GUI was introduced to the masses and because the GUI aligns better with the natural cognitive abilities of most of the population, that is where we see the exponential adoption of personal computing. Since then, we have been pushing for better user interfaces (e.g., WYSIWYG, Drag-and-Drop, Cut-and-Paste, Intellisense, etc). The LLM is the most significant upgrade in UI since the GUI because it elevates the UI to the highest form of human cognitive alignment - Natural Language.

An LLM interface provides the ability to use natural language to get the model to do things. No special syntax, format, programming ability, or even any experience in data science needed. For that matter, if you ask an LLM like ChatGPT using one of the *more than 40 languages supported*, it will understand what you are asking for, even if it is not able to provide the information or carry out the task.

LLMs' ability to converse in natural language is the main driver for adoption. No other technology was as accessible as an LLM. When ChatGPT was first introduced, consumers flocked to the site to ask it to generate dinner ideas, travel itineraries, poetry, letters, emails, party ideas, and almost everything imaginable. Realtors are leveraging it to create narratives for listing properties, government organizations use it to quickly understand and apply complex rules and regulations. Commercial organizations are using it to create advertising materials, marketing plans, and identify customer sentiment. Legal professionals and lawmakers use it to quickly understand legal documents and also create initial drafts of new legislation. Since the common skill needed to make use of this technology, in all these use cases, is the ability to communicate in natural language, the personal and professional personas of individuals overlap.

On the regulatory compliance front, the gap between the use of AI in government versus the commercial sector is also starting to close. This is mainly due to the maturity of cloud computing, better understanding of risks, and improvement in technologies and processes that make it more feasible to provide a common standard across all clouds. As such, many of the regulatory compliance for government versus commercial use cases have converged. For example, the Federal Risk and Authorization Management Program (FedRAMP) in the United States, perhaps the most stringent of regulatory compliance requirements, now applies to both Azure Government and Azure Commercial clouds.[4]

One special note about LLMs' penetration is in software engineering and development. Not only are LLMs capable of natural language, but they are also particularly adept at programming languages, logic, syntax, and even algorithms. This has led some to muse over the "death of Leetcode." In fact, Microsoft revealed that about 30% of code at the software giant is written by AI.[5] This is an often-overlooked point but it is of great importance, especially for this audience. Traditionally, with the introduction of new technologies and approaches that makes life easier for consumers and users, this does not necessarily mean that the software engineers' portfolio has gotten easier. LLMs, though, provide advancement for the user and creator of products and services. This can be seen through the increased excitement around Vide Coding,[6] which is the use of natural language to collaborate with LLMs for coding and software engineering purposes. Your journey in developing an AI-enabled product or service may very well involve some level of vibe coding, thereby shortening your go-to-market timeline and even reducing the challenge of finding enough skilled builders to join your team.

The productivity increase and replacement of humans with AI is unfortunate, but throughout history, that is what automation and advancement have done to transform the workforce. But the focus of this

---

[4] All US Azure regions now approved for FedRAMP High impact level | Microsoft Azure Blog

[5] `https://www.cnbc.com/2025/04/29/satya-nadella-says-as-much-as-30percent-of-microsoft-code-is-written-by-ai.html?msockid=3c3ae63a5af7666a3054f32b5b4d6779`

[6] `https://www.geeksforgeeks.org/techtips/what-is-vibe-coding/`

book is about productizing AI. Therefore, all the signals we have presented here should paint an exciting "Total Addressable Market" for your AI-enabled product or service.

Recognizing Your Audience – Accelerationists and Doomers

The group of people that advocate faster adoption and development of AI are known as accelerationists. On the other end of the spectrum, Doomers is the group convinced AI will destroy humankind and therefore are advocating slowing down development and increasing oversight, scrutiny, and defining more definite boundaries that restrict AI's encroachment, etc. Granted that the majority of people tend to fall somewhere in between, but if your target customer is an enterprise comprising several decision-makers, you will likely encounter the Accelerationists and Doomers.

It is widely believed that capitalists and commercial entities like Microsoft are extreme accelerationists. Prominent technology leaders like the vocal Mr. Elon Musk is a Doomer, even though he has spearheaded the development of Grok and an early backer of OpenAI. Mr. Sam Altman himself has famously claimed AI can destroy humanity and is urging governments to monitor and legislate AI. He co-founded OpenAI and was one of the designers of the board's structure, where members are not financially benefiting from OpenAI so that there is no conflict of interest when governing the technology developed by the company. Ironically, it was the very same board that ousted him. These are not what you would expect from an accelerationist.

Handling the objections of a Doomer and reigning in the over-enthusiasm of the Accelerationist is beyond the scope of this book, but we are mentioning it in this opening chapter because it is a psychological aspect of productizing an AI-enabled product or service that you need to address.

Emerging Technologies Enabling New AI Products (2025)

We will look at the emerging technologies and trends now, but bear in mind that everything is about facilitating creation of products. Specifically, AI-enabled products and services. This is what this book is focused on because we assume you, the reader, are interested in creating new products and services that are AI-enabled. It may not be a brand new product or service. Perhaps, it is an existing non-AI-enabled product or service that you are targeting to revamp.

Several **breakthrough technologies** have come to the forefront in 2025, unlocking new possibilities for AI-driven products and solutions. The most influential of these – **Model Context Protocol (MCP)**, **multi-modal and multi-model AI**, **autonomous AI agents**, and **AI avatars** – are what we will be examining in detail, as they provide the foundation for many of the latest applications.

For now, here is a brief overview of these key technologies that are foundational to the design of your product or service.

The Agentic Architecture

"Agentic" is the buzzword for much of 2025. It is the next iteration of Generative AI which took us from just conversations with AI to actual actions and tasks that can be carried out by AI. An agent is simply a representation of an LLM, which comprises its persona (role), its instructions (prompt engineering), the actual base model of the LLM (GPT-4o, GPT-5, DeepSeek, etc.), and the data it has access to.

There are several key concepts of an agentic architecture:

- Having many specialized agents with tighter prompt engineering and smaller scoped data produces better results and less hallucinations.

- Leveraging multiple agents allows for the use of multiple models for the specific request (e.g., some models may be better at deep reasoning versus others that may be better at math).
- Enabling Agent-to-Agent (A2A) collaboration.
- The ability to attach tools to Agents so they can carry out tasks.

Real-Time Data

One of the shortcomings of LLMs is the timebound data that is restricted to when the model was trained. The current Retrieval Augmented Generation (RAG) architecture that grounds the LLM with curated data sources is still based on time-bound data sources.

A compelling use case for using agents is the ability for the LLM to get real-time data from web services (or MPC, as we will see shortly). For example, with agents, the LLM can query a flight's status from web services to find out its flight schedule. An investment tracker application, when asked in natural language what the current top market movers for the day is can connect to web services to get that information and research on latest news that may have caused such a movement.

Perform Tasks

Aside from the tasks of retrieving information, creating content, or answering questions, the other benefit of using agents is to carry out tasks. For example, after looking up flight status and price, agents can initiate purchasing of an airline ticket, or book hotels, etc.

Autonomous AI Agents

We will explore the different types of agents - Embedded in applications as part of the application's functionality, as a Robotic Process Automation (RPA) workflow, exposed as a direct user-interaction UI, part of an Agent-to-Agent or Agent Chatgroup orchestration.

Despite the different types of implementations, the common ability for agents is the ability to now work *autonomously without oversight or interaction,* in a secure manner, will in effect make agents function like *digital employees* or *colleagues* that can execute multi-step processes effectively. See Chapter 8 for more details on digital employees when integrating Agents in Copilot. Autonomous agents essentially elevate AI from passive to active engagement.

From Passive to Active

Traditional AI assistants, like Siri and Alexa, or basic chatbots were reactive. They answered questions or executed single-step commands. In 2025, AI agents can handle objectives like "Plan my business trip" or "Monitor our website and fix any broken links" with minimal supervision. To accomplish these objectives not only involves multiple steps, each step would be reliant on outcomes from previous/other steps, which brings the concept of memory into the picture. Agents can break these requests into sub-tasks, decide which tools or data to use, and refine their approach if needed - behaviors that resemble problem-solving, planning, and deep reasoning. Being autonomous and going from passive to active leverages

- **Improved LLM reasoning**: Newer models are better at chain-of-thought reasoning, keeping track of intermediate steps.

- **Tool use frameworks**: Standards like MCP and libraries like LangChain allow models to use external tools (web search, databases, calculators) when needed, extending their capabilities beyond what's in the model's brain.
- **Long-term memory stores**: Integrations with vectorized databases or memory systems give agents continuity over time because they can now remember past interactions, user preferences, or prior outcomes.
- **Safety controls**: There has been a focus on guardrails so that autonomous agents act within tightly defined boundaries – for example, requiring certain checks or approvals before sensitive actions. This is crucial for enterprise trust in agents.

Building autonomous agents, enabling Agent-to-Agent (A2A) interactions, the tools, frameworks, and development platforms will be covered in detail in Chapter 4.

Model Context Protocol (MCP)

It should be of no surprise that data is the cornerstone for AI enablement. All the problems associated with AI and LLMs – Hallucination, laziness, accuracy – are all because of the lack of data and/or the quality of the data.

Therefore, it is of no surprise that one of the biggest leaps in AI integration is the rise of the Model Context Protocol (MCP), an open standard that has rapidly become the backbone of modern AI integration in 2025. The simplest way of describing MCP is that it is essentially the "USB-C for AI" – a universal, open connector for linking AI models to external systems and data. Developed by Anthropic and released in late 2024, MCP provides a structured, secure way for LLMs to interface with tools, databases, APIs, and real-time information.

Why is MCP a game changer? It solves the integration and accessibility issue. Traditionally, connecting an AI model to, for example, a company database or a SaaS platform, required custom code and bespoke APIs for each case – a slow and fragile approach because API endpoints oftentime change when updated. MCP replaces this fragile approach with one standardized protocol, eliminating integration silos and accelerating development. With MCP, an AI assistant can fetch live data ("What's our latest sales figure?") via a common interface instead of relying only on its training data or a custom plugin.

MCP's design is inspired by the Language Server Protocol (LSP) used in software development and leverages a mature, well-known architecture – the client–server architecture – where the AI application acts as a client sending requests, and MCP servers expose various data or actions (e.g., a finance database server providing revenue data, or a CRM server providing customer info).

All communication uses a standard JSON format with defined schemas for queries and responses, making it interoperable across programming languages and platforms. **Crucially, MCP includes secure authentication and role-based access controls (RBAC), so enterprises can manage exactly what an AI agent is allowed to see or do**.

Adoption and ecosystem: MCP has seen remarkably fast uptake. All major AI players – Microsoft, Google, OpenAI, Anthropic – now support MCP in their tools and APIs. According to industry reports, up to 90% of organizations will be using MCP by the end of 2025 as part of their AI deployments. The market for MCP-related tools is booming, projected to grow from ~$1.2 billion in 2022 to $4.5 billion in 2025. Already companies have built dozens of MCP servers for common services – from GitHub source control to Google Drive to SQL databases – and open-source communities maintain registries of connectors. This ubiquity means developers can "plug and play" AI capabilities into enterprise systems far more easily than before.

Using the earlier example of an agent using a web service to book an airline ticket, in which case the agent needs to understand the booking system's API, with MCP, it can call an authorized "Ticket MCP server" which retrieves the available flights from the database, then the AI can summarize them, all on the fly. The result is a precise, up-to-the-minute presentation of flight availability.

MCP does not just feed data into models - it also allows models to take actions externally in a controlled way. The AI agent can use MCP to execute functions like updating a record, sending an email, or triggering a workflow, under defined policies. Continuing with the airline ticket booking example above, the agent will be able to execute the entire reservation once a flight has been selected.

In summary, MCP provides the plumbing that turns isolated AI capabilities into integrated solutions, making AI far more useful in practical, productized scenarios. Companies prioritizing MCP find they can deploy AI features faster and with better accuracy. MCP is one of the major topics we will be focusing on in Chapter 5.

Responsible AI

Earlier in this chapter, we discussed the maturation of AI that is driving the discussions around governance, ethical use of AI, and security and safety. AI providers have also provided more transparency and assurances to the use of AI, both in their products and as stand-alone AI services and models that customers can incorporate when building products. The latter, of course, is the one that is applicable to us since we are trying to productize AI. As such, the product or service we build will inherit these characteristics. Here is a sampling of the a few of the principles put forth by major AI providers. Note how similar and aligned they are.

Amazon Web Services (AWS)

AWS highlights its Life Cycle Integration and Customization Guardrails[7] as its implementation of the responsible use of AI across the full development life cycle. It emphasizes fairness, explainability, privacy, and controllability as part of the governing principle.

AWS' Bedrock Guardrails[8] provide safeguards that are native but customizable and touts the ability to block as much as 85% more harmful content that traditional safeguards, filtering out 75% hallucinations, and providing deep insight into AI utilization for your applications.

Google's AI Principles

Google's AI Principles[9] emphasize beneficial use, safety, fairness, privacy, and accountability. Extending their original "do no evil" mantra, Google's AI Principles pledge to be socially beneficial and avoid creating or reinforcing bias. The company's stance is that safety and human oversight are mandatory through the AI life cycle of model development and pledges respect for privacy and intellectual property. That pledge is based on the company's Secure AI Framework, which governs the security and privacy across models.

Meta

Of all the major AI providers, Meta is perhaps the one with the most turbulent history, not through any direct or public incidents, but more because of its heavy involvement in social media. Meta's genesis as a social media platform creates a level of mistrust, but this was compounded when

[7] https://aws.amazon.com/ai/responsible-ai/

[8] https://aws.amazon.com/bedrock/guardrails/

[9] https://ai.google/principles

Meta dissolved their Responsible AI (RAI) team in 2023. Meta has also acknowledged shifting of risk assessments that include key topics such as privacy, bias, and misinformation, from human reviewers to AI.

But because Meta is a provider of LLaMa, an AI model, it published information on the responsible use of its models[10] and the details around how LLaMa is built and maintained. This is important because LLaMa is targeted at developers and product development. Therefore, since we are discussing AI productization in this book, and if you are considering using LLaMa as one of the models, this guideline will be of particular importance.

Microsoft Principles of Responsible AI

Remember that we mentioned many would consider Microsoft to be an Accelerationist? As a for-profit company, it is in a race to bring AI to market and this is being done by making AI the core component of the product portfolio. Through the Copilot branding, Microsoft is infusing AI in every product and service it offers. Like Google and AWS (and other technology heavyweights for that matter), Microsoft continues to pour billions of dollars in advancing AI and to stay in (ahead of) the race. It is not one company going off and doing its own thing, it is the entire software industry!

AI is not new to Microsoft, though. In fact, Microsoft has been in the AI space since at least 2016.

In 2016, Microsoft CEO, Satya Nadella laid down the 10 laws of AI.[11] A year is an extremely long time by technical standards. However, after 7 years, these laws have stood the test of time, demonstrating their continued *and growing* relevance. These laws have been, and continue to be, the foundation for Microsoft Principles of Responsible AI.

---

[10] `https://ai.meta.com/static-resource/responsible-use-guide/`

[11] Geekwire article – CEO Satya Nadella lays out the 10 laws of AI (and human behavior) for Slate Magazine

Since 2016, roles, committees, and processes that ensure the responsible use of AI at Microsoft has been formalized and put in place. For example, the AI and Ethics in Engineering and Research (Aether) Committee was established and comprised every product group, engineering, and leadership. It is an advisory board at Microsoft that deliberates about questions, issues, and challenges arising with developing and fielding applications of AI. The committee reports to Microsoft's senior leadership team.

In fact, prior to Generative AI, there are equivalent sensitive AI technologies that Microsoft had to address, like facial recognition[12] in 2018. Microsoft took the initiative to urge regulators to regulate the technology, and restrict the adoption of the technology by vetting use cases. Figure 1-1 shows the roadmap of responsible adoption at Microsoft since 2016. So, although Microsoft is a leaning accelerationist, it is without wild abandon, and history is on its side to support that claim.

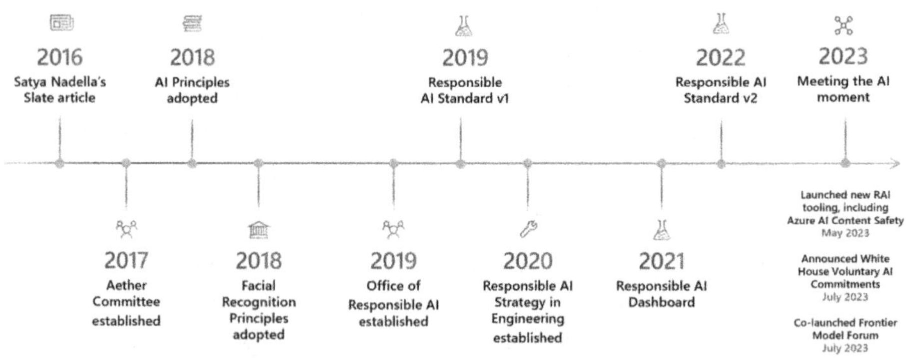

***Figure 1-1.** Microsoft Responsible AI journey*

Microsoft has a site dedicated to the company's AI principles at `https://www.microsoft.com/en-us/ai/responsible-ai`. In 2020, we wrote that Microsoft is a leader in charge to ensure ethics are deeply

[12] Microsoft blog – Six principles to guide Microsoft's facial recognition work

ingrained in the development of AI technologies. The most important aspect of Microsoft's AI principles is that it applies to AI at scale since the technology is built into every service and shared across its entire portfolio.

Intellectual Property (IP) Considerations

There are two aspects when discussing Intellectual Property as it relates to LLMs. First is the potential use of IP when training LLMs, and second, how would you protect the IP that goes into creating your AI-enabled products and services, or what does IP mean in this case.

With respect to the first issue, despite the numerous lawsuits with regard to whether copyrighted content can be used to train LLMs, there is still no definitive clarity but recent US court rulings have leaned toward the concept of "fair use[13]" – where the data was lawfully acquired and the outputs do not replicate the originals.

Because Generative AI models are trained on literary works, does any content derived from the models infringe on intellectual property? There is already legal precedent when the US Copyright Office ruled that images created by AI will not be protected by copyright laws because copyright laws apply only to content that has been created by humans.[14] Whatever source content that may be used in the creation of the content is unclear. Even though this may be unclear, it should not be mistaken for the lack of transparency of which sources are part of the model being used to generate the content. For example, part of Microsoft's Principles for responsible AI is the Transparency note for Azure OpenAI.[15] This note provides insight into the data sources and training methods for the AI models.

---

[13] Bartz v. Anthropic (June 2025) and Kadrey v. Meta (June 2025)

[14] CNET - Graphic Novel's AI generated art won't get copyright protections

[15] Transparency Note for Azure OpenAI

Consider this analogy – a person's educational journey involves studying materials that already exist in topics like literature, science, programming languages, algorithms, art, etc. Everything that is part of a well-rounded education. Any original content that this person creates is based on their education. It will be like trying to determine whether the original works that one creates infringes on IP because of their education.

Regarding the second scenario surrounding IP protection, it is interesting to note that the determination of the US Copyright Office in the case mentioned above that the decision was revisited and subsequently revised to include protection for *"the text and author's instructions to AI, but not the artwork the AI had produced."* Below examples form a sample checklist to assess product IP-specific risk:

- Verify rights/licenses for every data source.
- Add guardrails against copyrighted/trademarked content.
- Log prompts/outputs for audits.
- Clarify ownership of AI-generated content.
- Track risks with severity + mitigation owners.

The instructions to AI are known as prompt engineering. This means that the US Copyright Office has determined that prompts are subject to copyright protection, which is an important aspect when it comes to productizing AI. Instructions on *how* to use the content and *how* to respond to requests, including the *tools* to invoke, all forms the logic for AI. Therefore, the key to creating a product is the generation of value and differentiation. This creates the demand for our product and therefore requires protection.

In September 2023, Microsoft became the first company to provide customers protection against legal action stemming from the use of its AI technology when generating content. This is known as the Copilot

Copyright Commitment[16] for customers. The commitment states that if a *"third party sues a commercial customer for copyright infringement for using Microsoft's Copilots or the output they generate, we will defend the customer and pay the amount of any adverse judgments or settlements that result from the lawsuit, as long as the customer used the guardrails and content filters we have built into our products."*

This is a significant commitment to creators of products and services because of the legal risk related to IP violation.

Market and Technology Outlook

Investments in AI continue to grow at an astounding rate. For example, Nvidia Corp., the leading provider of GPUs, became the first $5 trillion dollar company, and Microsoft stands second at $4 trillion dollars, closely followed by AWS and Google. These companies are increasing capital expenditures tied to infrastructure expansion around the world. These current investments are a direct reflection of market sentiment on AI adoption even amidst concern about an "AI bubble" raised by different groups, none of which should deter our goal of productizing AI.

On the technology front, these are the development efforts, and pursuits:

Artificial General Intelligence (AGI)

Artificial General Intelligence (AGI), often referred to as "strong AI" or "human-level AI," is the aspirational end-point of artificial intelligence research. In fact, if you read the revised agreement[17] between OpenAI and Microsoft, AGI is prominently mentioned throughout the document, which is a clear indication of the industry's focus.

[16] Microsoft Copilot Copyright Commitment

[17] `https://blogs.microsoft.com/blog/2025/10/28/the-next-chapter-of-the-microsoft-openai-partnership/`

AGI is basically an AI system with the general learning and reasoning capabilities of a human being, or, likely beyond. AGI could understand context, transfer knowledge between application domains, and improvise solutions to new problems in a way that today's AI cannot. Today's (2025) AI is in the stage known as Artificial Narrow Intelligence (ANI) – which is highly skilled at specific tasks but cannot apply itself outside its trained domain.

Achieving AGI is exceedingly difficult. Human intelligence is the product of millions of years of evolution. To replicate this in silicon, researchers will need much bigger neural networks, new paradigms in learning, reasoning, and memory. Achieving AGI is a field of active study and spirited debate; academically, some think our current methods of simply scaling up deep learning models will eventually yield AGI, while others believe **entirely new breakthroughs** will be required. Philosophically, the Doomers, for example believe that AGI would be the beginning of the end for humankind.

Avatars

Avatars give LLMs a "physical" appearance. This elevates the user interaction experience. Now, not only can you use natural language, you can augment natural language with visual interaction. And we are not talking about the "animation-like" avatars that were previously on teams, but the use of *actual human likeness* and voices of real people. It is a combination of ANI models (specifically Text-to-Speech), LLMs, and the new Azure Avatar service.[18] Figure 1-2 shows the communication flow between a user and an Avatar.

[18] https://techcommunity.microsoft.com/blog/azure-ai-foundry-blog/text-to-speech-avatar-in-azure-ai-is-now-generally-available/4224708

Figure 1-2. *Text-to-Speech Avatar service with LLMs*

Microsoft has also started incorporating Avatar technology into Copilot[19] and touting this as the new era of personalized AI Assistance.

There are also third party companies that have been providing avatar technology for LLMs and these companies' Avatars, like those from Soul Machines,[20] will work with different types of platforms and LLMs.

One thing that we will mention, if you have not noticed, is that more companies are referring to Agent-based LLMs as Digital Workers, Digital Employees, Personal Assistants, etc. Avatar technology is a big contributor to humanizing Agents.

Robots and Humanoids

Nvidia is now the household name for AI but they are primarily known as the GPU providers. The hardware guys. On the other hand, OpenAI, Microsoft, AWS, etc., are more well known as the AI interface. However, it is natural to note that given Nvidia's DNA in silicon, they are pursuing the next iteration beyond Avatars - actual physical existence like robots and humanoids.

[19] https://windowsforum.com/threads/introducing-microsoft-copilot-avatars-a-new-era-of-personalized-ai-assistance.359414/

[20] https://www.soulmachines.com/

Nvidia envisions a future on a robot workforce.[21] Tesla is moving beyond just electric vehicle into AI and robotics,[22] which is somewhat ironic given Elon Musk's confusing stance on AI and humankind. Tesla Optimus[23] is already being deployed in limited fashion in Tesla's factory.

While AGI and humanoids may not be available yet, the amount of R&D investment is going to yield intermediate and usable advancements during the journey. Avatars can be viewed as one such milestone since the technology is available today, but market adoption in products and services are still considered fairly low.

A Look at What Is in Store

Now that we have an idea on what the AI landscape is, and the huge potential market for your product or service, let us take a look at what we will be covering in the following chapters:

Chapter 2: Cost and Pricing

In Chapter 2, we will go into the details of estimating the cost using AI models and tools. However, when building a product or service that leverages technology, the traditional cost of materials that are non-AI related is still valid. For example:

- **Storage**: The amount of space the solution and contents, such as knowledge sources, would consume.

[21] https://gizmodo.com/nvidia-bets-the-future-on-a-robot-workforce-2000677996

[22] https://www.tesla.com/AI

[23] https://www.teslaoracle.com/2025/09/07/the-golden-tesla-optimus-is-version-2-5-not-3-says-elon-musk/

- **Non-AI Compute**: If it is a Web Application, this would include the cost to host the application (e.g., web servers).
- **Databases**: Some of the storage that delivers content that the LLMs need may come in the form of structured data in databases.
- **Networking**: An entire slew of services fall in this category (e.g., Firewalls, DNS, network traffic, load balancers, etc.).
- **Security**: A solution that covers all the traditional security protections such as DOS attacks, hacking, etc., but also AI-specific security such as jailbreaking and content filtering.

These are generally topics that have been covered by other sources and thus will be excluded from this book. Instead, we will focus primarily on the AI-related cost aspects because this is still a new area and there are still a lot of uncertainty and confusion around costing and budgeting for AI projects.

In essence, we will be introducing and discussing tokens. Tokens are the core transactional currency of AI and the goal we will need to accomplish is to establish a good understanding on tokens and ideally come up with a conversion model between tokens and a pricing model for the AI-enabled product or service you are planning to build.

Chapter 3: Design and Prototyping

In Chapter 3, we will start exploring the tools that will help with the design and prototyping of your AI solution. An AI solution, as its name implies, would comprise AI technologies, the obvious one being LLMs. But there are other non-LLM AI technologies such as Computer Vision and Speech. All these technologies predate LLMs but are not obsolete. In fact, they are often used to augment LLMs.

Since we are focusing on the Microsoft platform in this book, we will explore the use of their latest AI studio – Azure Foundry. Azure Foundry is the online development and experimental platform for AI-related projects and is specifically designed for rapid prototyping.

Chapter 4: Building the Agentic Way

Agentic architecture is the recommended approach when building enterprise-scale LLMs. In this chapter, we will look at the rationale behind the agentic approach.

We will also examine the Orchestration Frameworks like LangChain, AutoGen, Semantic Kernel, and Agent Framework. Orchestration Frameworks are core to agentic architecture because it is the glue that binds agents together and facilitates their ability to utilize tools and communicate with other agents.

Chapter 5: Building with Model Context Protocol (MCP)

As we mentioned earlier in this chapter, MCP is one of the newest technologies that was introduced in 2025. It significantly contributes to the accuracy of LLMs by removing data silos. Remember that MCP is akin to a USB port for data sources that LLMs can access without special API definitions.

In this chapter, we will take a deeper dive into MCP through building an MCP server as well as discuss what an MCP strategy would look like.

Since the majority of analytical data resides in data warehouses and data lakes, we will also explore MCP technologies associated with analytical platforms like Azure Fabric and Databricks.

Chapter 6: Addressing Resiliency and Service Level Agreements (SLA)

In Chapter 6, we will take a step away from the core AI technologies and look at the immediate adjacent technologies that provide resilience to AI services. How do we load balance AI requests, handle errors and retries and logging.

Most importantly, we will discuss security for AI, which includes content filtering, identifying and preventing hacking attempts such as jailbreaking and prompt injection.

Chapter 7: Publishing on Azure Marketplace

In Chapter 7, we will look at a distribution channel for your AI product. Although we will use the Azure Marketplace as an example, the process is similar with other platforms on Google and AWS. These are known as certification processes that would enable publishing of your application for distribution. This is an important topic as it is a fundamental portion of your overall Go-to-Market strategy. By going through the actual process of navigating the Azure Marketplace requirement, it would provide you with guidance on how to leverage Microsoft's leadership role in AI as a channel, and a roadmap with reusable artifacts that can be used with other vendors should you choose to pursue publishing through multiple channels.

Chapter 8: Integration with Copilot

Since the introduction of Generative AI, OpenAI has branded their product as ChatGPT and Microsoft, using the same OpenAI technology, branded their offering as Copilot. Today, ChatGPT and Copilot are used synonymously with Generative AI but at the same time have caused a lot of confusion because these are essentially different types of implementation, even within the Microsoft ecosystem (Azure OpenAI, Microsoft 365 Copilot, Copilot Chat, GitHub Copilot, Copilot Studio, etc.).

Not only will we attempt to demystify the difference between all these terms, we will introduce the first glimpse of convergence as the AI landscape continues to mature. This convergence has an impact on how you should think about designing, marketing, and distributing your AI product or service.

Chapter 9: Go-to-Market Scaling and Measuring Success

In this final chapter, we will look at ways to monitor and measure the adoption of your AI product and service. We will look at utilization reports and how to take advantage of economies of scale. There are also programs and opportunities to co-market your AI product or service with the platform provider. Since we are using Microsoft as the platform provider throughout this book, we will explore Microsoft's programs and co-marketing tools.

Resources and Code Samples

Resources and code samples from this book will be shared through GitHub. The public GitHub site for this book will be located at `https://github.com/juliansoh/DataScienceSolutionsOnAzure-2ndEdition`.

Summary

In this chapter, we have highlighted all the current AI landscape in 2025, with a focus on the opportunities presented by the current market conditions. We also took a cursory look at the key topics when evaluating the market conditions – emerging technologies such as agents and MCP, identifying customers and types of customers, legal concerns such as IP, security, and responsible use of AI, and last but not least, an initial understanding on costing AI services in order to better develop a pricing model for your product or service.

Since we, as authors, work primarily in building Microsoft-based solutions, we will use Microsoft and Azure as the de facto technology provider., However, bear in mind that as far as Generative AI and Large Language Models go, there are other open-source LLM models as well as technologies offered by Microsoft's competitors, such as Google and AWS. Google Bard, PaLM2, Codey, and Imagen are alternatives and competitors to the Azure OpenAI stack, as is AWS' $4 billion investment in Anthropic AI.[24]

Regardless of the technology stack, the current state of Generative AI is such that all the core concepts that we cover in this book remain relevant, the technical concepts such as MCP, Orchestration Frameworks, and the agentic architecture are open source and therefore vendor agnostic. Furthermore, the variety of models available through the Azure Foundry model catalog is not restricted to OpenAI family of GPT models. In fact, at the time of writing, OpenAI and Microsoft agreed to end Microsoft's status as the sole provider of the[25] models, which led to developers being able to now use GPT models on AWS and other providers.

---

[24] CNN Business – Amazon invests up to $4 billion in Anthropic AI in exchange for minority stake and further AWS integration

[25] `https://blogs.microsoft.com/blog/2025/10/28/the-next-chapter-of-the-microsoft-openai-partnership/`

CHAPTER 2

Cost and Pricing

If we are going to build a product, these would be the important questions to ask:

- What is the market? We discussed this quite extensively in Chapter 1.
- What is our product or service? This is your homework and you probably already have a good idea of what this may be since you are reading this book.
- What will it cost to build and operate? This is what we will be covering in this chapter.
- How should I price my product or service? This is also what we will be exploring in this chapter.

Part of any business plan is going to be about cost. Therefore, before we start looking at all the tools and technologies, it is appropriate to have the discussion on cost. A better understanding on cost will in turn help us design a pricing and distribution model.

Although there are the traditional costs when developing and operating *any* technology-based product (e.g., web servers, databases, load balancers, security, networking, etc.), and keeping in mind that this also applies to AI-enabled products and services, we will only go into the details for the LLM. This is because it is the newest component in the

J. Soh et al., *Building and Distributing Agentic AI Solutions*,
https://doi.org/10.1007/979-8-8688-2586-6_2

product, with the largest amount of variability, and introduces the concept of *tokens*. Therefore, a good understanding of tokens will help with the cost and pricing model for your product or service.

Transacting with Large Language Models

In the Generative AI space, there are several LLMs to choose from. Here are the most popular ones:

- OpenAI GPT family of models (GPT-4o, GPT-5.x, o1-mini, etc.)
- Anthropic Claude
- Google Gemini
- DeepSeek[1]
- Meta Llama

Regardless of the model or the provider, one thing that all LLMs have in common is the "transaction currency." This currency, known as tokens, governs how much work the LLM must do in order to fulfill a request, and work is proportionate to GPU utilization. Therefore, tokens govern the cost of using LLMs. Model providers charge by token utilization.[2]

Tokens are also used to measure the *Context Window* of an LLM. As its name implies, context is "all the information necessary" to fulfill a request. It is the maximum amount of text that a model can consider in a single transaction. For example, if an LLM is asked to summarize a 15-page article versus a novel, the latter will obviously require a larger context window

[1] By Hangzhou DeepSeek Artificial Intelligence Basic Technology Research Co., Ltd.

[2] There are other methods that providers charge (e.g., dedicated GPU time, etc.), but these are all based on tokens as well. We will discuss these other charging methods later in the chapter.

because of the larger amount of text. If the amount of text exceeds the context window of a model, it will not be able to fulfill the request. In this case, the text will have to be broken into chunks that fit within the context window of the model and the LLM will have to execute the request over several transactions. *"Chunking"* is a method where text is broken into chunks, tracked to ensure order, sent to the LLM for processing, and the responses reassembled accordingly for a complete answer to be provided. Therefore, the smaller the context window, the more chunks would be needed, and this affects the performance of an LLM.

In summary, not only do tokens determine cost, when represented as the context window, they also determine the performance (generally measured by Tokens per second or TPS) of the LLM. Figure 2-1 below shows the performance (speed in TPS, not accuracy) of various models.

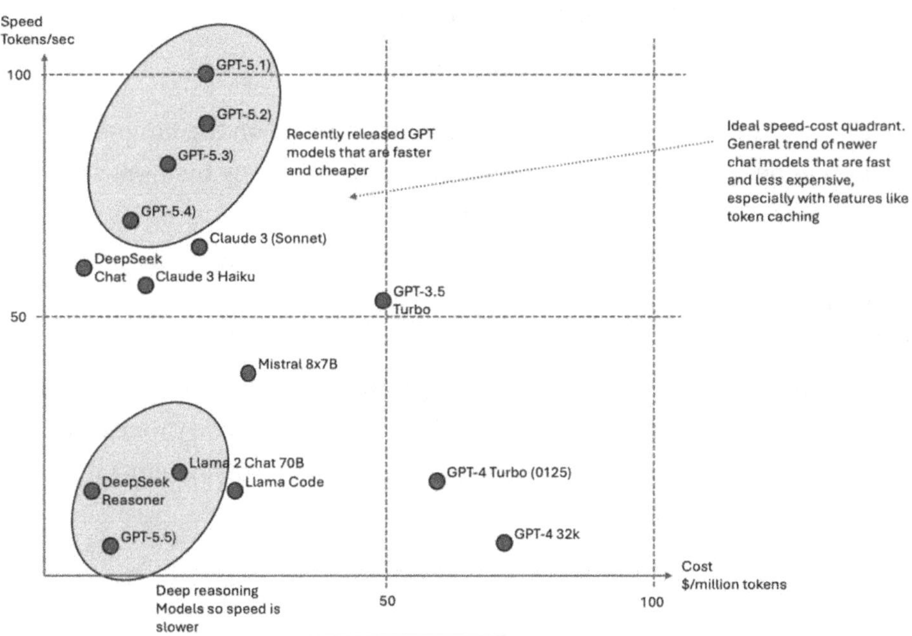

Figure 2-1. *Speed vs. cost of tokens*

Counting Tokens

In the next section, we will go into more detail on how tokenization works. But for now, in the general sense, you can view one token as

- Approximately four characters in English or
- ¾ of a word
- 1 Chinese character ≈ 0.6 tokens[3]

Conversely, we can use the following guidance. For Generative AI to process

- One to two sentences is approximately 30 tokens
- One paragraph is approximately 100 tokens
- 1,500 words is approximately 2048 tokens
- 75 words is approximately 100 tokens

The number of tokens needed is also dependent on the language, which is generally higher than English. Therefore, it may be more expensive to process non-English text.

The challenge with tokens is that it is cumbersome to come up with an estimate on how many tokens. Fortunately, there are several tools available. One such tool a Tokenizer tool[4] provided by OpenAI. It is a simple tool that allows you to copy and paste text into a text area, which will provide the number of tokens needed for the text to be processed by OpenAI. Figure 2-2 below shows the layout of the Tokenizer tool from OpenAI.

[3] Based on DeepSeek-R1

[4] `https://platform.openai.com/tokenizer`

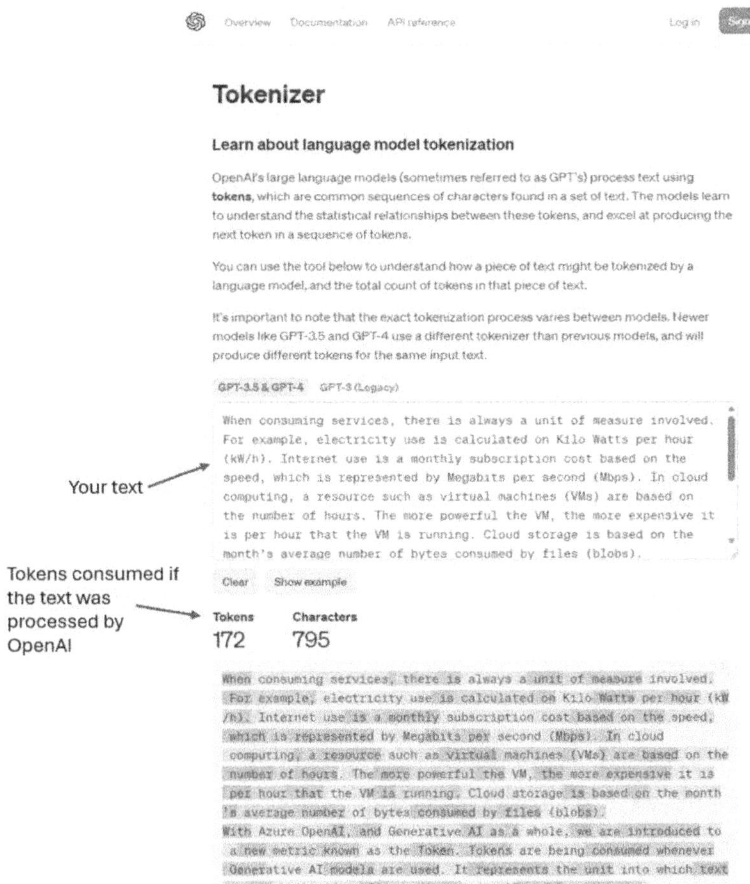

Figure 2-2. *Tokenizer tool from Azure OpenAI showing 172 tokens needed for a body of text*

This method of estimating tokens is a generalization, but the algorithm used in breaking up the text is not to just arbitrarily group strings into four characters from the beginning of the text to the end in a sequential way. Let us take a closer look at what happens during tokenization.

Tokenization

At a minimum, being able to determine how many tokens are needed to process a body of text provides you with the ability to select the best model for your product. During model selection, aside from determining the quality of responses, you will need to be able to optimize token utilization as well because it reduces your cost.

Tokenization[5] is technically an algorithm based on Byte-Pair Encoding (BPE) logic.[6] BPE identifies patterns in text and replaces the patterns with a token that uniquely represents the patterns. This happens iteratively until no more patterns can be identified.

For example:

```
Tokenize the text string "aabccabbbcccaabcc"
Identify pattern and frequency:
    "aa"
    "bcc"
    aa bcc abb bcc c aa bcc
Tokenizing the pattern by replacing them with text that
does not exist in the string:
    ZXabbXcZX
    Z=aa
    X=bcc
```

[5] Tokenization is also used for purposes other than processing by LLMs, for example, blockchain and data masking. As a general term, it is an action to mask/replace original content with unrelated numeric values, thereby making the original content unusable until the process is reversed.

[6] Medium/Towards Data Science – Byte-Pair Encoding – `https://towardsdatascience.com/byte-pair-encoding-subword-based-tokenization-algorithm-77828a70bee0`

```
Iterating:
    YabbXcY
    Y=ZX
    Z=aa
    X=bcc
```

The resulting tokenized text (YaabbXcY) is smaller than the original (aaccaabbbcccaabcc). The tokenized text is reversible and lossless, which means you can convert the tokens back into the original text.

The BPE algorithm is the basis of the tokenization logic in LLMs, except that instead of just contiguous pairs, tokenization identifies commonly used sequences in the language and uses a numeric representation of the text because the LLM only understands numbers. Hence, tokenization is also the process of converting text to numeric format, known as encoding. There are different encoding methods, such as o200k,[7] cl100k_base, p50k_base, r50k_base. Different model providers may also use their own customer tokenizer algorithms, such as DeepSeek and Llama SentencePiece, but they all leverage BPE as the base algorithm. Each contiguous body of text, letter, or word is represented by a unique number based on the model that is being used. Table 2-1 shows the different encoding techniques employed by different models.

[7] o200k_base is the latest OpenAI encoding method first used in GPT-4o and now in GPT-5.

Table 2-1. *Encoders used by OpenAI models*

Encoder	OpenAI models
o200k	GPT-4o, GPT-5
SentencePiece	Llama 4
Custom BPE over UTF-8	DeepSeek
cl100k_base	gpt-4, gpt-3.5-turbo, text-embedding-ada-002, text-embedding-3-small, text-embedding-3-large
p50k_base	Codex, text-davici-002, text-davici-003
r50k_base	gpt-3, davinci

The tokenizer uses both the encoder and the model to determine how contiguous text is selected. This combination is the vocabulary that the tokenizer uses for conversion purposes. In English, tokens are commonly grouped to form one character to one word (e.g., "t" or "meet"). Spaces are usually grouped at the *start* of a word (e.g., " an" instead of "an ").

For example:

```
Tokenizer vocabulary:

    "ing" = 341
    "is" = 45
    "an" = 85
    "Run" = 2256
    "Kick" = 2215
    "ic" = 18
    "sport" = 8459
    "even" = 7485
    "event" = 3258
```

```
Tokenize "Running is an Olympic sporting event"
Identify contiguous text based on the library:
    "Run", "ing", "ic", "sport", "event"
Tokenizing:
```

Run	n	ing	is	an	Olymp	ic	sport	ing	event	36 chars
2256		341	45	85		18	8459	341	3258	

```
Replacing non-matched strings or characters with unique
numbers:
n=25, Olymp=5126
```

Run	n	ing	is	an	Olymp	ic	sport	ing	event	36 chars
2256	25	341	45	85	5126	18	8459	341	3258	10 tokens

This example uses a hypothetical rudimentary vocabulary but with an LLM like GPT-5, the vocabulary is extensive so much fewer tokens would be needed. We are also using a hypothetical number in this example to represent how words are being converted into numeric values. Once a word or letter is converted to a numeric value, the value remains the same for every instance of the word or letter. Using the same body of text and plugging it into OpenAI's tokenizer, we get the results shown in Figure 2-3.

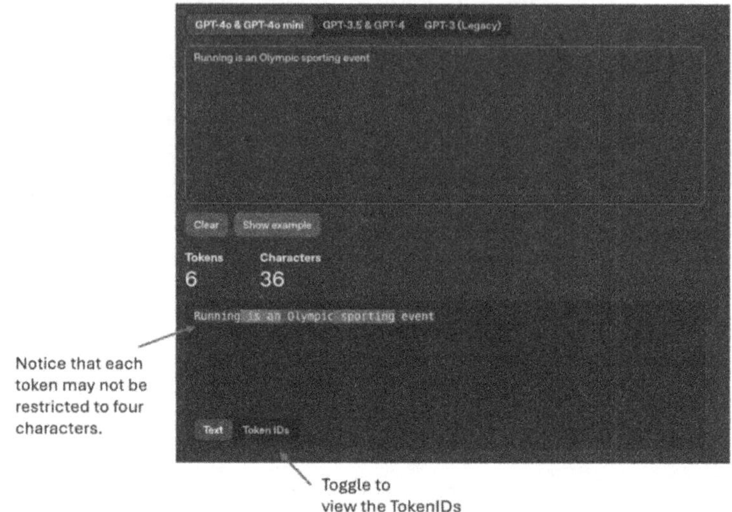

Figure 2-3. *How text is organized using OpenAI's tokenizer*

You might be wondering why the hypothetical example provided 10 tokens whereas the Tokenizer showed 6 tokens. The answer is the algorithm that is being used by OpenAI. The first example was for illustration purposes to show how tokens are generated from words, whereas the Tokenizer is an actual tokenizer tool. Simply put, Tokenizer is more optimized when it comes to selecting words/characters than our manual conversion! Hence a lower token count.

Comparing Models with Tiktoken

A better alternative to using the online Tokenizer is to use the *Tiktoken* library provided by OpenAI. You can use the Tiktoken[8] open-source tokenizer by OpenAI in a Jupyter notebook, as shown in Figure 2-4.

[8] GitHub – How to count tokens with tiktoken open-source tokenizer by OpenAI – `https://github.com/openai/openai-cookbook/blob/main/examples/How_to_count_tokens_with_tiktoken.ipynb`

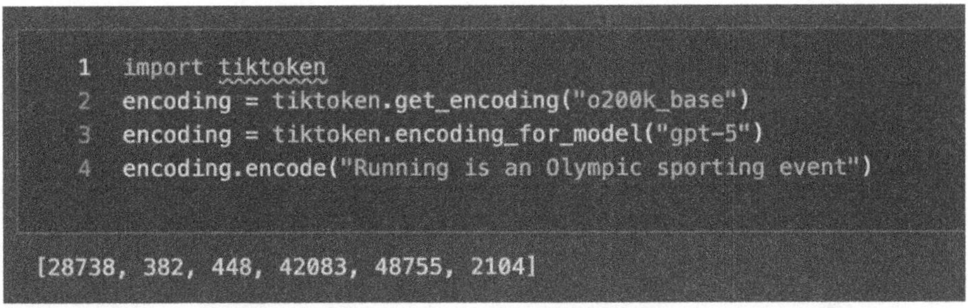

```
import tiktoken
encoding = tiktoken.get_encoding("o200k_base")
encoding = tiktoken.encoding_for_model("gpt-5")
encoding.encode("Running is an Olympic sporting event")
```

```
[28738, 382, 448, 42083, 48755, 2104]
```

Figure 2-4. *Code block in Jupyter notebook using Tiktoken to retrieve encodings*

Hands-On Exercise: Exploring Tokenization

For this hands-on exercise, and all the other exercises in this book, you will need to have a working understanding of git, python, and Linux. We will assume you have this level of skill and will not go into extensive details on configuration and tooling.

Recommended prerequisites:

- Visual Studio Code (recommended) or your preferred IDE installed.
- Git or GitHub desktop installed.
- Windows Subsystem for Linux (WSL) installed (if you are developing under the Windows OS).
- Install Python 3.8 or above.

Start of the hands-on exercise:

1. Clone this book's GitHub repo located at `https://github.com/juliansoh/Building_and_Distributing_AI-Enabled-Solutions`.
2. Launch Visual Studio Code.

3. Install the Jupyter notebook support extension from the Extensions marketplace, as shown in Figure 2-5.

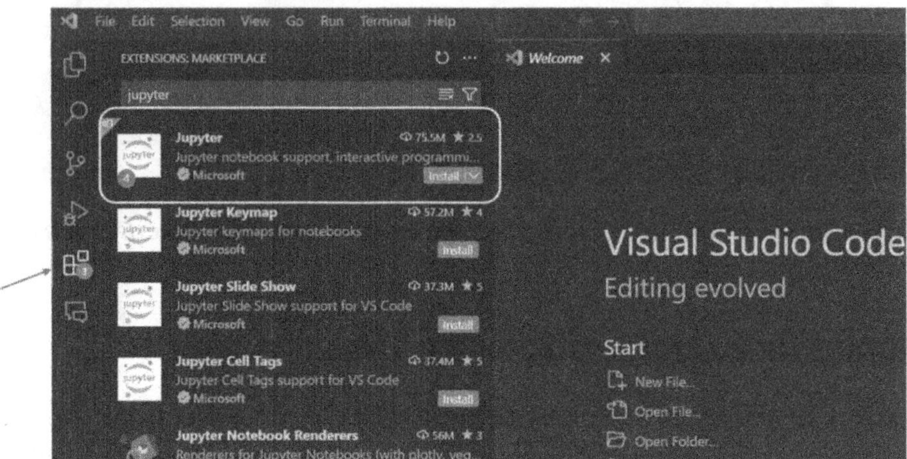

***Figure 2-5.** Install the Jupyter support extension in Visual Studio Code*

4. Select File ➤ Open Folder in Visual Studio Code and navigate to the local root directory of the repo you cloned in step 1.

5. Navigate to the folder named "Chapter_2/ Exercise_1" and open "exercise_1_tiktoken.jpynb," as shown in Figure 2-6.

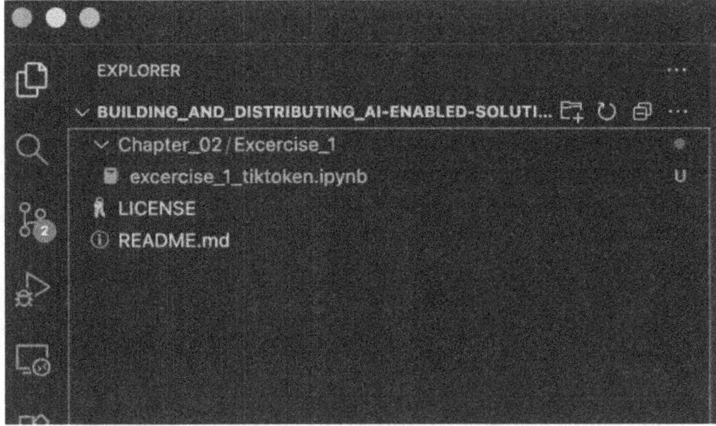

Figure 2-6. *Open Jupyter notebook "exercise_1_tokenizer.jpny" in the folder named "Chapter_02/Exercise_1"*

6. Read the comments in code blocks 1 and 2, then run them in sequence. Change the value of the variable "text" in code block 2 if desired.
7. Next, read the markdown comments in code block 4, then execute the code in block 5.
8. Execute the code in block 7 and observe the results. It should be similar to Figure 2-7.

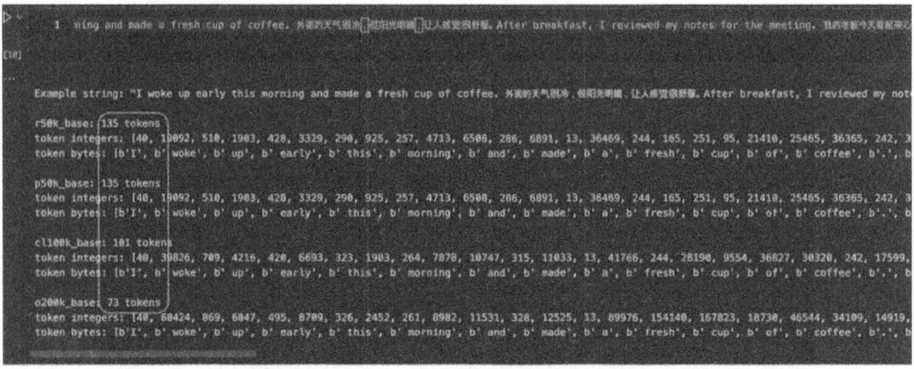

Figure 2-7. *The different number of tokens required by each model/encoder*

Notice that for this body of text, the o200k_base (GPT-4o/GPPT-5) requires 73 tokens compared to cl100k_base (GPT-4) of 101 tokens. Therefore, from a model selection standpoint, not (yet) taking into consideration the quality of the response, GPT-4o/GPT-5 is a more efficient model.

Prompt versus Completion Tokens

Tokens are classified into two categories:

- Prompt tokens
- Completion tokens

Prompt tokens are the tokens created based on the user input. For example, if you ask the question "Tell me more about this book," the seven tokens that are generated are called prompt tokens.

If the LLM generates the response to this question as "This book teaches us how to use create AI-enabled products and services and a go-to-market strategy," this equates to 19 tokens, and these tokens are called completion tokens.

In summary, prompt tokens are tokens associated to questions (prompts), and completion tokens are tokens associated to the LLM's generated response. Furthermore, in most interactions with LLMs, the number of prompt tokens consumed are usually higher than the completions tokens. The reason is because setting up the prompts require not only the question, but also the context of the question and all the relevant sources (e.g., knowledge base articles, etc.).

In a conversational setting, in order to provide the LLM with the context of all the previous conversation turns, each subsequent prompt would need to include the questions previously asked. Therefore, each subsequent prompt would consume more tokens than the previous as the conversation goes on.

For estimation purposes, Table 2-2 lists common use cases and the observed average number of tokens for each use case. So why is it important for us to distinguish between prompt and completions tokens? Because models have limits on the number of prompt versus completions tokens per transaction, not just the total number of tokens defined by the context window. Furthermore, some providers have different unit-charges for prompt versus completion tokens.

Table 2-2. *Use cases and their corresponding token utilization breakdown (estimates) based on GPT-5*

Use case	Prompt tokens	Completions tokens	Total tokens
Basic chat	500	100	600
Chat with your own data: Retrieval Augmented Generation (RAG) architecture[9]	3500	300	3800
Summarization (article)	5000	300	5300
Classification	3800	10	3810
Chat (summarization)	900	200	1100
Meeting (summarization)	1200	100	1300
Code completion/generation	1150	50	1200
Code explanation (summarization)	950	250	1200

Token Estimation in a Multi-agentic Scenario

Although Table 2-2 provided guidance for use-case scenarios, these numbers only indicate single transactions. As we incorporate more deep-reasoning models and multi-agent scenarios, the number of tokens significantly increases because of agent-to-agent collaboration. For example, if you have five agents collaborating to fulfill a request, simple extrapolation would dictate the number of tokens needed is five times the number of the initial estimate.

[9] Retrieval Augmented Generation (RAG) architecture will be discussed later in the book. For now, just know that RAG is a use case where you are using the LLM to answer questions sourced from your own Knowledge Base (KB).

With this in mind, we present Table 2-3, which is a representation of token consumption in multi-agentic scenarios. Multi-agentic architectures promise better quality responses and more manageable prompt engineering and knowledge sources. Therefore, your product will likely use this architecture and thus, the token estimates represented in Table 2-3 would be the preferred baseline.

Table 2-3. *Token consumption in multi-agent use case scenarios*

Source	Scenario	Prompt	Completion	Total
AgentTaxo[10]	Planner, reasoner, verifier roles	8k–15k	1k–2k	10k–17k
MultiAgentBench[11]	Coordination topologies (star, chain, tree, graph)	5k–12k	800–2k	6k–14k
Reliable Decision-making[12]	Redundant agent deployments (voting, decentralized)	10k–18k	1k–2k	12k–21k
MCP-enabled agents[13]	Multi-agent orchestration via Model Context Protocol	8k–20k	1k–3k	10k–25k

[10] AgentTaxo: OpenReview ICLR 2025 (`https://openreview.net/forum?id=0iLbiYYIpC`)

[11] MultiAgentBency: https://arxiv.org/abs/2503.01935 (`https://arxiv.org/abs/2503.01935`)

[12] Reliable Decision-Making: AAAI 2025 PDF (`https://multiagents.org/2025_artifacts/reliable_decision_making_for_multi_agent_llm_systems.pdf`)

[13] MCP-Enabled Agents: https://arxiv.org/abs/2511.07426 (`https://arxiv.org/abs/2511.07426`)

Token Caching

With newer models like GPT-4.1 and GPT-5, a token efficiency mechanism is built into the model known as cached input tokens. Token caching takes portions of your prompt from a previous request and re-uses it without re-computing. This caching mechanism reduces latency by speeding up inference, and reduces cost for long or repeated prompts.

Cost

Now that you understand of tokens and have the ability to estimate token utilization, we can translate that into cost. Cost for using LLMs usually falls into two categories:

- Pay by amount of token utilization
- Pay by Compute hours

The first option is self-explanatory. The second option is to pay by the runtime of the compute resources that host the model. Although both are ultimately token-based, the first option provides less predictability and potentially no upper limit to token utilization. The second option provides a mechanism toward more predictable cost, although it is less elastic in nature - users will usually get a service unavailable error message if there are insufficient compute resources to service requests. Table 2-4 lists the token-based and compute-based billing models by different providers.

Table 2-4. *Token-based vs. compute-based billing options by different providers*

Provider	Token-based billing	Compute-based billing
AWS	AWS Bedrock	AWS SageMaker
Google	Vertex AI	Dedicated endpoints
Microsoft	Pay-as-you-go	Provisioned Throughput Units (PTUs)
DeepSeek	On-demand (default)	Available via Microsoft PTUs and AWS SageMaker

To illustrate the concept behind these two billing models, we will use Microsoft Azure OpenAI as a basis to understand cost calculations:

- Consumption or Pay-as-you-go ("PayGo") model
- Provisioned Throughput Units (PTUs)

Microsoft Token-Based Billing

Sometimes known as "Pay-as-you-go," or simply, "PayGo", this billing model is straightforward - you are charged a price for blocks of *1000 tokens* being consumed. As with all Azure services, the pricing calculator is the tool to use to estimate the cost of using the Azure OpenAI service.

Hands-On Exercise: Exploring Cost

1. As shown in Figure 2-8, access the calculator at `https://azure.microsoft.com/pricing/calculator`, select AI + machine learning in the left menu, then select the Azure OpenAI Service. You will see a popup appear in the right corner of the screen that says Azure OpenAI Service added. Click on the View link.

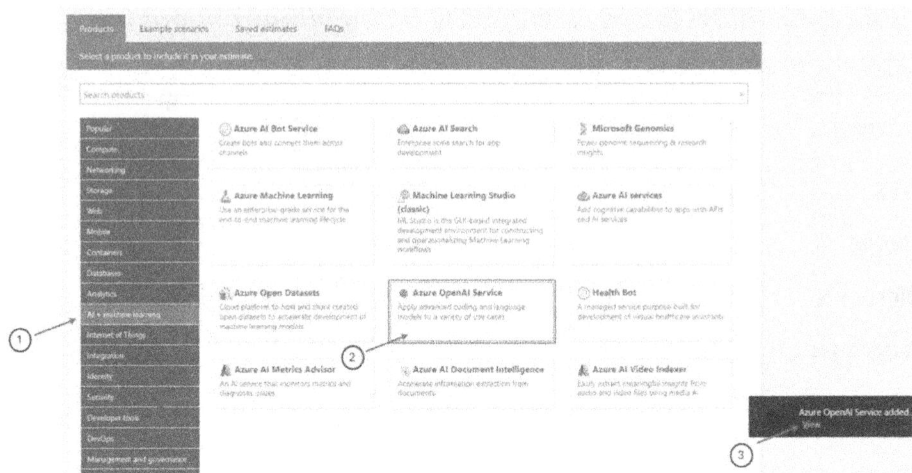

Figure 2-8. *Azure Online Calculator and selecting the Azure OpenAI Service*

2. Remember from earlier in this chapter where we differentiated tokens into Prompt tokens versus Completions token? Here is where it matters because there is different pricing for the types of tokens in the PayGo model. Refer to Table 2-2 and select a use case. Then provide the number of prompt and completion tokens for that use case in the calculator. Figure 2-9 shows the use of the calculator with GPT4.1 selected with “Global On-Demand” (PayGo) as the pricing model.

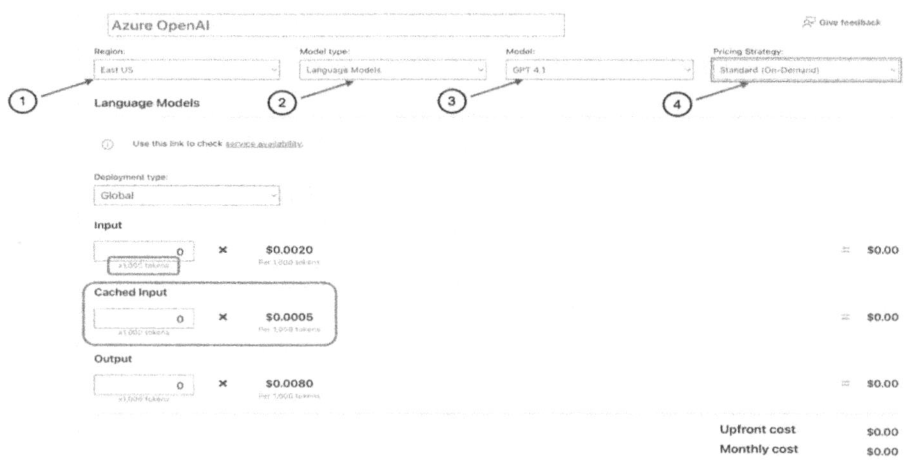

***Figure 2-9.** Estimating cost based on number AND types of tokens in the Azure calculator for GPT-4.1*

3. Note the following aspects from the calculator:

    a. We selected the East US region, but Azure OpenAI is not available in every region. So, if you select a different region, the service may not be available.

    b. Even if Azure OpenAI is available in a region, not all the models are available in that region.

    c. Depending on the model selected, the price per Prompt and Completion token is different.

    d. Depending on the model selected, the Cached Input option may not be available (e.g., only newer models like GPT4o and above have the ability to cache input tokens).

    e. The base unit cost is per **1000 tokens**.

f. For a list of Azure OpenAI and model availability by region, please refer to `https://learn.microsoft.com/en-us/azure/ai-foundry/foundry-models/concepts/models-sold-directly-by-azure?view=foundry-classic&tabs=global-standard-aoai%2Cstandard-chat-completions%2Cglobal-standard&pivots=azure-openai#model-summary-table-and-region-availability`.

Provisioned Throughput Units (PTUs)

Provisioned Throughput Units (PTUs) is a Microsoft Azure term for dedicated compute that runs the LLM. Think of a single PTU as a composite unit of compute (GPU), memory, and storage needed by the LLM. The more PTUs dedicated to an LLM, the more tokens it can process per minute.

There is a minimum number of PTUs needed for an LLM. This is dictated by the LLM type and version and the deployment type. There are three deployment types - Global, Data Zone, and Regional.

Although you specify the model that you intend to use the PTUs for, the concept of PTUs is that these are model-independent. As the service matures, dynamically assigning PTUs that are in your quota to different models is not yet available at the time of writing. You will need to request for new PTUs and specify the model you wish to use the PTUs for.

Not all models have the PTU deployment option. Currently, most Azure OpenAI gpt models and Deepseek models can be deployed using PTUs.

Global PTUs

Global PTUs mean that you will be provisioned PTUs from any data center in the world. Once those are provisioned, it will remain in that region. It is the broadest form of allocation and has the lowest minimal number of PTUs you can reserve, which is 15.

Data Zone PTUs

There are currently two Data Zone PTUs - EU and US. This means that PTUs are only provisioned within any region in the EU or the USA, depending on which Data Zone you specify. For example, if you only want PTUs provisioned within the USA, then select US Data Zone. This is foreseeably the most common type of deployment because it is a balance between availability and region flexibility. Like Global PTUs, the minimum number of PTUs for most models in Data Zone is also 15.

Regional PTUs

Region PTUs are the most narrowly defined PTU deployment type. You are specifying a distinct region that you want PTUs in, with zero flexibility. So if you request for Regional PTUs and select East USA as the region, then the PTUs provisioned to you will be in East USA. The minimum number of PTUs for most models for Regional deployment is 50. There are a few models that may have a minimum of 25 PTUs (e.g., gpt-4.1 mini regional deployment).

In addition to the minimum number of PTUs, there is also the minimum incremental number of PTUs. This is the minimum number of PTUs you can add to your existing pool of PTUs should you require to scale up. These are generally in increments of 5 PTUs.

Figure 2-10 shows the minimum number of PTUs required by the latest Azure OpenAI models, and you can view the minimum number of PTUs and minimum increment for previous models at `https://learn.microsoft.com/en-us/azure/ai-foundry/openai/how-to/provisioned-throughput-onboarding?view=foundry-classic#previous-azure-openai-models`.

Latest Azure OpenAI models

ⓘ Note

gpt-4.1, gpt-4.1-mini and gpt-4.1-nano don't support long context (requests estimated at larger than 128k prompt tokens).

Expand table

Topic	gpt-5	gpt-5-mini	gpt-4.1	gpt-4.1-mini	gpt-4.1-nano	o3	o4-mini
Global & data zone provisioned minimum deployment	15	15	15	15	15	15	15
Global & data zone provisioned scale increment	5	5	5	5	5	5	5
Regional provisioned minimum deployment	50	25	50	25	25	50	25
Regional provisioned scale increment	50	25	50	25	25	50	25
Input TPM per PTU	4,750	23,750	3,000	14,900	59,400	3,000	5,400
Latency Target Value	99% > 50 Tokens Per Second*	99% > 80 Tokens Per Second*	99% > 80 Tokens Per Second*	99% > 90 Tokens Per Second*	99% > 100 Tokens Per Second*	99% > 80 Tokens Per Second*	99% > 90 Tokens Per Second*

* Calculated as p50 request latency on a per 5 minute basis.

Figure 2-10. *Minimum PTUs needed by LLM and by deployment type*

Benefits of Using PTUs

Instead of paying for the number of prompt and completion tokens being consumed, the PTU model is a monthly fixed cost for "unlimited" number of tokens. However, although it is unlimited, the maximum number of tokens that can be consumed is still constrained by the underlying physical infrastructure - compute, memory, storage, etc. In contrast, the PayGo model can potentially rack up a lot of tokens if you do not have a throttling or metering mechanism in place.

The benefits of using a PTU deployment model is predictable cost and performance. With some modeling, you will have a very good idea on what your service limits are. Performance is therefore also predictable. ***PTUs are recommended for enterprise deployments of LLM-enabled solutions.***

Knowing the peak requests per minute is an important metric because this gives you an idea how many users you can service simultaneously. We will discuss this in detail under the section titled "Peak users and TPM in PTU model" later in this chapter.

Performance and Service Limits

Performance and service limits are different for PTUs and PayGo, so we will discuss these separately. However, before doing so, we need to introduce two concepts - Tokens per minute (TPM) and Requests per minute (RPM).

Tokens per Minute (TPM) and Requests per Minute (RPM)

Tokens per minute (TPM) is the throughput measure of how many tokens from *all users* are being transacted each minute. Each user is likely consuming different number of tokens because no two conversations are likely to be the same.

Requests per minute is the total number of requests, which can be loosely interpreted as number of users utilizing the service each minute. We say "loosely interpreted" because a user may be invoking multiple agents that run parallel requests, or instead of a user, it may be a workflow that consists of multiple parallel requests. Therefore, keep this in mind because if you know your solution has a high tendency of running parallel requests with each user interaction, the number of actual users may be lower.

Figure 2-11 depicts a hypothetical scenario where capacity is represented as a pipe through which user requests, in the form of tokens, are being processed. In the figure, for a particular one-minute window, there are four requests. Therefore, the RPM = 4. These four requests/users have different prompt and completion lengths. As such, each user/request is consuming different number of tokens. Assume that if they are making a request during the same one-minute time window, the total number of tokens for the four requests is 9500. Therefore, the TPM = 9500.

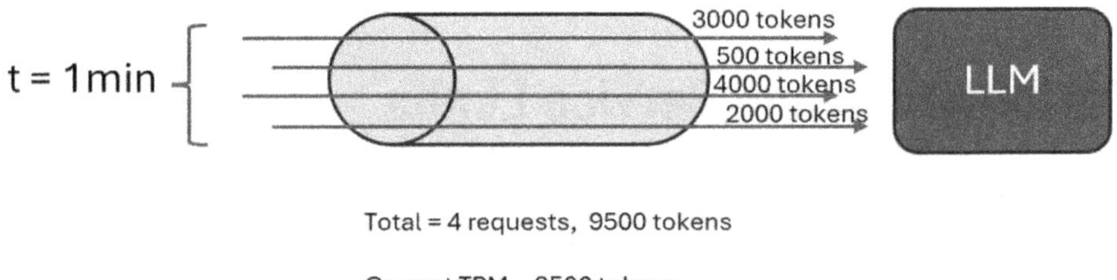

Figure 2-11. *Graphic depicting TPM and RPM*

Quotas and Service Limits (PayGo Only)

Now that we understand TPM and RPM, visit the Azure OpenAI in Microsoft Foundry Model quotas and limits page.[14]

[14]https://learn.microsoft.com/en-us/azure/ai-services/openai/quotas-limits

Azure OpenAI service limits are primarily by model, model version, deployment type, and region. The quota and limits page lists the limits for the PayGo deployment model. We will discuss PTU limits in the next section.

First, look for the LLM you are using for your product. For the sake of discussion, we will select the latest model, which is gpt-5.1 and locate it[15] in the Azure OpenAI in Microsoft Foundry Model quotas and limits page mentioned above.

As you can see from Figure 2-12, gpt-5.1 (and any LLM for that matter) has a service limit bound by requests per minute (RPM) *and* tokens per minute (TPM). Exceeding the RPM or TPM limits will result in a 429 response error from the service. These limits are higher for Enterprise and MCA-E[16] customers. Because there are more data centers that can be leveraged in a Global deployment versus Data Zone, it is not surprising to see higher RPM and TPM limits accordingly.

[15] `https://learn.microsoft.com/en-us/azure/ai-foundry/openai/quotas-limits?view=foundry-classic&tabs=REST#gpt-51-series`

[16] MCA-E stands for Microsoft Customer Agreement for Enterprise, which is the new Enterprise Agreement (EA). All EA customers will eventually be transitioned to the new MCA-E agreement.

GPT-5.1 series

Expand table

Model	Deployment Type	Default RPM	Default TPM	Enterprise and MCA-E RPM	Enterprise and MCA-E TPM
gpt-5.1	DataZoneStandard	3,000	300,000	30,000	3,000,000
gpt-5.1	GlobalStandard	10,000	1,000,000	100,000	10,000,000
gpt-5.1-chat	GlobalStandard	10,000	1,000,000	50,000	5,000,000
gpt-5.1-codex	GlobalStandard	1,000	1,000,000	10,000	10,000,000
gpt-5.1-codex-mini	GlobalStandard	1,000	1,000,000	10,000	10,000,000

Figure 2-12. *GPT-5.1 PayGo service limits by RPM and TPM*

Model-Specific Limits (Applies to PayGo and PTUs)

Next, look at the quotas and limits reference[17] and find the limit named "Maximum prompt tokens per request," as shown in Figure 2-13. Aside from RPM and TPM limits, there is a maximum token per request that a model can handle. This is ***model-specific*** and therefore applies to PayGo and PTUs.

[17] https://learn.microsoft.com/en-us/azure/ai-services/openai/quotas-limits#quotas-and-limits-reference

Limit Name	Limit Value
OpenAI resources per region per Azure subscription	30
Default DALL-E 2 quota limits	2 concurrent requests
Default DALL-E 3 quota limits	2 capacity units (6 requests per minute)
Maximum prompt tokens per request	Varies per model. For more information, see Azure OpenAI Service models
Max fine-tuned model deployments	5
Total number of training jobs per resource	100
Max simultaneous running training jobs per resource	1
Max training jobs queued	20
Max Files per resource (fine-tuning)	30
Total size of all files per resource (fine-tuning)	1 GB
Max training job time (job will fail if exceeded)	720 hours
Max training job size (tokens in training file) x (# of epochs)	2 Billion
Max size of all files per upload (Azure OpenAI on your data)	16 MB
Max number or inputs in array with `/embeddings`	2048
Max number of `/chat/completions` messages	2048
Max number of `/chat/completions` functions	128
Max number of `/chat completions` tools	128
Maximum number of Provisioned throughput units per deployment	100,000
Max files per Assistant/thread	20
Max file size for Assistants & fine-tuning	512 MB
Assistants token limit	2,000,000 token limit

Figure 2-13. *Token limits of the model (context window)*

This is the maximum number of tokens that the model can process per request, and we referred to it as the context window size earlier in this chapter. Context window = Prompt Tokens + Completion Tokens. Click on the Azure OpenAI Service models link[18] in the Limit Value column and locate your model.

Find the section that describes the model availability and region that you will be using. For example, if you looked at gpt-5.1, you will see that the model is available in the US East and Sweden regions, as shown in Figure 2-14. Furthermore, you will find the context window size for the model, in this case, it is 400,000 tokens. The 400,000 tokens are further categorized by prompt tokens versus completion tokens. These token limits are model-specific, therefore, you need ensure that your prompts fall within the input token limit. As for completion (output) tokens, the response will automatically be fitted into this limit.

[18] https://learn.microsoft.com/en-us/azure/ai-foundry/foundry-models/concepts/models-sold-directly-by-azure?view=foundry-classic&tabs=global-standard-aoai%2Cstandard-chat-completions%2Cglobal-standard&pivots=azure-openai#gpt-51

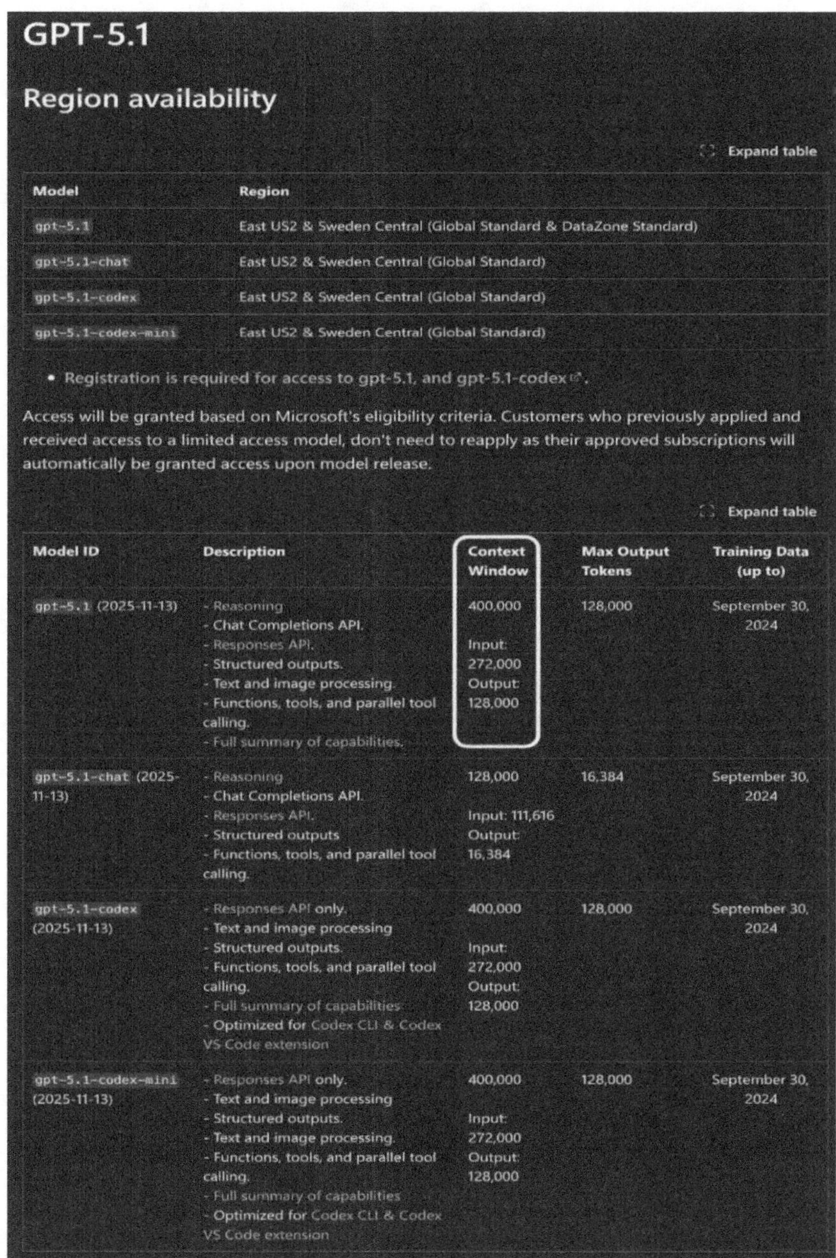

GPT-5.1

Region availability

Expand table

Model	Region
gpt-5.1	East US2 & Sweden Central (Global Standard & DataZone Standard)
gpt-5.1-chat	East US2 & Sweden Central (Global Standard)
gpt-5.1-codex	East US2 & Sweden Central (Global Standard)
gpt-5.1-codex-mini	East US2 & Sweden Central (Global Standard)

- Registration is required for access to gpt-5.1, and gpt-5.1-codex.

Access will be granted based on Microsoft's eligibility criteria. Customers who previously applied and received access to a limited access model, don't need to reapply as their approved subscriptions will automatically be granted access upon model release.

Expand table

Model ID	Description	Context Window	Max Output Tokens	Training Data (up to)
gpt-5.1 (2025-11-13)	- Reasoning - Chat Completions API. - Responses API. - Structured outputs. - Text and image processing. - Functions, tools, and parallel tool calling. - Full summary of capabilities.	400,000 Input: 272,000 Output: 128,000	128,000	September 30, 2024
gpt-5.1-chat (2025-11-13)	- Reasoning - Chat Completions API. - Responses API. - Structured outputs - Functions, tools, and parallel tool calling.	128,000 Input: 111,616 Output: 16,384	16,384	September 30, 2024
gpt-5.1-codex (2025-11-13)	- Responses API only. - Text and image processing - Structured outputs. - Functions, tools, and parallel tool calling. - Full summary of capabilities - Optimized for Codex CLI & Codex VS Code extension	400,000 Input: 272,000 Output: 128,000	128,000	September 30, 2024
gpt-5.1-codex-mini (2025-11-13)	- Responses API only. - Text and image processing - Structured outputs. - Text and image processing. - Functions, tools, and parallel tool calling. - Full summary of capabilities - Optimized for Codex CLI & Codex VS Code extension	400,000 Input: 272,000 Output: 128,000	128,000	September 30, 2024

***Figure 2-14.** gpt-5.1 region availability and context window size*

However, consider this scenario: Your solution implements a traditional Retrieval Augmented Generation (RAG) architecture where the applicable source content is large. There may be a risk where the response may become too generalized or, in some instances, truncated or seem disjointed because the LLM is trying to fit too much into a response. This is a great example where using multiple agents and making each agent and their respective prompt and source knowledge smaller and more targeted would improve the quality of the response.

For comparison, the context window for gpt-4o is 1,047,576 tokens, as shown in Figure 2-15. This is the result of the race to a million tokens that took over headlines for several months in the summer of 2025. But large context windows are not just for bragging rights. This is a key milestone[19] for modern agentic workloads.

[19] A good discussion regarding the significance of 1M tokens – `https://therelaymag.com/1m-token-context-race-long-context-agents`

Model ID	Description	Context window	Max output tokens	Training data (up to)
gpt-4.1 (2025-04-14)	- Text and image input - Text output - Chat completions API - Responses API - Streaming - Function calling - Structured outputs (chat completions)	- 1,047,576 - 128,000 (provisioned managed deployments) - 300,000 (batch deployments)	32,768	May 31, 2024
gpt-4.1-nano (2025-04-14)	- Text and image input - Text output - Chat completions API - Responses API - Streaming - Function calling - Structured outputs (chat completions)	- 1,047,576 - 128,000 (provisioned managed deployments) - 300,000 (batch deployments)	32,768	May 31, 2024
gpt-4.1-mini (2025-04-14)	- Text and image input - Text output - Chat completions API - Responses API - Streaming - Function calling - Structured outputs (chat completions)	- 1,047,576 - 128,000 (provisioned managed deployments) - 300,000 (batch deployments)	32,768	May 31, 2024

Figure 2-15. *Context window of gpt-4.1*

To summarize our discussion thus far, if we were going to deploy a gpt-5.1 AI-driven solution in eastern United States using PayGo, we must

- Confirm that the model is available in the east region (in this case it is available in East US2).
- Ensure we prompt engineer the solution such that prompt tokens do not exceed 272,000 tokens.
- Completion tokens, observed during testing, are generally less than 128,000 tokens.

- The prompt tokens from *all* requests must not add up to more than 300,000 tokens per minute (TPM).
- The number of users/requests per minute (RPM) must not exceed 3,000 or a 429 error will occur.

Planning PTU Capacity

If you need a more consistent and predictable performance coupled with a fixed cost, all of which are important requirements if you are going to market with your AI-driven product or solution, then the PTU model is the recommended implementation type. Remember, the PTU model is based on provisioned compute so each PTU has a known capacity. Refer again to Figure 2-10[20] and this time, locate "input TPM per PTU." For gpt-5, we see that the value is 4,750 tokens.

However, remember from our discussion above that there are minimums for PTUs (and increments). For regional PTUs, it is 50 and for Data Zone or Global provisioned PTUs, the minimum is 15. Therefore, depending on the deployment type, the minimum TPM is 237,500 tokens and 71,250 tokens, respectively. Table 2-5 summarizes and compares the TPM between gpt-5 and gpt-4.1, depending on the number of PTUs provisioned.

[20] Also at `https://learn.microsoft.com/en-us/azure/ai-foundry/openai/how-to/provisioned-throughput-onboarding?view=foundry-classic#latest-azure-openai-models`

Table 2-5. TPMs driven by PTU deployment

Model	TPM per PTU	Minimum PTUs	TPM(TPM per PTU x Minimum PTUs)	Incremental PTUs	TPM increase per increment (Incremental PTU x TPM per PTU)
gpt-5	4,750	15 (Global/ Data Zone)50 (Regional)	41,250237,500	5 (Global/ Data Zone)50 (Regional)	23,420237,500
gpt-4.1	3,000	15 (Global/ Data Zone)50 (Regional)	45,000150,000	5 (Global/ Data Zone)50 (Regional)	15,000150,000

During experimentation while building your AI product, you need to have a baseline average of the prompt, completions, and total tokens per transaction. Then it will be a simple extrapolation of

- Given the number of anticipated users/requests, the number of PTUs you will need and/or
- With the minimum number of initial PTUs (15 or 50 depending on deployment), how many users/requests can you service

Note that for PTUs, there is no limit on RPMs, so TPMs are the only throttle. This makes sense because *all* the PTUs belong to you so you can/should maximize their utilization, whereas in the PayGo model where you can consume as many tokens as possible, notwithstanding the model-specific token-per-request limit, there needs to be a secondary throttling mechanism, hence the need for RPM limits.

If you do not wish to do the math, there is a PTU Capacity calculator in Foundry.[21] If you are already using Foundry, you can access the calculator, as shown in Figure 2-16. But do not worry if you have not started experimenting with Azure Foundry yet because we will revisit this again in detail in Chapter 3.

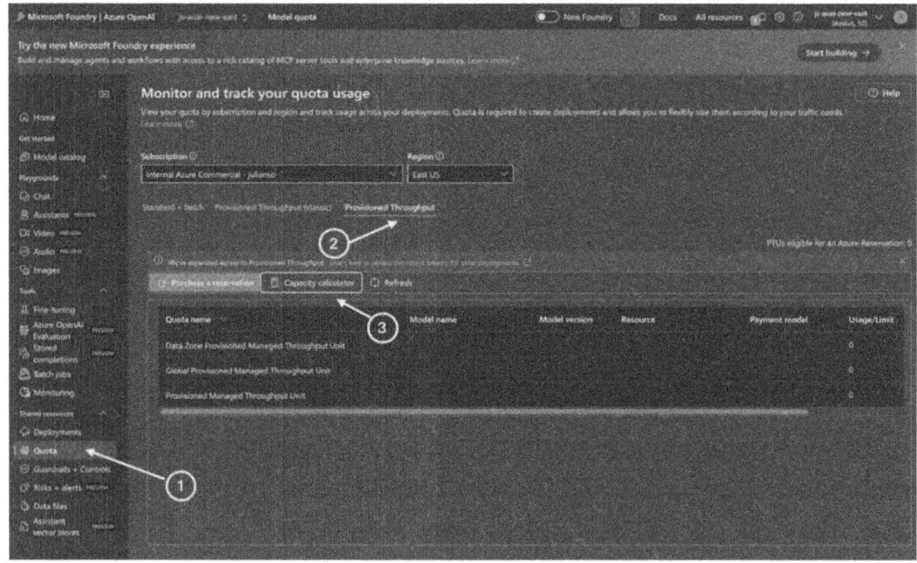

Figure 2-16. *Accessing the PTU capacity calculator in Azure Foundry*

The PTU calculator in Foundry is quite self-explanatory. It is loaded with estimated token values for different types of workloads (RAG chat, Basic Chat, Summarization, Classification), as shown in Figure 2-17.

[21] At the time of writing, the new Foundry User Interface announced at Ignite. microsoft.com is currently under preview and the calculator is NOT in the preview UI.

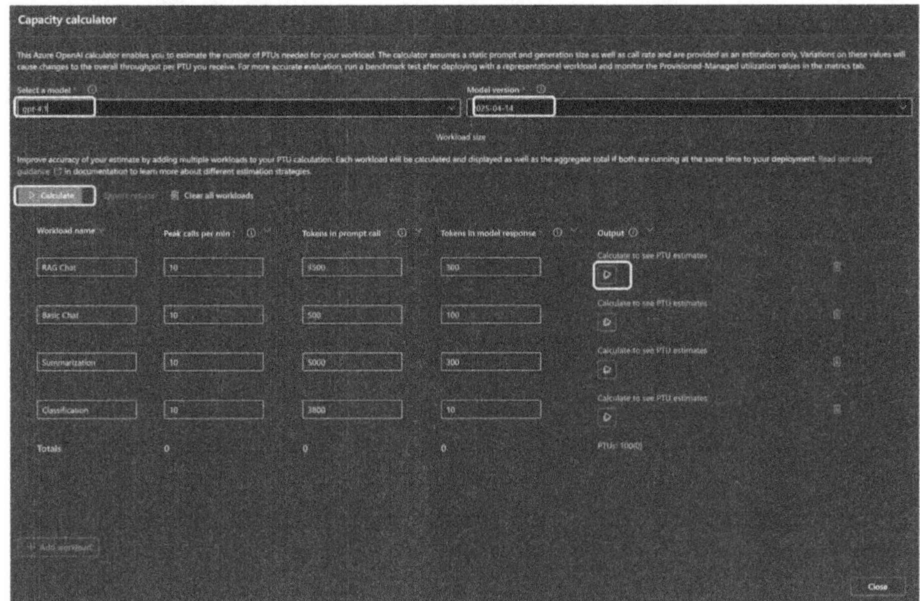

***Figure 2-17.** PTU calculator in Azure Foundry*

Choose the model and version, then either click on ▷ Calculate to calculate all the four workloads or the individual ▷ buttons to calculate the number of PTUs needed only for one workload. You can change the number of peak users.

The number of tokens populated in Foundry are based on generic estimates and we highly recommend using *actual numbers* derived during experimentation. Also note that these are for single transactions and likely to be much too low for multi-agentic workloads.

When you surpass the TPM limit, Azure will return a 429 error, as shown in Figure 2-18. We will look at ways to handle this error in later chapters.

***Figure 2-18.** 429 error when TPM limit is exceeded*

Non-linear Cost Modeling in Multi-agentic Scenarios

Understanding the dynamics of AI adoption is critical not only for forecasting market penetration but also for optimizing deployment strategies, licensing models, and infrastructure provisioning. These are all essential for the successful deployment of your AI product and something you will need to include in your business plan. However, up until this point, aside from understanding concepts like TPMs, RPMS, PTUs, and tokens, cost models have traditionally been linear in nature. This approach fails to capture the complex, nonlinear nature of user uptake, which is often influenced by network effects, saturation thresholds, external campaigns, and churn. In this section, we will explore a mathematical framework to simulate the adoption trajectory of an AI solution. By leveraging the logistic growth model and extending it with token and compute consumption, we aim to provide a data-driven and mathematical approach to making informed decisions regarding resource allocation and pricing strategies.

Methods

We begin by introducing the canonical logistic growth equation and then progressively extend it to reflect the impact on tokens and/or compute. The resulting approach serves as a reusable template for forecasting, scenario planning, and strategic rollout of AI services in enterprise and consumer contexts.

When extending the analysis to incorporate token consumption, we will take token caching into account so we take advantage of the new token optimization capabilities of newer models.

Logistic Growth Model

We propose a growth model that reflects user adoption over time. Furthermore, the model needs to capture the fundamental dynamics of user adoption and is expressed as follows:

Let

- $A(t)$ be the number of active users at time t
- K be the carrying capacity, representing the maximum potential user base
- r be the intrinsic growth rate, reflecting the natural adoption speed

Then:

$$\frac{dA}{dt} = rA\left(1 - \frac{A}{K}\right) \tag{1}$$

Assumptions and Limitations

To avoid an overly complex model involving a higher order differential equation, we make the following assumptions:

- We will use a Heuristic model for estimating Cached Input Tokens (for GPT-4.1 and above).
- We will base usage scenarios on multi-agent environments using A2A and/or MCP as communication protocols because this will
    - More accurately reflect the direction of agentic implementations
    - Reflect a more realistic scenario for enterprise implementations of AI services
- We will use data from AI adoption, not just LLM based, to model the parameters K and r.

Calculating Cached Input Tokens

Estimating reuse patterns require observation of historic data from user interaction. However, this data may not be available and/or practical to analyze. As such, we will use a heuristic model to estimate the number of cached input tokens. The Heuristic model for estimating cached input tokens is as follows:

- P = average number of prompt tokens
- C = average number of completion tokens
- T_{cached} = average number of cached input tokens

Caching only comes into effect when

$$P \geqslant 1024$$

If not, then

$$T_{cached} = 0$$

Furthermore, the reuse rate of tokens, known as the reuse ratio, R is dependent on the system's configuration:

- Static System prompt + reusued instructions: R = 0.8
- Semi-dynamic prompts (e.g., templated prompts): R = 0.5
- Highly dynamic prompts: R = 0.3

Using the values of P, C, and R, we can estimate the average number of cached input tokens, T_{cached} as follows:

Caching occurs at 128-token blocks B beyond 1,024 tokens.

Thus

$$T_{cached} = \begin{cases} 0, & \text{if } P < T_{min} \\ B \cdot \left\lfloor \frac{\min(R \cdot P, P)}{B} \right\rfloor, & \text{if } P \geqslant T_{min} \end{cases} \quad (2)$$

Expected Adoption Rate

The expected adoption rate from this model is one that describes an initial slower start, followed by exponential adoption before reaching equilibrium, as depicted in Figure 2-19. The factors contributing to this characteristic of equilibrium are

- **Retraction from initial hype**: As the novelty of the new service wears off, there may be an over-correction in adoption rates that led to the peak.

- **Recovery**: A recovery due to re-engagement and/or late adopters.
- **Stabilization**: The final plateau representing a stable core of user base.

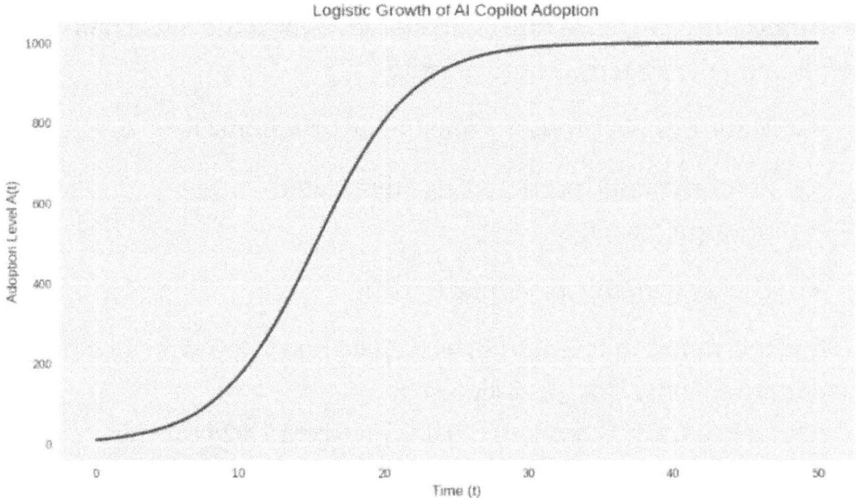

Figure 2-19. *Non-linear ideal adoption rate*

However, in reality, we expect a deviation from this ideal model at the equilibrium (maximum adoption) phase, which, starting near saturation, dipping due to early churn or fatigue, then rising again and stabilizing. It mimics a damped sinusoidal pattern, as depicted by Figure 2-20.

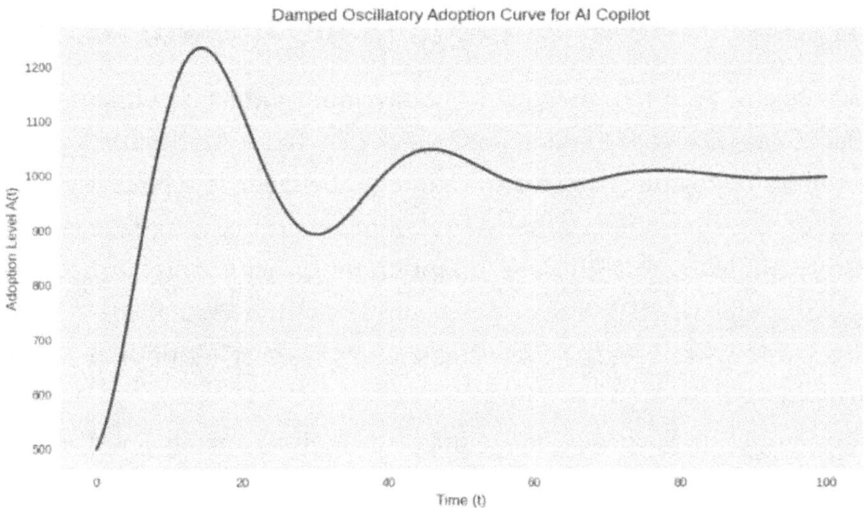

Figure 2-20. *Non-linear adoption rate (predicted actual)*

Model Application

Let us now apply the model to a hypothetical AI adoption scenario, demonstrating its utility in forecasting user growth and compute/token requirements. Consider a new AI product aimed at software developers, with a total target of 350,000 users. We will use our model to project user growth over the first year, taking into account the factors identified in our analysis.

As mentioned in our assumptions, we will benchmark our model using multi-agent environments with A2A and/or MCP communication protocols. The observed token usage per interaction in a multi-agent, multi-protocol scenario was shown in Table 2-3.

Parameterization of the Logistic Growth Model

To simulate AI adoption dynamics, we base our model on publicly available data from the Federal Reserve's FEDS Notes (February 2025). This report aggregates 16 surveys conducted between late 2023 and mid-2024, offering a comprehensive view of generative AI uptake across US firms and workers. Firm-level adoption rates vary widely, with the US Census Bureau's BTOS survey reporting less than 5% of firms using AI in the prior two weeks, while other sources suggest adoption levels as high as 40%.

For modeling purposes, we define the carrying capacity K as the maximum potential user base. In our primary simulation, we set K = 350,000 to reflect a large-scale deployment scenario. The initial adoption level A0 is set at 5% of K, yielding A0 = 17,500 users.

This conservative estimate is grounded in the lower bound of observed adoption from the BTOS survey and ensures the model captures the steep acceleration phase typical of early-stage technology uptake.

The adoption level after six months is taken as 40% of K, consistent with upper-bound estimates from aggregated survey data, giving A[6] = 140,000 users. To estimate the intrinsic growth rate r, we derive the closed-form solution of Equation 1.

$$A(t) = \frac{K}{1 + \left(\frac{K - A_0}{A_0}\right) e^{-rt}} \qquad (3)$$

Given

A0 = 17,500 (initial adoption)

A(6) = 140,000 (adoption after 6 months)

K = 350,000 (carrying capacity)

Solving numerically for r using Equation 3, we obtain

$r \approx 0.4232$ per month

For comparison, if we instead use the BTOS sample size as the carrying capacity - approximately 1.2 million firms[22] - the same adoption trajectory yields a slightly higher growth rate of $r \approx 0.446$. While both values are close, we adopt the lower r value in our model to reflect a more conservative adoption rate. This choice allows for cautious forecasting and avoids overestimating infrastructure demand in early rollout phases.

This model provides a reusable framework for forecasting AI service demand, correlating user growth by month modeled using the BTOS survey data, as shown in Figure 2-21.

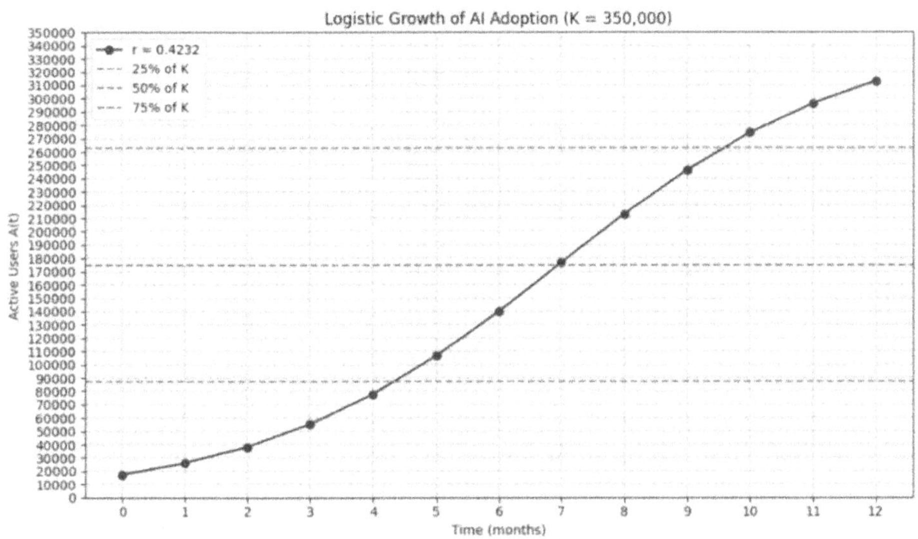

***Figure 2-21.** Adoption Rate for k=350,000*

[22] While the US Census Bureau's BTOS survey defines the total population K as the number of employer firms (approximately 1,200,000), our model uses K = 350,000 to represent the number of individual users or seats within a specific deployment context. Although these definitions differ - firm-level versus user-level - the logistic growth structure remains valid, as the model is scale-invariant under consistent adoption ratios. This distinction does not materially affect the shape or interpretability of the adoption curve, provided that A0 and A(t) are defined proportionally within the chosen reference frame.

Express Users As a Function of Time

Table 2-6 presents the monthly adoption levels and corresponding daily average user counts derived from the closed-form logistic growth model with $K = 350{,}000$ and $r \approx 0.4232$.

Table 2-6. *Number of users by month*

Month	Number of users $A(t)$
0	17,500
1	26,033
2	38,248
3	55,218
4	77,837
5	106,377
6	140,000
7	176,548
8	212,962
9	246,225
10	274,285
11	296,408
12	312,941

This shows, for example, that on initial launch to 350,000 potential users, we should expect that potentially17,500 users will access our service per day. By month 6, this increases to 140,000 users, and by month 12, we reach approximately 312,941 users.

Putting It All Together

As an example, let us use the token estimates from Table 2-3 and average the prompt tokens for our multi-agentic AI-enabled product to be 10,000 tokens, and completion tokens to be 2,000 tokens. Now let us also assume we will be using the newer models that have token caching capabilities and that we are using a semi-dynamic prompt, so R=0.5 for Equation 3.

This will set us up as follows:

- Prompt tokens (minus cached tokens) = 5,000 per transaction
- T_{cached} = 5,000
- Completion tokens = 2,000

At launch to 350,000 users, we should be ready to at least be able to service 17,500 users. If we spread those users across an 8-hour work day, for example, then that will be 2,188 users per hour, or 36 users per minute, which is our TPM. Therefore

36 users x 5,000 prompt tokens = 180,000 prompt tokens

36 users x 5,000 cached tokens = 180,000 cached tokens

36 users x. 2,000 completion tokens = 72,000 completion tokens

From Table 2-5, if we were to select gpt-4.1 as our model of choice in order to service 17,500 users with the above token consumption calculation, we would need approximately 60–120 PTUs (depending on the efficiency of T_{cached}).

Using the Azure Online Calculator, we can price out 60 PTUs in Data Zone, as shown in Figure 2-22.

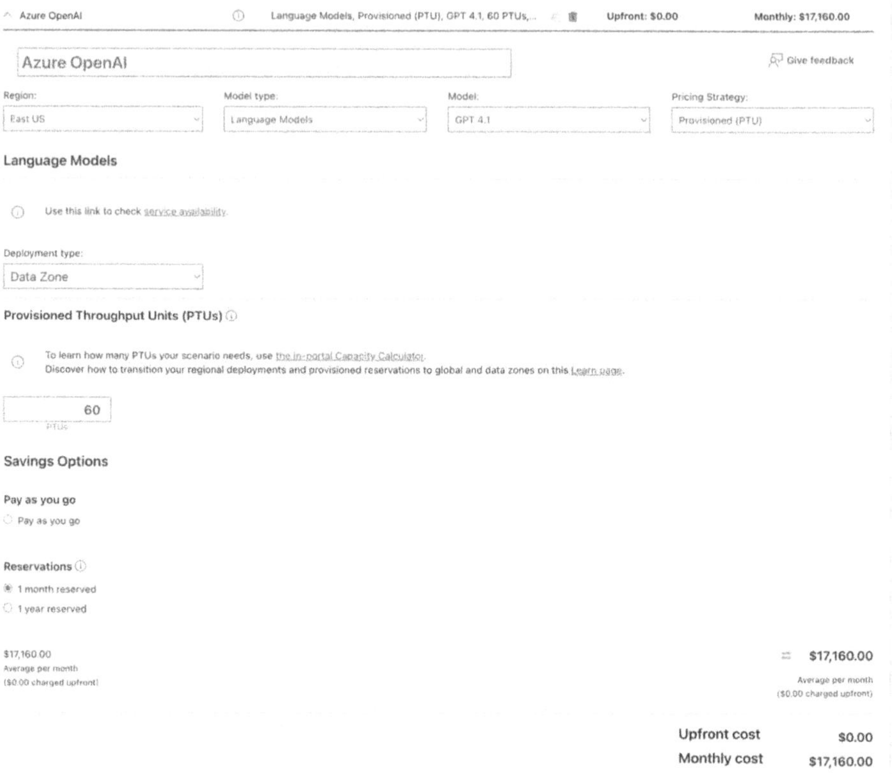

Figure 2-22. Pricing out 60 PTUs with the Azure Online Calculator

Let us compare PTUs to PayGo with this same scenario. Once again, we know that the potential at launch is 17,500 users/requests per day. If we only consider work days in a month to be approximately 21 days, then there are 367,500 requests per month.

367,500 x 5,000 prompt tokens = 1,837,500,000 prompt tokens

367,500 x 5,000 cached tokens = 1,837,500,000 cached tokens

367,500 x 2,000 completion tokens = 735,000,000 completion tokens

Using the Azure Online Calculator and inputting the tokens above, we get the cost as shown in

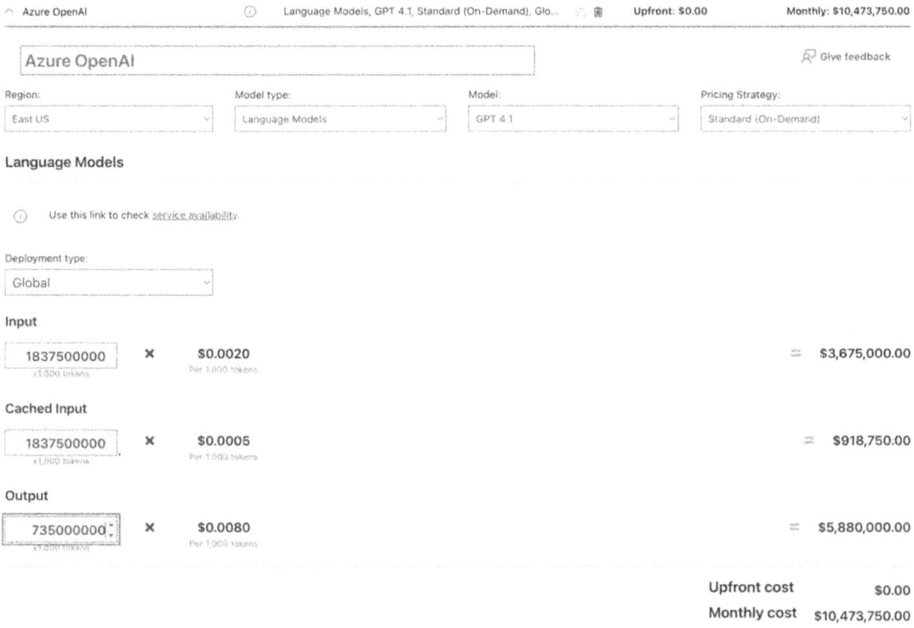

***Figure 2-23.** Pricing based on token utilization (PayGo) instead of PTUs (Figure 2-22 above)*

When PayGo Seems Less Expensive

Like our example, as you model your cost, you may run into this same scenario where PayGo seems to be less expensive. However, there are factors you want to consider:

- If you know that the starting PTUs are the absolute minimum you need and it will likely grow from that point onward, or remain the same, then select the "1 year reserved" option. This option will provide you with more savings and will bring down your monthly cost. Even with a 1 year reservation, you still pay monthly.

- PTUs are predictable in performance and in cost. There is no risk like the PayGo model where there is no upper limit on utilization. If it turned out that there is a wide variance between your estimate and the actuals, then your cost will go up.

Summary

In the chapter, we went into great detail on how LLMs are billed. We first introduced tokens, which is the transactional unit of generative AI. Then we introduced TPMs and RPMs, which are performance limits at the model level and at the service level. Next, we looked at two different types of cost modeling – linear and non-linear. Along the way, we learned about new capabilities such as caching input tokens and what impacts multi-agentic solutions have on token consumption.

Lastly, we brought it all together into a cost model by exploring a hypothetical scenario of deploying an AI product to 350,000 users and how to estimate adoption rate, and incorporating that back into our cost model.

CHAPTER 3

Building and Prototyping

Introduction

This chapter moves from opportunity selection and pricing into implementation. The objective is to help Microsoft ISV Partners produce a working AI agent prototype quickly, using Azure AI Foundry (new) end to end, while preserving a path to production. Chapter 1 framed productization opportunities. Chapter 2 sets cost and pricing constraints. This chapter turns those decisions into a prototype workflow you can run, measure, and iterate.

What This Chapter Covers

You will define a narrow prototype scope, create an Azure AI Foundry project, deploy a model, create and test an agent in the Azure AI Foundry portal, and then validate the same project and deployments from code using the Azure AI Foundry projects API. You will add the minimum set of tools needed for the task, run evaluations using Azure AI Foundry

J. Soh et al., *Building and Distributing Agentic AI Solutions*,
https://doi.org/10.1007/979-8-8688-2586-6_3

evaluators and agent evaluators, apply responsible AI controls that are hard to retrofit later, and package the prototype for handoff. The intent is a single coherent toolchain and a repeatable set of steps.[1]

A prototype is not only a technical exercise. It is the first validation of your cost model. Make the model choice explicit and treat it as provisional. Set limits on prompt size, tool usage, response length, and concurrency. If you ignore these constraints during prototyping, a successful demo can still fail as a product because unit economics do not hold up in real-world usage.

Microsoft Azure AI Foundry is designed to build, manage, and operate multi-agent applications in a project-centric experience. Azure AI Foundry projects group your models, agents, tools, evaluations, and operational signals so that prototype work can carry forward into later hardening work. Microsoft Azure AI Foundry is positioned as a unified platform for AI application development and operations, and the Azure AI Foundry Agent Service documentation describes a platform that combines models, tools, frameworks, and governance into a single system for building agents, with Azure AI Foundry Agent Service at the center for operating agents across development, deployment, and production. That platform framing matters for ISVs because it allows prototype work to begin in the same ecosystem that later supports evaluation, monitoring, and hosted runtime paths.

This chapter also aligns with the staged model used by Microsoft in the Agent Framework documentation. The Agent Framework tutorials are organized as a progression that starts with a first agent and then adds tools, multi-turn conversation, memory, workflows, and hosting. This progression is a good fit for ISV prototyping because it encourages teams to validate behavior before expanding capabilities. It also reinforces an important design discipline that runs through this chapter. Early success should come from reliably solving a narrow task, not from assembling the largest possible agent stack.

[1] https://learn.microsoft.com/en-us/azure/foundry/what-is-foundry

This chapter covers a practical sequence that works for most ISV teams. You begin by defining the scope of the first prototype in product terms, not model terms. You then set up an Azure AI Foundry project, deploy a model, and use the playground to validate instruction style and a small prompt set before writing application code. Next, you build a minimal code prototype using the Microsoft Agent Framework or an Azure AI Foundry project client pattern, depending on the task shape and the level of control you need in the first implementation. From there, you test tool behavior, turn prompt experimentation into repeatable runs using scripts or prompt flow, define evaluation before feature expansion, and add responsible AI controls that are difficult to retrofit later. Finally, you package the prototype for handoff so another engineer can run it, test it, and extend it without recreating your environment by trial and error. This sequence is intended to produce a prototype useful to engineering, product, and commercial teams simultaneously.

The chapter also assumes that prototyping is the first real test of the business case, not a separate technical exercise. Chapter 2 emphasized the cost drivers that shape AI product economics, including model choice, token usage, throughput, and usage patterns. Those factors do not become important later. They become visible during prototyping. A prototype that ignores cost and usage constraints can produce a convincing demo yet fail as a product because its unit economics do not hold under realistic workloads. This is why the workflow in this chapter repeatedly returns to constraints. Model selection should be explicit. Prompt size should be controlled. Tool usage should be tied to the product task rather than demo novelty. Response length should be bounded. Concurrency assumptions should be stated, even if they are provisional.

At this stage, the best way to preserve both technical focus and economic realism is to define a single primary task and a single target user role. A support triage agent for operations analysts is a good prototype shape. A claims document summarization agent for case workers is another. A broad "general assistant for the whole business" is usually a poor prototype shape because it makes success hard to define and cost hard to estimate. A narrow prototype gives the team something more valuable than a broad promise. It gives them a measurable answer to one real workflow question, with evidence on quality, latency, cost, and risk. That evidence allows the next product investment decision to be made on facts rather than enthusiasm.

There is also a process reason for using this approach. In many ISV teams, product managers, engineers, architects, and customer-facing teams all touch the prototype in different ways. The product team needs a way to validate the user task and expected outcome. Engineering needs a reproducible code path and baseline tests. Architecture and security need evidence on tool use, risk controls, and logging. Commercial teams need confidence that the prototype can support pricing and positioning discussions without overpromising. A prototype built in the sequence described in this chapter produces artifacts for all those audiences. It produces prompt and instruction baselines, a minimal runnable code implementation, tool behavior evidence, evaluation results, and a handoff package. That is why this chapter is not only a build chapter. It is the chapter where the first cross-functional evidence base is created.

You should also read this chapter with one boundary in mind. The objective here is not to decide the final architecture for a multi-agent production system. The objective is to establish a stable, measurable baseline to support subsequent design work. By the end of this chapter, the target outcome is a useful, measurable, and reproducible prototype. It should be useful because it solves a real task for a specific user role with credible quality. It should be measurable because the team has defined a prompt set, evaluation criteria, and baseline results before feature expansion.

Step 1. Create the Project and Deploy a Model

Prerequisites[2]

Prerequisites [2]

TECH REVIEW: Formatting: The prerequisite items below are currently styled as Heading 2 paragraphs with manual bullet symbols. Convert them to a normal bulleted list (and nested bullets where needed) so document structure/TOC isn't polluted with non-headings.

- An Azure account with an active subscription. If you don't have one, create a free Azure account, which includes a free trial subscription.
- If you're creating the project for yourself:
  - Access to a role that allows you to create an Azure AI Foundry resource, such as Azure AI Account Owner or Azure AI Owner on the subscription or resource group. For more information about permissions, see Role-based access control for Microsoft Foundry.
- If you're creating the project for a team:
  - Access to a role that allows you to complete role assignments, such as Owner. For more information about permissions, see Role-based access control for Microsoft Foundry.
- A list of user email addresses or Microsoft Entra security group IDs for team members who need access.

[2] https://learn.microsoft.com/en-us/azure/foundry/tutorials/quickstart-create-foundry-resources?tabs=portal#prerequisites

Use the Azure AI Foundry quickstart for setting up resources as the source of truth for the current sequence. In the new Azure AI Foundry experience, you create an Azure AI Foundry resource and an Azure AI Foundry project, deploy a model, and then share the project endpoint and deployment name with the team. The quickstart supports both portal and Azure CLI paths.

The CLI path is useful for repeatability because it makes the project and deployment steps explicit in code, including the flag that enables project management on the Azure AI Foundry resource. The allow-project-management flag enables project creation within the resource.

Start this step in Microsoft Azure AI Foundry with a single project, a single model deployment, and a narrow goal. The point is not to build the application yet. The point is to create a controlled place where product, engineering, and business stakeholders can test whether the proposed agent behavior is worth coding. Microsoft describes Azure AI Foundry as a unified Azure platform for agents, models, and tools with built-in enterprise capabilities such as tracing, monitoring, and evaluation, so the same environment used for prototyping can carry forward into later hardening work.

Create a project

Create a Foundry project to organize your work. The project contains models, agents, and other resources your team uses.

Azure CLI | Foundry portal

1. Go to Microsoft Foundry.
2. Sign in with your Azure account.
3. Select the project name in the upper-left corner, and then select **Create new project**.
4. Enter a project name, such as `my-foundry-project`.
5. Select **Advanced options** to configure the resource group and location:
   - **Resource group**: Create a new resource group or select an existing one. If you create a new resource group, you can more easily manage the project and all its resources together.
   - **Location**: Select the region closest to your team.
6. Select **Create project**.

   Wait for the project to be created. When the project overview page appears, your project is ready.

Figure 3-1. *Create a project in Azure AI Foundry portal as shown in Figure 3-1*

Create and deploy the first model as a single deployment inside the project. For the first prototype, choose any available model, document the selection, and treat it as provisional. Do not optimize for the "best" model in the abstract. Choose the model that is sufficient to validate the workflow and produce a baseline for cost, latency, and quality. Treat naming as part of the prototyping discipline. Your deployment name becomes the stable identifier used by code examples and evaluation runs. Use a name that reflects purpose and version rather than a default label. Also, record region- and capacity-specific assumptions early, as quota and throughput are enforced per model deployment and region and may differ by model family. Prototype instability is often caused by quota assumptions and environmental mismatches rather than by prompt quality, hence always make sure to confirm from Azure AI foundry portal.

Step 2. Create and Test an Agent in the Azure AI Foundry Portal

In Azure AI Foundry, create your first agent in the same project where you deployed the model. An agent is the simplest way to make your prototype repeatable because it lets you define core behavior once and reuse it across tests. Microsoft's Azure AI Foundry quickstart[3] helps create instructions used in every call, and it also shows the end-to-end path of chatting with a model, creating an agent with instructions, and validating multi-turn behavior.[4]

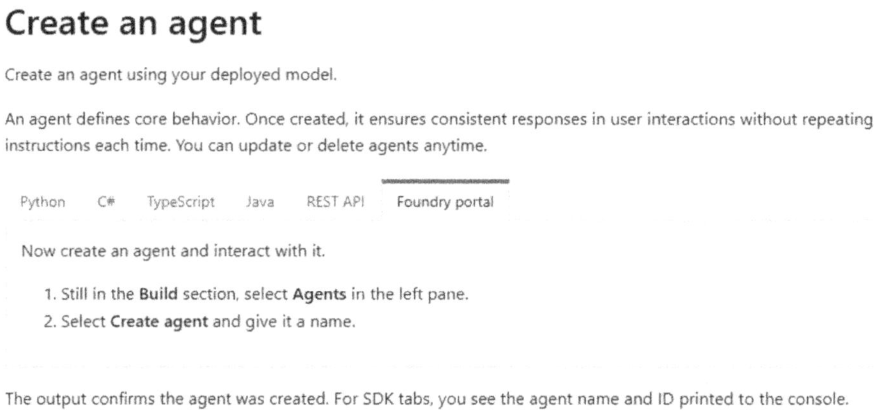

Create an agent

Create an agent using your deployed model.

An agent defines core behavior. Once created, it ensures consistent responses in user interactions without repeating instructions each time. You can update or delete agents anytime.

Python C# TypeScript Java REST API Foundry portal

Now create an agent and interact with it.

1. Still in the **Build** section, select **Agents** in the left pane.
2. Select **Create agent** and give it a name.

The output confirms the agent was created. For SDK tabs, you see the agent name and ID printed to the console.

Figure 3-2. *Create an Agent in Azure AI Foundry portal*

In the Azure AI Foundry portal flow described in the quickstart, you stay in the Build section, select Agents from the left navigation, then select Create agent and provide a name. Name the agent as if it will survive beyond the first demo. Treat the agent name as a stable identifier and plan to revise behavior through versions rather than renaming the agent

[3] https://learn.microsoft.com/en-us/azure/foundry/quickstarts/quickstarts

[4] https://learn.microsoft.com/en-us/azure/foundry/quickstarts/get-started-code?tabs=python

repeatedly. The quickstart uses an environment variable like AGENT_NAME="MyAgent" and then references that name when it chats with the agent. A stable name makes later steps easier because you can keep the integration constant while you improve instructions and tools. Azure AI foundry portal also provides Agent version and it's up to developers to ensure correct version in the code.

Keep the first agent simple on purpose. At this stage, you are proving that the single task you defined can be completed reliably, not proving that you can assemble every agent feature. Use one short instruction set that covers role, boundaries, and expected output format. The instructions should read like a product requirement, not like a long policy memo. The quickstart uses an intentionally simple instruction string to show the pattern, which is a good reminder that clarity matters more than length early on.

Write the instruction so it supports the evaluation you will do in later steps. If the prototype success measure includes format compliance, specify the format now. If the prototype success measure includes task completion, specify what "done" means. If the prototype has boundaries, state them plainly. A short instruction that is easy to review line by line is also easier to audit and iterate. When stakeholders disagree about behavior, the best place to resolve the disagreement is in the instructions and test set, not in a larger codebase.

After you create the agent, validate multi-turn behavior in the same project rather than treating it as a later feature. The quickstart includes a "Chat with an agent" section that demonstrates multi-turn continuity by creating a conversation and then making multiple calls that reuse the same conversation context. In the portal, you should mimic the same concept. Run an initial prompt that exercises the core task, then follow with a prompt that depends on the previous turn. Your goal is to confirm that the agent behaves consistently across turns and does not drift from the instruction when context accumulates.

Be deliberate about what you are testing in the portal. The portal is the right place to validate that the agent's baseline instruction produces acceptable results without extra code and without hidden local configuration. It is also the right place to validate that your prompt set is realistic. If the agent looks good only when you phrase the question in one particular way, that is a signal that the instruction and prompt contract are still unstable. Tighten the instruction, adjust the prompt set, and retest until the team can agree that the behavior is acceptable for the bounded task.

A practical way to keep portal testing honest is to treat the prompt set as a shared artifact rather than a live improvisation. Use the same small prompt set you set in Step 1 and rerun it after each instruction change. This prevents the prototype from turning into a performance where the prompt is quietly adjusted to fit the last response. It also makes later evaluation easier because you already have a fixed baseline set of prompts that the agent can pass before you add tools, memory, or broader scope.

When portal tests are stable, capture the agent definition as part of your prototype record. In Azure AI Foundry, agent behavior is defined by its instructions and model choice. The quickstart emphasizes that you can update or delete agents, which implies you should track changes so you know which version of the instructions produced which outcomes. In practice, record the agent name, the model deployment name, the instruction text, and the date of the last portal run in your repository runbook. That one page of documentation can prevent confusion later.

This step is complete when three things are true. You have an agent in the Azure AI Foundry project that represents the intended role and task. You can run the baseline prompt set and get consistent output that the team agrees meets the provisional success threshold. You can demonstrate one multi-turn interaction where the agent stays within the instruction and carries the right context forward, using the same multi-turn concept described in the quickstart.

Step 3. Validate the Same Project and Deployment from Code with Azure AI Projects SDK 2.x

Once your agent behavior is stable, validate the same project and deployment from code. The purpose of this step is not to start building your full application. The purpose is to confirm that the basic wiring works outside the portal and that your prototype can be reproduced through a documented, scriptable path. Microsoft's Azure AI Foundry quickstart uses the Azure AI Projects SDK >=2.0.0 with DefaultAzureCredential and the project endpoint copied from the[5] Foundry portal welcome screen. Use the official quickstart as the source of truth for exact package versions and imports. Ensure you sign in using the CLI az login and correct tenant id is passed to authenticate before running your Python scripts.

Before writing code, make sure the project and deployment identifiers are explicit. The quickstart sets PROJECT_ENDPOINT and MODEL_DEPLOYMENT_NAME as environment variables. That is good practice for prototypes because it makes the configuration visible and easy to change without editing source files. It also avoids a common failure mode in which developers hardcode endpoints and later forget which environment they used during a successful test. In Azure AI Foundry, the project endpoint is intended to be shared with team members so they can connect to the same project from code. That creates a consistent boundary between portal testing and script-based testing.

Use the same authentication path described by Microsoft. For local dev, quickstart uses DefaultAzureCredential and requires that you authenticate before running scripts, typically with az login, and that the signed-in identity has permissions on the Azure AI Foundry project, while

[5] https://learn.microsoft.com/en-us/azure/foundry/quickstarts/get-started-code?tabs=python

for enterprise environments, you may be required to select the correct tenant/subscription. This aligns with the RBAC model you used when you created the project and granted access. The point is to keep the prototype aligned with how the target customers will run it in a real tenant, where identities and role assignments matter. Avoid key sharing for this step. If the script works only with a shared key, you have not validated the enterprise access path.

Keep this validation step narrow. The goal is to confirm three things. Authentication works. The project endpoint is correct. The deployment name resolves to the model you expect. The quickstart's "Chat with a model" code path is designed for exactly that. It creates an AIProjectClient using the project endpoint and credentials, then requests an OpenAI client with get_openai_client(), then calls responses.create(...) using your deployment name. If this runs successfully, you have proven that your environment variables, identity, and project wiring are correct. That is the baseline you need before you add more moving parts.

There are a few checks that make this step more useful without expanding scope. First, log the endpoint and deployment name at runtime, like the quickstart does, so you can see which environment you are hitting. Second, run two prompts. One should be a simple sanity prompt, such as a factual question, to confirm the model responds. The other should be a prompt from your prototype prompt set, to confirm the portal behavior is not an artifact of the playground UI. Do not tune prompts in this step. If the output differs from portal testing, treat it as a configuration or instruction mismatch and resolve it before you proceed. Your purpose is to validate a consistent baseline, not to discover new prompt variants.

This step is also the right place to align your code test with the actual model deployment you intend to use. In Azure AI Foundry, the model argument in responses.create(...) is typically the deployment name you created. Confusion here is common because teams sometimes mix up model family names and deployment identifiers. The quickstart pattern reduces that risk by storing the deployment name in MODEL_

DEPLOYMENT_NAME and printing it before calling the API. Follow that pattern and keep the names consistent across portal and code so you can trace results back to the same deployment.

Figure 3-3 shows the model call pattern from the official quickstart. Treat it as a validation harness, not as a production integration.

```
import os
from dotenv import load_dotenv
from azure.identity import DefaultAzureCredential
from azure.ai.projects import AIProjectClient

load_dotenv()

print(f"Using PROJECT_ENDPOINT: {os.environ['PROJECT_ENDPOINT']}")
print(f"Using MODEL_DEPLOYMENT_NAME: {os.environ['MODEL_DEPLOYMENT_NAM

project_client = AIProjectClient(
    endpoint=os.environ["PROJECT_ENDPOINT"],
    credential=DefaultAzureCredential(),
)

openai_client = project_client.get_openai_client()

response = openai_client.responses.create(
    model=os.environ["MODEL_DEPLOYMENT_NAME"],
    input="What is the size of France in square miles?",
)
print(f"Response output: {response.output_text}")
```

Figure 3-3. *Chat with a model*

This script should live in your repository as a simple entry point that any engineer can run to verify configuration. It should not contain business logic, tool wiring, or evaluation. Once it works, you can branch into agent calls, tool testing, and evaluation with confidence that the base plumbing is correct.

This step is complete when you can run the script from a clean environment using only documented prerequisites, authenticate with an identity that has project access, and get a valid response from the deployed model. When that works, you have confirmed that the Azure AI Foundry (new) portal deployment and the Azure AI Foundry projects API path are aligned. That is the right point to add agent versions and multi-turn testing from code in the next step.

Step 4. Create an Agent Version and Test Multi-turn Conversations from Code

After the model call works, the next step is to move from plain model prompts to an agent that has a named identity and a versioned definition. In Azure AI Foundry, that definition is created in your Azure AI Foundry project and can be referenced consistently across runs. This matters for ISVs because most prototype failures come from drift. One developer changes the instruction text in a script, another tests a different prompt, and a third tries to reproduce the behavior but cannot tell which configuration produced the result. Creating an agent version gives you a fixed baseline to reference and compare.

Microsoft's Azure AI Foundry quickstart shows both required parts of this step. First, it shows how to create an agent using the Azure AI Projects SDK >=2.0.0 by calling project_client.agents.create_version(...) with a PromptAgentDefinition that binds your deployed model and your instruction text. Second, it shows how to chat with that agent using a conversation ID to preserve multi-turn history. Use the Microsoft Learn quickstart as the source of truth for exact imports, object names, and package versions (use python version 3.9 or later).[6,7]

Think of the agent version as the prototype contract. It captures the instruction text and the model deployment binding in a named configuration that your team can point to. That configuration can then be used in the portal and in code. This is different from Step 3, where you were only calling the model deployment directly. Direct model calls are useful for confirming that the deployment wiring works, but they do not preserve a consistent definition of behavior. An agent version does. Microsoft's quickstart describes the same point in practical terms by explaining that the agent defines core behavior, so you do not need to repeat instructions each time.

For ISVs, this concept becomes important when multiple teams touch the prototype. The Product team wants a stable behavior to review. Engineering wants a stable configuration to test. Solution engineering wants a stable artifact for internal demos and early customer conversations. A versioned agent definition is the simplest way to provide all those groups with the same baseline.

If you followed Step 2, you already created and tested an agent in the Azure AI Foundry portal. Step 4 is where you ensure your code operates on the same principle. Use the same agent's name and keep the instruction consistent. If you need to adjust the instruction, create a new version rather than silently editing the existing definition in multiple places. A prototype becomes hard to measure when the instruction changes are not tied to a new version or recorded in a scorecard.

---

[6] `https://learn.microsoft.com/en-us/azure/foundry/agents/quickstarts/quickstart-hosted-agent?pivots=python`

[7] `https://learn.microsoft.com/en-us/azure/foundry/quickstarts/get-started-code?tabs=python`

The quickstart pattern is also explicit about configuration. It reads the agent's name and deployment name from environment variables. This is useful in a prototype because it allows you to test multiple agent versions or deployments without editing code, while keeping the runbook simple. Readers should be able to change MODEL_DEPLOYMENT_NAME to compare capabilities and costs, or change AGENT_NAME to point to a different agent configuration.

Multi-turn behavior is where many prototypes start to break down. The first answer looks good. The second answer is wrong because the agent loses context, or the conversation accumulates irrelevant details. The quickstart demonstrates multi-turn continuity by creating a conversation once and then using the same conversation ID for subsequent calls. That is the correct baseline test. It proves that your code can maintain a shared conversation context across calls and that the agent's behavior is stable across turns.

In this step, do not try to "show" multi-turn by asking two unrelated questions. Make the second question depend on the first question or on a piece of context introduced in the first answer. The quickstart uses "size of France" followed by "capital city," which is a simple example of a dependent follow-up. In your product prototype, use a follow-up from your own workflow, such as "now format that as JSON" or "now apply the same rule to this second ticket." The test is not whether the model can answer a second question. The test is whether it can carry the right context forward while remaining consistent with the instructions.

The quickstart uses the responses.create(...) method and passes an extra_body with an agent_reference that includes the agent's name. This wiring is important because it shows that the same Responses API call can be used for both plain-model interactions and agent interactions, with the difference being the agent-reference metadata. That is a practical design feature for ISVs. It means you can keep one core client path in your prototype and choose whether the call is an agent call or a direct model call based on configuration.

Keep this step limited to what the quickstart demonstrates. Create one agent version. Create one conversation. Make two calls in the same conversation. Confirm both calls return output. If you add tools or attempt evaluation here, you will not know whether failures come from agent definition, conversation wiring, or tool configuration. The goal is to isolate multiturn and agent-reference behaviors first.

Treat this script as the second prototype harness after Step 3. Step 3 proved that you can call the model deployment. Step 4 proves that you can create a versioned agent configuration and chat with a multi-turn context. Both should be runnable by another engineer with only environment variables and a documented auth step. That is why it is worth keeping the script small and keeping output visible.

A useful practice in this step is to print the agent ID and version after creation. The quickstart prints agent metadata, which helps confirm what was created and allows you to trace later behavior back to a specific agent version. In a prototype, this is more useful than it seems. It prevents confusion when multiple versions exist and makes it easier to connect evaluation results to a specific configuration.

Use the full Microsoft Learn sample as the runnable reference because the SDK is actively evolving during the beta period. This shortened example is intended to show the shape of the prototype harness, not to replace the official quickstart sample.

Python C# TypeScript Java REST API Foundry portal

Python Copy

```
import os
from dotenv import load_dotenv
from azure.identity import DefaultAzureCredential
from azure.ai.projects import AIProjectClient

load_dotenv()

project_client = AIProjectClient(
    endpoint=os.environ["PROJECT_ENDPOINT"],
    credential=DefaultAzureCredential(),
)

agent_name = os.environ["AGENT_NAME"]
openai_client = project_client.get_openai_client()

# Optional Step: Create a conversation to use with the agent
conversation = openai_client.conversations.create()
print(f"Created conversation (id: {conversation.id})")

# Chat with the agent to answer questions
response = openai_client.responses.create(
    conversation=conversation.id, #Optional conversation context for multi-turn
    extra_body={"agent_reference": {"name": agent_name, "type": "agent_reference"}},
    input="What is the size of France in square miles?",
)
print(f"Response output: {response.output_text}")

# Optional Step: Ask a follow-up question in the same conversation
response = openai_client.responses.create(
    conversation=conversation.id,
    extra_body={"agent_reference": {"name": agent_name, "type": "agent_reference"}},
    input="And what is the capital city?",
)
print(f"Response output: {response.output_text}")
```

Figure 3-4. *Create an agent version and chat with multi-turn history*

This step is complete when you can run the agent script from a clean environment, create an agent version, and carry context across at least two turns in the same conversation. If you get correct answers but the agent violates your instruction boundaries, fix the instructions now. If the first answer is fine and the second answer drifts, that is a signal to tighten the instruction and reduce ambiguity in your prompt set before you add tools or a broader scope.

Once Step 4 is stable, you are ready to add tools in a controlled way. At that point, you have validated three foundations in order: deployment wiring, project wiring, and agent multi-turn wiring. That sequence prevents tool work from being blocked by simple configuration issues and gives you a stable baseline for later evaluation.

Step 5. Add Tools That Match the Product Task

Prototype tools before you expand the agent into complex orchestration. In most ISV prototypes, failures first appear in tool use. The agent might produce a reasonable response in the playground, but it fails when it needs to retrieve grounded content, call a business function, or use an external API. The root cause is often tool selection and tool-call reliability, not planning logic. In Azure AI Foundry, tools are managed through the Azure AI Foundry tool catalog experience and then attached to agents as capabilities. Treat tool selection and tool-call correctness as part of the prototype baseline, in the same way you treat instruction adherence and output formatting.

The Azure AI Foundry tool catalog is the management surface for the tools your agents can use. Microsoft describes it as a catalog that includes both public and private tools, so teams can connect agents to capabilities without hardcoding everything directly into the prompt text. This is useful for prototypes because you can keep your "agent behavior contract" stable while you experiment with a small set of capabilities. It is also useful because it supports a repeatable configuration story for handoff. An agent with a defined set of tools is easier to reproduce than one that relies on developers remembering which endpoints or services were wired during a demo.[8]

The catalog framing also helps ISVs keep tool scope under control. A common mistake is adding tools because they look useful rather than because the product task requires them. In prototypes, adding tools increases the number of ways the system can fail. It increases ambiguous tool-choice decisions. It increases the number of parameters and schemas that must be correct. It increases the number of external dependencies that can break. The catalog makes adding tools easy. Your job in this step is to add only the tools that directly support the single task and single user role you defined at the start of the chapter.

Tool selection should start from the task, not from the demo you want to show. For most ISV agent products, early tools fall into two categories. The first category is knowledge grounding tools, where the agent needs access to enterprise or customer data and must cite sources. The second category is action tools, where the agent must call deterministic business logic, create or update records, or trigger workflows. Microsoft's tool catalog concept emphasizes connecting tools into your agent as capabilities and supports both public catalog tools and private tool catalogs, which fit these two categories well.

If your use case is grounded retrieval over enterprise content, start with the knowledge source that matches your real product. For example, if your prototype is "support triage," the first grounding source might be an indexed set of past tickets and known resolutions. If your prototype is "claims summarization," the first grounding source might be a document repository of policy guidance and sample claim forms. In this stage, the

[8] https://learn.microsoft.com/en-us/azure/foundry/agents/concepts/tool-catalog?view=foundry

tool goal is not broad coverage. The tool goal is consistent grounding behavior on a small evaluation set so you can measure whether the agent uses the knowledge source properly.

If your use case depends on deterministic business logic, expose that logic through a tool interface and test parameter correctness. In practice, deterministic logic often includes CRUD operations, eligibility checks, calculations, routing decisions, or status transitions that the product must perform consistently. In a prototype, that logic should not be reimplemented in prompts. It should be called through a tool so you can validate the contract between the agent and the application. This is where many prototypes fail. The agent calls the right tool but sends the wrong parameters, or it calls the wrong tool because the tool descriptions overlap. Your measurement plan in this step must include parameter correctness, not just response text.

Start with one tool, then add a second only if the task requires it. When a prototype starts with many tools, the agent's job becomes ambiguous. The agent must decide which tool to use and when. Ambiguity leads to inconsistent behavior and slows debugging. A small tool set makes it easier to understand why a tool was called or not, and whether its output was used correctly. The Azure AI Foundry tool catalog supports managing a large tool set, but your first prototype should not. The purpose is validation, not completeness.

Write tool descriptions so they are clear and non-overlapping. A good tool description states what the tool does, what inputs it requires, and what output shape it returns. Avoid describing multiple actions in one tool. Avoid duplicate tools that differ only slightly. If you need a read and an update operation, keep them separate. If you need search and retrieval, keep them separate unless the platform tool already treats them as a single operation.

This step only adds value if you treat tool behavior as measurable. For each prompt in your tool test set, you should be able to answer four questions:

Did the agent call the tool when it should have?

Did it select the correct tool?

Were the parameters correct and complete?

Did the final response reflect the tool output?

Tool work often fails at the third and fourth questions. The agent might correctly decide that it needs a tool, but it sends an incomplete identifier or passes an invalid filter. Or it receives a correct tool result and then ignores it, continuing with a plausible but ungrounded response. This is why the prototype baseline should include tool-call checks, not just the text-answer quality checks you used in earlier steps.

In Azure AI Foundry, this is also where you should begin using the platform's traces and run outputs to review what happened during each run. The goal is to show evidence that a specific run invoked a specific tool with specific parameters and returned a specific output, and that the response used that output. If you cannot show that evidence, the prototype is still in demo territory.

Your tool test set should be a subset of your overall prompt set, designed to force tool usage. If your product needs retrieval, include prompts that cannot be answered correctly without using the knowledge source. Include prompts that contain ambiguity where retrieval must disambiguate. Include at least one prompt that should result in "not found" or "insufficient information," because a grounded agent must handle gaps safely.

If your product needs deterministic logic, include prompts that require exact numeric or structured outputs that must come from a function result. Include at least one prompt in which the tool should reject the request due to missing required parameters and verify that the agent requests the missing information rather than guessing. This is a common enterprise requirement, even in early pilots, because guesswork in business processes creates operational risk.

If you plan to deploy a containerized hosted agent later, keep the hosted agent quickstart as a reference for later chapters, not as a required step for the first prototype. The hosted agent quickstart shows a sample path that uses tools such as web search and optional MCP tools, tests locally, deploys to Azure AI Foundry Agent Service, and then validates the deployed agent in the Azure AI Foundry playground. It is useful as an example of how tool use and deployment can come together in a hosted runtime, but it should not be part of the first prototype path unless your immediate goal is deployment validation.

The practical reason to defer hosted deployment is scope control. Tool correctness and grounding quality are hard enough to validate within a single environment. Adding containerization, deployment wiring, and runtime differences introduces new failure modes that are not necessary for the first decision gate. This chapter's objective is to build a prototype that proves value and can be measured. Hosting is a decision made later, once you have baseline results.

This step is completed when the prototype has a small tool set attached to the agent, the team can run a tool-focused prompt subset, and you can demonstrate tool-call reliability with evidence. For a retrieval tool, that evidence should include citations or grounded references in the answer and a clear alignment between the retrieved content and the response. For a deterministic tool, that evidence should include correct tool selection, correct parameters, and an output that matches the tool results. When those checks pass, the prototype is ready for evaluation planning and scoring, because you have validated that the agent can act, not only talk.

Step 6. Define Evaluation Before Feature Expansion

Prototype quality should be measured before you add features. If you expand the scope first, your team will not know whether the prototype improved or simply changed. This is a common failure mode in ISV agent projects. The early demos look good, then the team adds tools, more prompts, changes the model, and introduces new instructions, making the system harder to reason about. Azure AI Foundry provides evaluators and agent evaluators to define a baseline and track changes against it. Agent evaluators are designed for agent-specific concerns, such as intent resolution, task adherence, and tool-call accuracy, which usually determine whether an agent is usable in a business workflow. Use the Azure AI Foundry documentation as the source of truth and treat evaluation as part of the prototype workflow, not as an optional later step.[9]

A prototype can generate fluent output and still fail the task. That is why evaluation should include more than text quality. For a business prototype, measure at least four dimensions and keep the definitions simple. Task success means the agent completed the requested work for the target role. It is not a score for "sounds correct." It is a score for whether the outcome is usable. If the prototype is a support triage agent, task success might mean it was categorized correctly and produced the expected escalation outcome. If the prototype is a summarization agent, task success might mean it extracted the required facts and produced the expected output structure.

Instruction adherence means the response stayed within the role and boundaries you defined and followed the required format. If you require a specific response structure or a refusal pattern, adherence should measure

[9] https://learn.microsoft.com/en-us/azure/foundry/concepts/evaluation-evaluators/agent-evaluators

that. This is also where you catch silent drift, such as the agent becoming verbose, adding unsupported claims, or ignoring formatting constraints. Tool call quality means the agent used the tools correctly when the tools were needed. This includes selecting the right tool, passing correct parameters, handling tool errors correctly, and incorporating tool outputs into the final response. This is the main dimension that separates "good chat" from "reliable workflow."

Safety means the system behaved within acceptable risk boundaries for the intended use. In prototypes, safety is often tested with a small set of misuse prompts and injection attempts. This is not a full production safety program. It is a baseline check that your agent does not violate obvious safety constraints when expanded later. Azure AI Foundry's agent evaluators are useful here because they make intent resolution, task adherence, and tool call accuracy explicit evaluation targets rather than hidden assumptions.

Keep the first evaluation set small enough that your team will run it often. A good starting point is 10 to 30 cases, depending on task complexity and the number of tools involved. The set should represent the real workflow, not just generic prompts. Include straightforward requests, ambiguous requests, and a few cases that should trigger refusals or safe redirects. If tool use is required, include prompts that cannot be answered correctly without using the tool.

Write each evaluation case so it can be rerun. For each item, record the user input and the expected outcome. The expected outcome can be one of three forms. It can be an exact answer, which is useful for classification or structured outputs. It can be a bounded set of acceptable answers, which is useful for summaries and natural language responses. Or it can be a checklist, which is useful for task adherence, where the response must include specific elements.

Avoid expanding the evaluation set every time you see a failure. Keep a stable baseline set and add a separate "exploratory" set for new failure patterns. The baseline is the comparison anchor. The exploratory set is where you collect new cases for later inclusion. At this stage, you do not need a complex scoring pipeline. You need repeatable scoring. Azure AI Foundry's documentation provides evaluator concepts and agent evaluator building blocks, and Microsoft also provides notebook examples and samples for end-to-end evaluation pipelines. The SDK and evaluators can change during preview periods, so pin the package versions you use in your repository and record them in the runbook and requirements file.

A practical pattern for ISVs is to combine automatic scoring with a small human review pass. Use evaluators to score every run consistently, then review a handful of cases manually, focusing on failures and borderline cases. This avoids the two extremes that slow teams down. Pure manual review does not scale and produces inconsistent judgments. Pure automated scoring can hide failure patterns that matter in the target workflow. A blended approach gives you speed and control.

This is the core discipline of the step. Run the evaluation set against the current configuration and record the results. Then treat the results as your baseline. Do not change prompts, tools, or models until the baseline is recorded. When you do change something, run the same evaluation set again and compare the results.

A prototype scorecard should be stored in source control. It should record the prompt or instruction version, the model deployment name, the agent's name and version, the tool set attached to the agent, the evaluation dataset version, and the metric outputs. Keep this record short and consistent. The goal is not to build a reporting system. The goal is to prevent confusion when stakeholders ask why the configuration changed or why quality seems different in a later demo.

This is also the point where you connect back to Chapter 2. If you track cost and latency alongside quality, you will see the trade-offs early. A prototype can improve task success by using a larger model, calling tools more often, or generating longer answers. Those changes may violate your pricing assumptions. Evaluation plus basic telemetry keeps you honest.

Agent evaluators focus on agent behavior rather than generic text quality. The Azure AI Foundry agent evaluators documentation highlights intent resolution, task adherence, and tool call accuracy as first-class concerns. This matches how business prototypes fail. They fail because the system misinterprets user intent, skips required steps, misuses a tool, or produces a response that does not meet process requirements. Agent evaluators are a way to measure those concerns consistently. (learn.microsoft.com)

Start with one or two agent evaluators that map to your most expensive failure modes. If your system routes requests, start with intent resolution. If your system must follow a checklist, start with task adherence. If your system uses tools, start with tool call accuracy. Add more evaluators only when the baseline is stable and you have a reason to measure more dimensions.

Figure 3-5 shows the shape of an evaluator call and is useful for confirming you can construct and run an evaluator with your chosen configuration. For prototype scoring at scale, use Azure AI Foundry's cloud evaluation capability, which runs evaluations in the service, stores results in your Azure AI Foundry project, and supports Microsoft-curated built-in evaluators as well as custom evaluators managed in the evaluator catalog under the same project-scoped RBAC. Cloud evaluations are intended for pre-deployment testing, CI/CD integration, and larger test sets without managing local compute, and you can also schedule recurring runs or set up continuous evaluation.[10]

[10] `https://learn.microsoft.com/en-us/azure/foundry/how-to/develop/cloud-evaluation?tabs=python`

Get started

Install the SDK and set up your client:

Bash Copy

```bash
pip install --pre "azure-ai-projects>=2.0.0b4"
```

Python Copy

```python
import os
from azure.identity import DefaultAzureCredential
from azure.ai.projects import AIProjectClient
from openai.types.eval_create_params import DataSourceConfigCustom
from openai.types.evals.create_eval_jsonl_run_data_source_param import (
    CreateEvalJSONLRunDataSourceParam,
    SourceFileContent,
    SourceFileContentContent,
    SourceFileID,
)

# Azure AI Project endpoint
# Example: https://<account_name>.services.ai.azure.com/api/projects/<project_name>
endpoint = os.environ["AZURE_AI_PROJECT_ENDPOINT"]

# Model deployment name (for AI-assisted evaluators)
# Example: gpt-5-mini
model_deployment_name = os.environ.get("AZURE_AI_MODEL_DEPLOYMENT_NAME", "")

# Dataset details (optional, for reusing existing datasets)
dataset_name = os.environ.get("DATASET_NAME", "")
dataset_version = os.environ.get("DATASET_VERSION", "1")

# Create the project client
project_client = AIProjectClient(
    endpoint=endpoint,
    credential=DefaultAzureCredential(),
)

# Get the OpenAI client for evaluation API
client = project_client.get_openai_client()
```

Figure 3-5. *Cloud evaluation using the Microsoft Azure AI Foundry SDK*

This step is complete when you can run a small evaluation set and produce a baseline scorecard across the four dimensions. You should be able to point to results for task success, instruction adherence, tool call quality, and safety, and you should be able to rerun the evaluation after a change and explain what improved or regressed. That makes the next prototype iteration a controlled experiment instead of another demo.

When this baseline exists, feature expansion becomes safer. You can add tools, refine instructions, change models, or introduce new workflows and still understand the impact. Without it, you will be making changes based on impressions, and the prototype will become harder to defend as it grows.

Step 7. Build Responsible AI Controls into the Prototype

Responsible AI should not wait for production hardening. In Azure AI Foundry, responsible use guidance treats trustworthy development as an end-to-end life cycle, not a final checklist. The guidance emphasizes risk discovery, protection, and governance across the build, test, deploy, and operate phases. Even in a prototype, your job is to make the risks visible and to prove that basic controls are feasible in the same environment where you are building the agent. This improves delivery by preventing late redesign when a security or compliance review occurs after a demo. It also improves commercial readiness because enterprise buyers often move faster when they see evidence of risk controls early.

This step has three goals. First, define the boundaries of intended use so reviewers can judge whether the behavior is acceptable. Second, add protections that reduce predictable failure modes such as unsafe content and instruction overrides. Third, set up governance and monitoring signals to explain what happened when something goes wrong. In Azure AI Foundry, those goals map directly to the platform's life cycle framing and project-level management features such as RBAC and policies.[11]

Start with a one page "prototype use statement." Keep it short and specific. It should include the intended user role, the primary task, the allowed data inputs, and the expected output type. It should also include

[11] https://learn.microsoft.com/en-us/azure/foundry/responsible-use-of-ai-overview

any limitations relevant to your workflow. Examples are "the agent does not make eligibility decisions," "the agent summarizes but does not approve," or "the agent requires retrieval citations for policy answers."

Azure AI Foundry's responsible use guidance emphasizes that risk discovery begins with understanding the scenario and identifying what the system is and is not meant to do. This is also practical engineering control. A clear scope reduces the chance that you accidentally build features through prompt drift, and it helps you evaluate task success correctly. A prototype without a written intended-use statement often grows into a general assistant by accident, increasing risk and making quality harder to measure.

Document known limitations as observations, not aspirations. If retrieval grounding is incomplete, say so. If the agent struggles with a certain document type, say so. If the model sometimes produces uncertain answers, record the conditions where that happens. This becomes the seed for your evaluation set and your mitigation plan. It also helps you avoid overselling the prototype to internal stakeholders.

A responsible prototype does not only test happy paths. It tests how the system behaves when a user tries to push it outside its role. The responsible use guidance in Azure AI Foundry calls out end-to-end risk discovery and protections across the life cycle, which includes identifying misuse and abuse scenarios for the system. For an ISV prototype, misuse cases should be drawn from the product context. Examples include a user asking the agent to expose internal data, ignore policy, generate content that violates workplace standards, or perform an action it should not.

Keep this list short and specific. Five to ten misuse cases is enough for a prototype baseline. The important thing is to include at least one case for each category that matters to your product: data-leakage attempts, policy-override attempts, unsafe-content requests, and tool-misuse attempts. If your agent can call tools that modify data, it includes prompts that try to trigger unauthorized changes. If your agent is grounded in enterprise content, include prompts that try to force disclosure of sensitive records.

In a prototype, the most important safety control is to configure content filtering and verify how it affects real prompts and responses. Azure AI Foundry's responsible use guidance frames protections as part of the life cycle, and this protection affects user experience early. Configure content filtering settings on the deployment and then run your baseline prompt set again. Observe what is blocked, what is allowed, and what the fallback experience should be.

In practice, the key question is not whether filtering exists. The key question is whether filtering behavior aligns with your product requirements. For example, a support workflow may include user text that contains profanity or harassment. Filtering should not break legitimate classification or summarization tasks, but it should still enforce safety boundaries. A prototype should test this directly so you can tune instructions and user messaging early rather than discovering the problem during pilot. If the deployment supports adjustable safety configuration, record the setting in your scorecard. A reviewer should be able to answer "what is the safety posture of this prototype" without having to hunt through portal screenshots.

Prompt injection and jailbreak testing should be part of the prototype evaluation, not a later security add-on. This is especially important once the agent is connected to tools or enterprise content. Injection attempts often aim to override instructions, extract hidden system prompts, or coerce the agent into calling tools with unsafe parameters. Your prototype needs a small set of these cases to measure whether your instruction and tool configuration are resilient.

Add these cases to the same evaluation set you use for task success, instruction adherence, tool call quality, and safety. That keeps the results comparable across iterations. The point is not to create a full red-team program in Chapter 3. The point is to ensure that obvious injection attempts fail silently, and that failures become visible and measurable. If the agent fails these tests, fix the instruction and tool boundaries before you expand features.

A practical approach is to create three tiers of injection tests. Tier one is a direct "ignore your instructions" attempt. Tier two is an attempt to extract system or tool details. Tier three is a tool misuse attempt that tries to force unsafe action. These tiers align well with how real-world injection attacks tend to progress.

In Azure AI Foundry, access control should be enforced at the project level so the right people can build and test without giving everyone broad access to prompts, outputs, and datasets. Responsible Use guidance emphasizes governance throughout the life cycle, and access boundaries are the most concrete governance control you can implement early on. Decide which roles need access to the project and assign the minimum required permissions.

At a minimum, define who can do each of the following:

- **View and edit agent instructions**
- **View prompt and response logs**
- **Access evaluation datasets and results**
- **Modifying model deployments**
- **Attach or change tools**

If you do not make these decisions early, prototypes tend to share secrets by accident. Prompt sets and evaluation data often contain customer-like content. Output logs can contain sensitive information. A responsible prototype should assume that these artifacts are controlled assets and must be protected the same way as other project data.

Use role assignments to enforce the boundary rather than relying on informal agreements. If your prototype is being prepared for broader review, create a read-only path for stakeholders who need to see results but do not need to modify configuration.

Azure AI Foundry includes preview and prerelease capabilities, and many organizations want to keep production-like environments focused on general availability features. Azure AI Foundry supports suppressing preview surfaces via organizations' chosen Azure tags and provides role-based guidance to limit preview exposure. If your organization uses an environment separation model, apply these controls during prototyping in the environment intended to represent production readiness. This prevents the prototype from accidentally depending on preview-only features that will not be allowed later.

This also helps keep the chapter's message consistent for ISVs. You can still experiment in a sandbox project that allows preview features, but the prototype you plan to hand off should have a clear statement about which preview features it uses, if any. If the answer is "none," say so. If the answer is "some," record them and include a mitigation plan.

This step is complete when the prototype has a written intended-use and limitations statement, a small set of misuse and injection tests integrated into the evaluation, safety settings configured and recorded for deployment, and access boundaries enforced through project-level role assignments. If your organization requires it, preview exposure is controlled with tags, so production-like environments remain focused on general availability capabilities. Together, these controls make the prototype reviewable and reduce the likelihood that you will need to redesign the system after early stakeholder or customer feedback.

Step 8. Package the Prototype for Handoff

A prototype is ready to move forward when another engineer can run it, test it, and extend it without reconstructing your environment by trial and error. This matters to ISVs because prototypes are rarely owned by a single developer for long. Solution engineers need a repeatable demo. Product teams need consistent results for review. Implementation teams need to validate behavior with customer data. Security teams need evidence of controls and logging. If the prototype cannot be reproduced on a clean machine, it is not a scalable prototype. It is a local experiment.

This step is about packaging, not adding features. Your goal is to turn what you already validated in the Azure AI Foundry portal and with the Azure AI Projects SDK into a small, repeatable repository. The package should capture configuration, test inputs, evaluation, and run instructions in a way that survives team handoff and normal version churn.

Keep the repository structure small and predictable. You want a layout that makes it obvious where to find code, prompts, evaluation inputs, and results. A practical structure looks like this:

- **src**/for prototype scripts
- **prompts**/for instruction text and prompt sets
- **eval**/for evaluation scripts and evaluation datasets
- **docs**/for a short runbook and change log
- **.env.example** for environment variable template
- **requirements.txt or pyproject.toml** for pinned dependencies

Do not optimize this structure for the final product architecture. Optimize it for clarity and reproducibility. You can restructure the repository for production needs later. The handoff package should keep the next engineer's cognitive load low. If you are using multiple scripts, keep them narrowly scoped to the steps in this chapter. For example: one script for model wiring validation, one for agent creation and multi-turn chat, one for tool tests, and one for evaluation runs. Narrow scripts help with debugging because failures are easier to isolate.

Use the Azure AI Foundry quickstarts as the canonical reference for required environment variables. The Azure AI Foundry "get started in code" quickstart shows a small environment setup that includes

PROJECT_ENDPOINT, MODEL_DEPLOYMENT_NAME, and AGENT_NAME, and it uses those values consistently across the model call, agent creation, and agent chat sections. Use the same variable names in your prototype so your readers can map the book to the official documentation without translation.

Create a **.env.example** file that lists required variables with placeholder values and short comments. Keep it simple. For example:

- **PROJECT_ENDPOINT=** copied from the Azure AI Foundry project welcome screen
- **MODEL_DEPLOYMENT_NAME=** the deployment name you created in Azure AI Foundry
- **AGENT_NAME=** the agent's name used in the portal and code

If your prototype includes optional settings such as "stream responses" or "use tool X," include those as optional variables with defaults. Do not hide configuration inside code constants unless it is stable and not environment-dependent. The purpose of **.env.example** is to make environment setup a single visible step.

If you are using python-dotenv, make that explicit in the runbook and scripts. The Azure AI Foundry quickstart uses load_dotenv() in the Python examples and suggests setting environment variables before running scripts. Follow that pattern so a reader can use the same method locally.

A practical runbook section is a simple "known-good baseline" header that records

- **Date of last validated run**
- **Azure AI Foundry portal version used (Azure AI Foundry new)**
- **azure-ai-projects version and related package versions**

- **Model deployment name**
- **Agent name and latest agent version ID output**

This one block of metadata saves hours of troubleshooting later.

Your prompt and evaluation sets should not consist only of prose. Store them as files. Use a small JSON or YAML format that is easy to read and edit. If your output format matters, include notes on the expected output structure for each test case.

At a minimum, include

- **A baseline prompt set used for portal testing**
- **A tool-focused prompt subset used in Step 5**
- **An evaluation dataset used in Step 6, with expected outcomes**

This allows another engineer to rerun the same tests after making changes. It also supports consistent review conversations because everyone is looking at the same inputs.

Include a small evaluation script that runs the baseline evaluation set and prints or saves results in a consistent format. The script does not need to implement every evaluator on the platform. It needs to produce a repeatable output that can be compared across changes. Save results to a file under **eval/results/**with a timestamp and a configuration header.

Even if you plan to run cloud evaluations later, a local evaluation harness is still useful for quick checks. The important part for handoff is that the evaluation method is documented and runnable without guesswork.

If you do use cloud evaluation, record the evaluation configuration and how to run it so another engineer can reproduce the same run in the Azure AI Foundry project. Include links or commands used and record any required permissions.

Keep the runbook short and procedural. It should include

- **Prerequisites:** Azure account, access to the Azure AI Foundry project, and required tooling
- **Authentication step:** az login and confirmation of tenant
- **Environment setup:** Copy **.env.example** to **.env** and fill values
- **Install step:** Create **venv** and install pinned requirements
- **Smoke tests:** Run the model call script and confirm output
- **Agent test:** Run the agent script and confirm multi-turn behavior
- **Tool test:** Run the tool prompt subset if tools are enabled
- **Evaluation:** Run the evaluation script and confirm a scorecard file is produced

The runbook should also include "what to do if it fails" for common problems. For example, missing permissions, an incorrect endpoint, a wrong deployment name, or a missing prerelease package version. This is not a full troubleshooting guide. It is a short set of checks that reduces time lost during handoff.

If you later deploy a hosted agent, the deployment guidance provides an incremental path from local code to a containerized agent in Azure AI Foundry Agent Service. Microsoft's hosted agent deployment documentation describes how to deploy hosted agent code to the Azure AI Foundry Agent Service and keep the agent managed on the platform. Treat that as a later chapter activity but align your repository early so deployment becomes an incremental change rather than a rewrite. That mainly means keeping code in a predictable folder, externalizing configuration, and providing a clear entry-point script or service module.

This step is complete when a second engineer can

- **Clone the repository**
- **Authenticate with an identity that has project access**
- **Set environment variables using the template**
- **Install pinned dependencies**
- **Run the model validation script**
- **Run the agent multi-turn script**
- **Run the tool tests if applicable**
- **Run the evaluation script and produce a scorecard**

If they can do that without direct help, your prototype is ready to move into the next phase. If they cannot, fix the packaging and documentation before you add more features. This discipline is what keeps an ISV prototype from turning into a fragile demo that only one person can run.

Conclusion

In this Chapter, we established a single, repeatable prototype path that stays inside Microsoft Azure AI Foundry from initial setup through evaluation, risk controls, and handoff. The central idea is that a prototype is not a demo. A prototype is an evidence artifact. It proves that the use case is worth building, that the cost and latency assumptions from Chapter 2 are plausible, and that the team can reproduce results without relying on a single person's machine or memory.

The workflow began with project setup and a single-model deployment to test a narrow task in a controlled environment. From there, you created an agent in the Azure AI Foundry portal to define behavior once and validate multi-turn interactions against a shared prompt set. You then validated the same project and deployment from code using the Azure AI Foundry Projects API and the Azure AI Projects SDK 2.x, confirming that authentication, endpoint wiring, and deployment wiring are correct outside the portal. That sequence reduces the most common early failure mode, where teams treat a successful portal run as proof that their integration path is ready.

Once the agent was stable, you attached only the tools that matched the product task and treated tool behavior as part of the baseline. This matters because many agent prototypes fail not due to reasoning, but because tool calls are inconsistent or incorrect. Tool selection, parameter correctness, and the correct incorporation of tool outputs are behaviors that determine whether an agent can operate within a real workflow. Validating tool behavior early prevents you from building orchestration on a fragile foundation.

You then defined evaluation before feature expansion. The chapter's evaluation approach is intentionally small and repeatable. It uses a limited evaluation set and a small set of metrics that align with business outcomes. Task success confirms that the agent produces usable outputs for the target role. Instruction adherence confirms the agent stays within the defined boundaries and formats. The tool call quality confirms that the agent can act reliably when tools are required. Safety confirms the agent can resist common misuse and injection patterns. Recording baseline results before changing prompts, tools, or models turns iteration into controlled change rather than continual rediscovery. If you use Azure AI Foundry cloud evaluation, you also gain a path to run larger test sets and integrate evaluation into a build pipeline without maintaining local evaluation compute.

Responsible AI controls were built into the prototype rather than deferred. The chapter treated responsible AI as a set of concrete prototype deliverables. You defined intended use and limitations, identified misuse cases, configured safety and content filtering for the deployment, added injection and jailbreak prompts to evaluation, and enforced access boundaries using project-level role assignments. These controls are not "production hardening" in disguise. They are the minimum set of decisions and artifacts that prevent late redesign and speed up security and customer review cycles.

The chapter ended with packaging for handoff. The handoff standard is simple. Another engineer should be able to run, test, and extend the prototype without having to guess. This requires a small repository structure, an environment template aligned to the Azure AI Foundry quickstarts, pinned SDK versions, a prompt set and evaluation set stored as files, and a short runbook that documents the known-good baseline. This packaging discipline turns your prototype into a team asset and makes later deployment work incrementally rather than as a rewrite. At this point, you have a useful, measurable, and reproducible prototype.

CHAPTER 4

The Agentic Approach to AI Design

The Agentic Approach

AI has evolved in many ways and incorporating many technologies. Each of these may have their own architecture, like the well-known Retrieval Augmentation Generation (RAG) architecture. As such, it would be inaccurate to define agentic as a single architecture. Therefore, we are calling the agentic design as an approach rather than a single reference architecture – The Agentic Approach to designing AI.

In this chapter, we will cover the foundational architectural components of agentic AI design. A good understanding of these foundational components will help when we go deeper into these topics from Chapter 5 onward. Agentic AI design will also help make your product more agile and easier to manage and scale as you incorporate more AI capabilities in the future.

To design your AI-driven product, there are several capabilities you will likely incorporate, examples of which may include

- Retrieval Augmented Generation (RAG) to provide customized and/or more current knowledge sources
- Codex capability to generate or understand code

J. Soh et al., *Building and Distributing Agentic AI Solutions*,
https://doi.org/10.1007/979-8-8688-2586-6_4

- Vision to provide the ability to analyze images and identify objects and people
- Document intelligence to extract key-value pairs from documents such as forms
- Speech capabilities for speech-to-text, text-to-speech, transcription, and translation

Starting in 2025, the term "Agentic" started getting popular and as mentioned in Chapter 1, it was a key milestone in LLM advancement.

The Agentic approach was introduced to address two key shortcomings of LLMs:

1. As we added more and larger data sources, which is a natural evolution of LLM adoption, we ended up with knowledge articles within the sources that may contradict each other if proper context is not provided.
2. Introduction of specialized and possibly more efficient models, for example, the mini and nano models of the GPT series, Small Language Models (SLMs), and codex-efficient models like Claude paved the way for multi-model utilization. Having different agents grounded on different models would allow the output quality of a task or sub-task to be more refined. Therefore, how do we use the best model at the right time and not be stuck with a single model throughout a session?

In this chapter, we will provide foundational knowledge for Chapters 5 and 6. These next two chapters will dive into the technologies involved in the agentic approach, but first let us understand the concepts and the technologies involved.

Foundational Concepts and Design Considerations

To be agentic, we need to leverage agents. Agents are representations of AI models, regardless whether the model is an LLM, SLM, or a non-language model like Vision or Speech. Think of agents as the atomic level of AI model representation in a solution so the goal is to create combinations of such agents to come up with a multi-agent (and therefore also a multi-model) solution that will provide the best results.

Quality and Efficiency Through Specialization

As an analogy, consider a need to build a team of engineers whose goal is to design an autonomous vehicle (e.g., a Mars Rover). We would not go out and hire an uber know-it-all engineer (if one even exists, or at least one that is good at every engineering discipline). To that effect, at a minimum, the makeup of the team would include

- Product/Project Manager (PM) specialized in
    - Project Management
    - Quality Assurance
    - Budget
- Electrical and electronics engineers specialized in
    - VLSI and Chip Design
    - Electrical Systems
    - Embedded Computing

- Mechanical engineers specialized in
    - Robotics and Control Systems
    - Power and transmission
    - Mechatronics
- Materials engineers
    - Software engineers specialized in
    - AI and Machine Learning
    - Operating Systems

We may not need Mechanical Engineers with an emphasis on HVAC or Full Stack Software engineers, assuming we are not worried about the environment inside the autonomous vehicle or the software user interface. We will also not need any Civil Engineers since there are no structures or bridges where this autonomous vehicle will be going (Mars). Therefore, including engineers with deep expertise in these areas may be redundant. But that is exactly what an LLM would represent - engineering knowledge that is all encompassing. One of the side effects of broadly applying an LLM with vast general knowledge is hallucination. Narrowing down the breadth of knowledge and applying that knowledge into sub-tasks will significantly reduce the risk of hallucination.

We can then proceed and divide these teams into the Propulsion Team, the Controls Team, Manufacturing Process Team, etc. Each of these teams will be responsible for a certain aspect of the vehicle design and makeup of each team may comprise some or all of the different types of engineers mentioned above. In fact, every one of the teams may likely need their own team PM. Another benefit of specialization is the ability to form teams that can work independently but still have inter-team collaboration when needed, thereby promoting efficiency. Figure 4-1 shows the possible makeup of the different teams tasked with the development of the different aspects of the autonomous vehicle. This is a classic example of any organization and the goal here is to replicate this organizational efficiency as part of the agentic design.

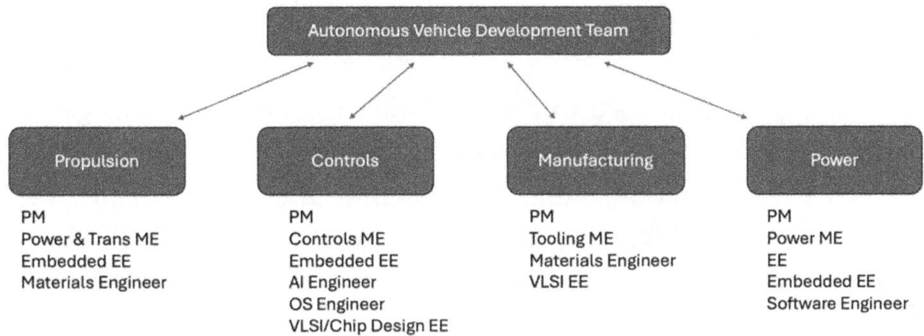

Figure 4-1. *Sub-teams that form the Autonomous Vehicle Development Team*

Agents

Based on our detailed analogy above, suppose we want to augment the engineering teams above with AI. We would build specialized AI agents that are focused *specifically* on the needs of the individual teams. Alternatively, we may decide to build and deploy specialized AI agents specific to the area of expertise. For example, a controls agent.

Let us also explore another scenario where a function can be automated using an AI agent. One of the roles missing, but crucial in any system design, is a test engineer. In some projects, the role of testing may be part of a job function instead of a dedicated role. The benefit of this is the familiarity of the engineer to test their work product. On the other hand, making testing part of an engineer's job focus may not give it the rigor or completeness (e.g., testing inter-team product dependencies). If that is the case in this scenario, we could develop a test agent that has the ability to holistically and completely test across all teams' deliverables. When designing agents, there are primarily two types of agents – knowledge-based agents and action-based agents.

Knowledge-Based Agents

The central component of a knowledge-based agent is the knowledge base (KB), and this is generally represented by the now well-known Retrieval Augmented Generation (RAG) architecture. KBs are grounding sources for your LLM-based agent. In most agentic designs, it is almost certain that there will be at least one agent, in a multi-agent workflow, that relies on RAG to carry out their assigned role. A failure of such an agent would potentially affect the decisions by other agents in the agent group. As you will see shortly, we can have action-only agents or knowledge-based agents.

Action-Based Agents

Another important feature of agents is the ability to extend LLMs into actionable tasks. Prior to Agents, LLMs were restricted only to inferencing roles. In fact, LLM's claim to fame is ChatGPT, a chat bot.

Instead of just being able to answer questions very well, with the agentic approach and using agents, if the request is to "develop a correspondence email," for example, instead of just crafting the email, the agent can invoke tools that allow it so send the email as well. "Sending the email" is the actionable task of the "develop a correspondence email" NLP that the agent can execute. We will visit this example in Chapter 6 when we discuss function tools.

Another example is leveraging the codex capability of LLMs to translate an NLP request into an SQL statement-given knowledge of the schema of a database. Taking this a step further, the agent can then call on tools to connect to the database and execute the SQL statement, retrieve the records, and either present it verbatim as a table or summarize the results back to NLP. We will visit this example in Chapter 5 when we discuss Model Context Protocol (MCP).

Agents that carry out tasks are often referred to as Action-based agents. We do so to differentiate them from the knowledge-based agents.

Knowledge Bases (KB)

As mentioned earlier, KBs are the source of truth that grounds the AI model. KBs are scoped to enhance, restrict, or override the general knowledge that LLMs possess. Following the "garbage in, garbage out" adage, failures in agentic systems often stem from the inadequate design of KBs.

KB inadequacies can occur when there is

- Too little information
- Too much information
- Conflicting information

The first occurrence is quite self-explanatory. When there is too little information, the LLM would either not be able to answer, or would rely on its training data (sometimes known as general knowledge), which may be inaccurate or outdated.

The second occurrence can occur when insufficient context is provided. One simple example is information regarding contact information. If there are multiple different contact information in a single KB, these could lead to LLM confusion, thereby leading to unpredictable responses. This is very common whenever the design leverages a single general purpose KB.

Knowledge Engineering

The third occurrence regarding conflicting or contradictory information in a KB can be addressed through a process called knowledge engineering.[1] Through knowledge engineering, KBs are created and scoped to specific domains. Therefore, instead of general KBs, part of an agentic approach would involve the development of specific-purpose KBs.

Using the Mars Rover engineering team scenario unveiled earlier, a large KB may contain conflicting engineering terms if we did not have specific-purpose KBs. For example, the mechanical engineers on the project may need to factor in losses due to friction and damping. These are essential for controllability and are sometimes deliberately introduced as part of the design. In electrical engineering, loss is almost aways a bad thing (e.g., heat generation due to loss, power losses, etc.). The design intent may be contradictory (is loss good or bad), depending on the context. Therefore, just as agent specialization provides better overall system quality, developing and incorporating specific-purpose KBs through knowledge engineering is also an important factor to take into consideration in agentic design.

Incorporate Structure in Prompt Engineering

By now, everyone knows about prompt engineering, which are the instructions for the agent. In most cases, prompt engineering can be accomplished through NLP and incorporating strategies such as few-shot learning.[2] Going into detail on prompt engineering is beyond the scope of

---

[1] Stuart Russel and Peter Norvig - Artificial Intelligence, a modern approach. Fourth Edition.

[2] Julian Soh and Priyanshi Singh - Data Science Solutions on Azure, the rise of Generative AI and Applied AI. Second Edition.

this book and furthermore, there are many resources that cover this topic in detail (see our other book referenced in the footnote below).

There are also less common, advanced prompt engineering techniques that can further govern the actions of agents. For example, we can leverage concepts from propositional logic[3] in prompt engineering. Although prompt engineering does not use propositional logic in a strict, formal, and mathematical sense, and LLMs do not evaluate truth tables or execute symbolic logic, the structure of propositional logic can be used to effectively constrain and guide agent behavior. Therefore, leveraging the structure of propositional logic as a design analogy for your agents can remove ambiguity, enhance inference, and thus improve the quality of your agents. An elegant and effective prompt is usually a combination of natural language and structured syntax.

Model Context Protocol (MCP)

Closely related to Knowledge-based agents and RAG is the Model Context Protocol (MCP). We will be exploring MCP in greater detail in Chapter 6, but we are introducing MCP here because it is a key feature of knowledge-based agents. As its name implies, it is a communication protocol that facilitates the access to external tools and data sources. MCP is extensively used when databases are involved, which can be seen as a variation of RAG for structured data. Agents and MCP often go together as part of the agentic architecture.

[3] Propositional Logic – the use of logical words like AND, OR, NOT, and IF-THEN, which will then lead to reasoning output (e.g., Truth Tables).

Physical AI

In Chapter 1, we discussed the rapid emergence of robots, which in essence is the fusion of AI with machines. There is a category for this in agentic AI design, and it's called Physical AI.

Physical AI is an extension of AI actions that we discussed above. Instead of just carrying out tasks, these tasks are translated to actuators, servos, cameras, and any input/output device in the physical realm. The integration of Grok in Tesla vehicles is a great example of Physical AI.

Therefore, when designing your AI product or service, you are no longer limited to a purely software solution. You may decide to partner with device manufacturers to enable your AI solution to physically interact with the real world. In an Agentic approach, you may designate specific agents that specialize in the interaction and control of different machines.

Ambient AI

Ambient AI is a close relative to Physical AI and is sometimes categorized as a subset of Physical AI. Ambient AI refers to intelligent systems that operate on a continuous basis in the background. It uses sensors and other input devices such as cameras and microphones to proactively assess their environment. Ambient AI is also seen as the natural evolution from the IoT era with AI overlayed on top of traditional IoT devices. The defining goal of Ambient AI is to make technology feel invisible and supportive, thereby allowing people to focus on their primary tasks which AI augments their efforts seamlessly. Just like Physical AI, because of the uniqueness of devices, specialized agents would need to be associated with such devices. Looking at it in a different way, Ambient AI agents rely primarily on inputs from physical devices, and may in turn collaborate with other agents that are connected to output-based devices (e.g., actuators). Figure 4-2 below is a simple illustration of a weather agent serving as an Ambient AI agent that incorporates data drawn from a weather service via an API, combining the data from a weather sensor, and then collaborating with the automation agent serving as a Physical AI agent that controls irrigation.

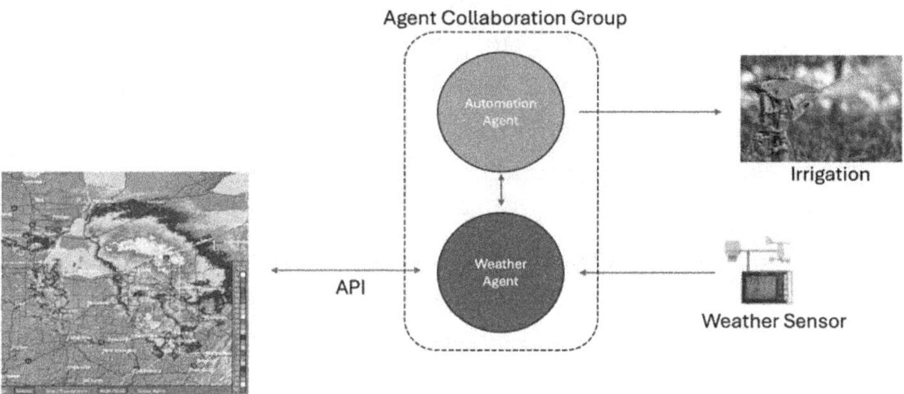

Figure 4-2. *Agent collaboration incorporating physical and ambient AI*

Declarative vs. Procedural

Agents are knowledge-based entities. A knowledge base contains sentences that represent facts the agent believes to be true about the world. Knowledge bases had to be written in formal syntax but any unstructured content can now be ingested by LLMs. Therefore, inserting a language model between an agent and a knowledge base is foundational to the agentic approach.

The knowledge-based approach is declarative in nature. An agent asks a knowledge base and figures out the response, or the actions to take if it is task-based. The declarative approach creates flexibility and the language model extends that flexibility to NLP. For example, if the knowledge base contains information about US states and roads, a declarative approach would allow a user to issue a request to travel from Seattle to San Francisco by car without prescribing a route. The LLM will be able to recommend a route based on the desired prompts (e.g., shortest path, no tolls, most scenic, etc.).

Compare this to traditional development where the approach is generally procedural in nature. The procedural approach requires program behaviors to be directly and specifically expressed. Reusing the above example for comparison, specific routes from Seattle to San Francisco would need to be categorized and then programmed into the system. New routes will need to be explicitly added or changed because the procedural approach would not be able to infer these new routes dynamically.

Therefore, a declarative knowledge-based approach makes it easier to modify and extend applications. When implementing an AI product or solution, modernizing legacy applications that were built based on procedural statements may provide the quickest and/or highest return on investment (ROI).

Orchestration Frameworks

Out of all the foundational concepts for agentic AI, Orchestration Frameworks play an oversized role. Think of these frameworks as the "glue" that defines the agent-to-agent relationships. Since one of the main goals of creating multiple agents is to improve performance and quality, there needs to be a way to coordinate the work of these agents. That is the job of orchestration frameworks.

LangChain

LangChain is an open-source Python-based framework that comes bundled with toolkits (sometimes referred to as packages) that integrate with different services and applications. Creating an LLM-powered application takes the form of connecting actions, like building blocks, into an orchestrated workflow, hence the term "chains" in LangChain, where chains refer to the orchestration of actions into a workflow. As such its name was derived from "Lang," to represent the Language models the framework supports, and "Chain" representing its core functionality of linking services. LangChain supports models from OpenAI, Cohere, HuggingFace, Anthropic, and more.

AutoGen

AutoGen is one of several orchestration frameworks introduced by Microsoft. Like LangChain, it is an open-source framework for building agentic AI systems with a particular focus on multi-agent collaboration. Developers can create AI agents that can communicate with each other and use tools and APIs to solve complex tasks through structured iterations. AutoGen is designed to support both experimentation and real-world applications but is not recommended for enterprise grade, mission critical applications.

Semantic Kernel

Semantic Kernel is another orchestration framework from Microsoft. It is an alternative framework to LangChain and is also open source. It is available as an SDK in Python, C#, and Java. Semantic Kernel is positioned as the enterprise grade orchestration framework compared to AutoGen, which is a very important differentiator.

Instead of chains, Semantic Kernel revolves around a kernel that invokes events using plugins and functions to complete a task. It included a Planner that can automatically decide which plugins and functions to use given a prompt, but the planner was later replaced with Automatic Function Calling in newer models of Generative AI models. Again, to emphasize, between Semantic Kernel and AutoGen, the former is considered the enterprise-ready framework, whereas the latter is for research-focused or less critical workloads.

Microsoft Agent Framework

The Microsoft Agent Framework is the third orchestration framework from Microsoft and, like all the others, is also an open-source framework. It is the newest addition to the orchestration framework category and it moved from preview to production release in April 2026. The official name of this release is the Microsoft Agent Framework 1.0 for .Net and Python. Having said that, the Microsoft Agent Framework continues to rapidly evolve with many preview and experimental features being dropped every week. The Microsoft Agent Framework is an enterprise-grade orchestration framework and combines the best of AutoGen with Semantic Kernel. Think of the Microsoft Agent Framework as the next generation and the go-to framework to use.

Which Framework to Use?

Selecting which framework depends on your project. First and foremost, for enterprise-grade applications, you should consider LangChain or the Microsoft Agent Framework. If you do not have any dependencies on Semantic Kernel (e.g., the need to support Java) or AutoGen, then do not consider these frameworks because their features are being combined into Microsoft Agent Framework.

LangChain predates the Microsoft Agent Framework. It also has a broader community support. It currently has more packages than the Microsoft Agent Framework and is most suited for Python, although it does support other languages like JavaScript/TypeScript. On the other hand, because the Microsoft Agent Framework is from Microsoft, it has tighter integration with the .Net and with the Microsoft ecosystem, including Azure. Changes and updates to the Microsoft Agent Framework are less frequent and more controlled than LangChain and this is sometimes viewed positively for production-level workloads, but the preview and experimentation features are introduced very rapidly, thereby achieving the best of both worlds - production stability and rapid prototyping of new features. It supports Python, C#.

Therefore, choosing between the two frameworks depends on the features required by the project, preferred programming language, and the level of integration with the Microsoft ecosystem. In this book, we will be using the Microsoft Agent Framework as the orchestration framework in later chapter and exercises.

Design for Performance and Efficiency

Agent performance and efficiency describes how an AI agent's resource usage - time, cost, and memory - scales as the problem size grows, and Big-O notation provides a useful way to reason about this growth for agentic systems.

For example, an agent that scans every document in a repository to answer a question has O(n) behavior with respect to the number of documents, while an agent that first builds an index or embedding store and then queries it may shift most work to a one-time O(n) preprocessing step and achieve O(log n) or near-constant-time retrieval at runtime. Therefore, when designing agents in this example, we may have two agents - one that is responsible for indexing[4] and another that uses the index and embeddings to better respond to a request.

Similarly, a multiagent "debate" pattern where each agent responds to every other agent can drift toward $O(n^2)$ message exchanges as the number of agents increases, whereas a manager-worker pattern often keeps coordination closer to O(n) by routing communication through a single

[4] In a real-world implementation, some of these may not require agents but may be built into services. For this example, indexing and embeddings can be incorporated in the search service. Nonetheless, this is a good example of how we include performance and efficiency as part of the agentic design.

orchestrator. This is an example of the Magentic Pattern in the Microsoft Agent Framework, which we will cover in Chapter 6. While Big-O does not capture model latency constants or token-level costs, it is still valuable for comparing agent designs: lower order growth (e.g., O[log n] vs. O[n^2]) generally correlates with more scalable, predictable agents as inputs, tools, or collaborators increase.

Choosing the Right Development Option

One of the challenges with today's AI landscape is the myriads of options and tools. This is even more so with the Microsoft portfolio – Microsoft Copilot, Copilot Studio, and Foundry.

To put it simply, if you are building a distributable AI product or service like a SaaS, then your selection should always be Foundry. Microsoft Copilot and Microsoft Copilot Studio are deliberately optimized for internal productivity and line of business enablement, whereas Azure AI Foundry agents, combined with orchestration frameworks (such as Microsoft Agent Framework), are designed to support distributable, production grade, and productized AI systems, and the difference becomes increasingly visible as complexity rises.

Azure AI Foundry agents paired with orchestration frameworks explicitly target productization scenarios: they decouple agent logic from UI, support agent-to-agent communication (A2A), shared context via MCP, deterministic workflows, retries, approvals, human-in-the-loop gates, advanced observability, and multi-model routing, and can be deployed as managed services or embedded into SaaS products, APIs, or external channels without assuming a Microsoft 365 user or license boundary. Foundry provides a control plane for model selection, evaluation, and governance, while the Agent Framework provides a pro-code runtime for orchestrated, multi-agent systems that scale from prototype to production - something explicitly called out as a gap in Copilot-centric approaches when developers attempt to ship externally consumable agents or complex autonomous workflows.

Summary

In this chapter, we introduced the design concepts and foundational knowledge when developing agents. You should be able to leverage this knowledge to determine the number and types of agents and KBs needed for your product or service. This chapter also sets the stage for a deeper dive into the technologies covered in the following chapters.

CHAPTER 5

Building with Model Context Protocol (MCP)

In Chapter 4, we learned all about Agents and the Agentic Architecture. We introduced the concept of delegating smaller tasks to multiple LLM agents rather than a single bloated LLM prompt. With multiple agents, knowledge sources can be smaller and targeted, and prompts can be more precise. This will all lead to better execution performance and less hallucination.

What Are We Trying to Achieve?

In this chapter, we are going to achieve two things:

- Extending the capabilities of agents
- Getting agents to collaborate with each other

J. Soh et al., *Building and Distributing Agentic AI Solutions*,
https://doi.org/10.1007/979-8-8688-2586-6_5

First, we will take a look at extending the abilities of the agents. Specifically, we will be looking at two important abilities:

- The ability to look up real-time data
- The ability to execute tasks

These are commonly referred to as tools. Although quite intuitive and self-explanatory, let us take a look at the benefits of enabling agents with these tools.

Real-Time Data

One of the shortcomings of LLMs is the timebound data that is restricted to when the model was trained. We are all familiar with the Retrieval Augmented Generation (RAG) architecture that grounds the LLM with curated data sources. However, this is still based on time-bound data sources.

A compelling use case for an agentic tool is to allow the LLM to retrieve real-time data from web services, or look up a structured data source like a database. For example, with a tool, the LLM can look up a flight's status from web services to find out its flight schedule. An investment tracker application, when asked in natural language what the current top market movers for the day are can connect to web services to get that information and research on latest news that may have caused such a movement.

Perform Tasks

Aside from the tasks of retrieving information, creating content, or answering questions, the other benefit of using Semantic Kernel is to carry out tasks. For example, after looking up flight status and price, Semantic Kernel can initiate purchasing of an airline ticket, or book hotels, etc.

At this point, you may be wondering what difference agents are making. Are we not able to do this via web Application Programming Interfaces (API) today? Real-time lookups via APIs can be done with a

GET request to an endpoint. Likewise, we can execute tasks by making a POST request to API endpoints that invoke actions. In fact, APIs are so ubiquitous and provide the foundational interoperability between disparate systems on the internet.

The value of the Model Context Protocol (MCP) is that it further streamlines and simplifies the use of APIs.

Model Context Protocol (MCP)

As its name implies, MCP is a protocol. It was founded by Anthropic to make it easier for AI systems to interact with capabilities of the computing world, such as

- Carrying out tasks
- Easier access to structured data sources

But the *most important* differentiator between APIs and MCP is the latter's capability to

- Dynamically advertise its capabilities
- Dynamically ingest the metadata of structured data sources

MCP is an open-source protocol and has rapidly become the standard of connecting data sources and tools to LLM agents. The architecture of MCP is essentially a Client-Server architecture. The primary components of the MCP architecture are

- The Host
- The Client
- The Server

Figure 5-1 below depicts the MCP architecture. At the top of the architecture is the host. The host is the User Interface (UI) that could take the form of a chat interface, an Integrated Development Environment (IDE) like GitHub Copilot, an application, or a workflow.

The MCP Host will contain an MCP client and the MCP client will then communicate to MCP Server via the MCP protocol transport layer.

MCP Servers have access to databases, APIs, and or code. This access layer is often referred to as the tools that MCP servers can invoke. The capabilities of these tools and how they can be invoked are advertised by the MCP Servers to the MCP Clients.

The MCP architecture takes advantage of the Codex capability of language models because it translates natural language requests into code or query for execution.

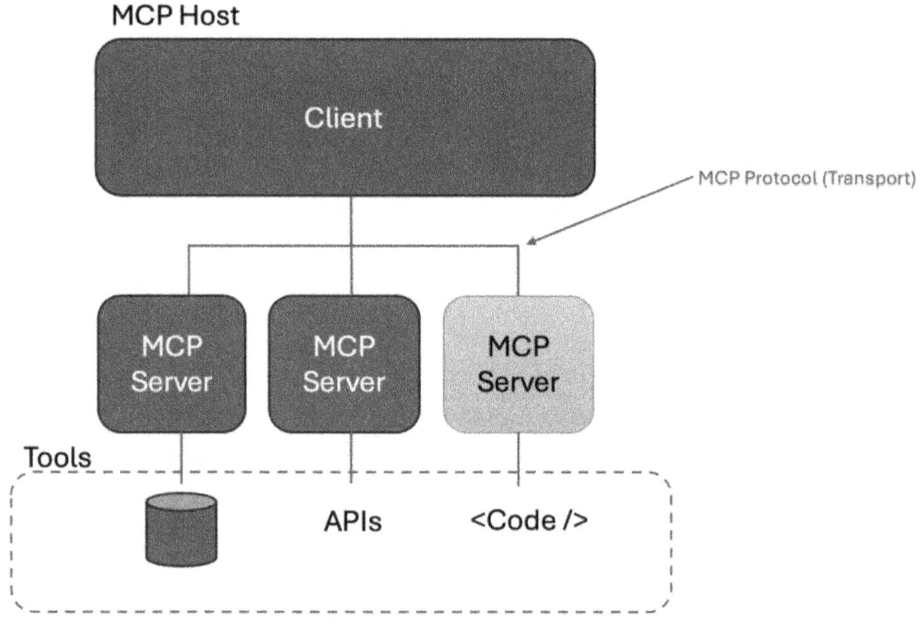

Figure 5-1. *MCP architecture*

MCP and LLM integration

Figure 5-2 below depicts the conversation flow from a user to an AI system that comprises MCP servers and an LLM.

For the sake of simplifying the architecture, we are omitting the agent from the diagram and depicting a direct communication to the LLM. In reality, the LLM is represented by an agent because that is where the prompt engineering layer resides.

The conversation flow as depicted in Figure 5-2 is as follows:

1. Assume a question is submitted from a suer to an MCP host, in this case, a chatbot.
2. The MCP host uses its MCP client to query the MCP servers to retrieve information on available tools.
3. The MCP client then sends the question *together with* information of the available tools to the LLM.
4. The LLM assesses the question and determines the best tool(s) to use, then sends the instructions on specific tool(s) to use back to the MCP client.
5. The MCP client communicates directly with the MCP server(s) that can execute the specific tools.
6. The MCP server(s) executes the tool and gets the results.
7. The result is returned to the MCP client that then forwards it back to the LLM.
8. The LLM incorporates and formats the results into a response to the original question and sends the completed response back to the MCP client, which then returns it to the MCP host for the user.

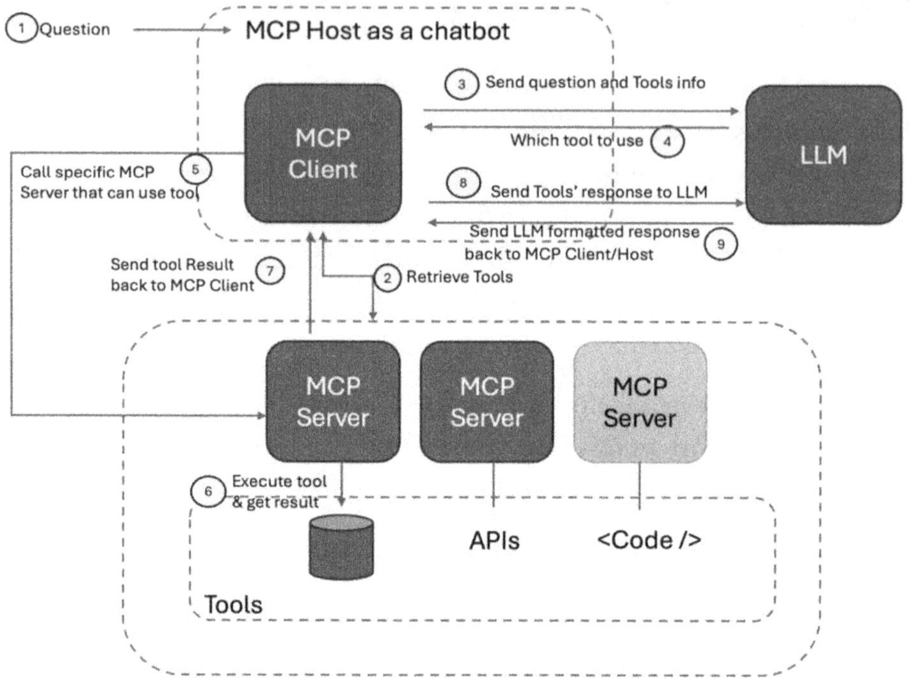

Figure 5-2. *Conversation pathway between MCP and LLM*

Next, to help better understand this flow, we will rephrase it via the specific examples below.

Dynamic Consumption of APIs Using MCP

Developers often need to understand what an API can do and the right way to invoke it. So, they often rely on a set of documentation-related terms, and Swagger, for example, is one of the most common toolsets. Swagger is so popular that it is sometimes used as a verb, although it is not the only tool in this space. Tools like Swagger describe how an API is defined, documented, and understood before anyone writes a line of integration code. When someone says "Check the Swagger," they usually mean "look at the API's interactive documentation to understand the endpoints, parameters, and models. Figure 5-3 below shows the API reference for ServiceNow. Making a REST GET request from the API endpoint and passing it the "/now/account/{id}" will return a response containing the account information tied to the "id". The response is usually in JSON format.

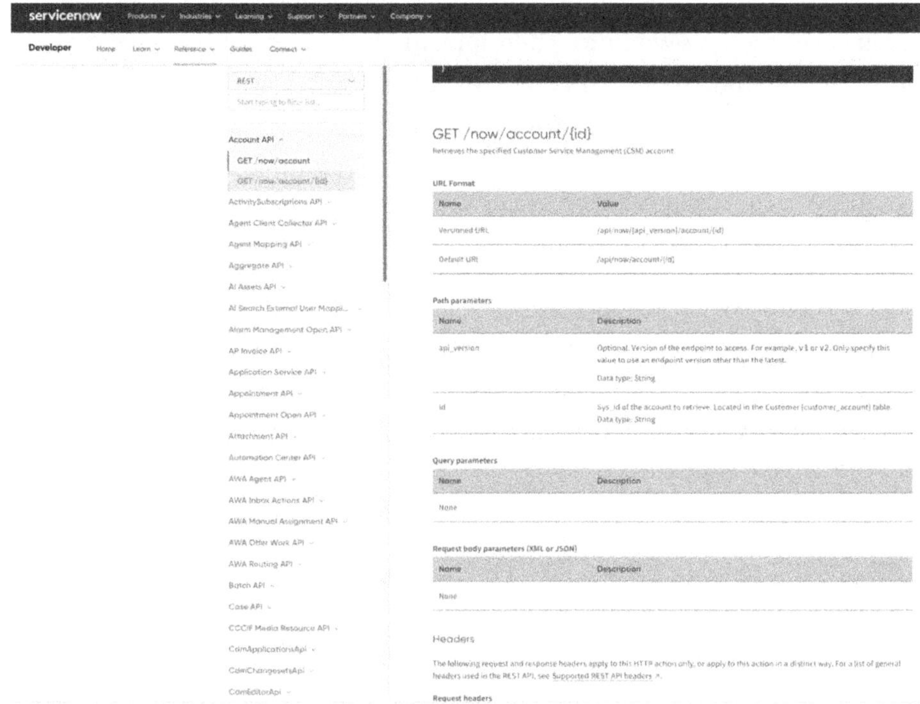

Figure 5-3. *API reference for ServiceNow*

The problem with APIs though is that new capabilities would be introduced and old capabilities removed. The parameters and format on how the API is being called would thus also need to be modified. Therefore, like applications, APIs also have version numbers and need to be maintained.

There are two sides to the API consumption equation. The first side of this equation, as described above, is the ongoing maintenance of APIs. This is unavoidable. The second side of this equation is the consumption of the APIs within applications and workflows. Whenever there are changes to APIs, developers who are consuming services exposed by these APIs will need to update their code. If they do not do so, then the system would break, thereby leading to down time. Therefore, in an ideal scenario, developers will always be informed of API changes, and that they are able to implement the changes in a timely fashion, which, unfortunately is not always the case.

Since AI Agents use APIs to extend their capabilities, what if there is a way for them to dynamically learn about the capabilities exposed by the API? This will solve the issue of breakage whenever APIs change, not to mention the ease of consuming APIs in the first place. This is what MCP solves for the world of APIs and we will explore this further in our hands-on exercises later in this chapter. Essentially, by putting MCPs in front of APIs, the agents and LLMs will not directly interact with the API first, but with the MCP to dynamically discover capabilities exposed as tools.

Dynamic Schema Understanding

Semantic Models are a higher level abstraction of the traditional Entity-Relationship (ER) between tables in a database as well as the overall schema of the tables. A semantic model describes the meaning of the data, not just its structure, and it focuses on

- Business concepts
- How those concepts relate
- Logic behind relationships
- Rules that govern the domain
- How data should be interpreted by humans or analytics tools

An example of an ER model is – "Table A links to Table B via foreign key X," whereas a semantic model says "A Customer places Orders, and an Order contains Products."

The idea behind using MCP as a dynamic schema-understanding tool is to help the LLM translate a natural language request into a query that the application or workflow can execute against the database. Then taking the results from that query and running it through the LLM again to refine the final response. The LLM, using MCP to understand the queries it can execute, should be able to ingest the schema and ultimately the construction of the query without the need of a Semantic Model.

Next, we are going to do four hands-on sessions to demonstrate the MCP architecture and concepts we have discussed so far:

- **Hands-on exercise 5.1**: Adding an existing MCP server to an IDE (VSCode). Pre-requisite: GitHub Copilot.
- **Hands-on exercise 5.2**: Creating an MCP server and testing it locally. Pre-requisite: GitHub Copilot.
- **Hands-on exercise 5.3**: Use MCP as a data connector.
- **Hands-on exercise 5.4**: Publishing the MCP server to a Web Application and testing via Foundry.

Aside from GitHub Copilot as a pre-requisite, since these examples leverage the Microsoft Azure Cloud, an Azure subscription would be required. If you are a developer but have not used GitHub Copilot before, it is a difference maker. Even though this book is not focused on GitHub or in-depth development, it does have sufficient development topics to warrant having exposure to GitHub Copilot. That is why we designed these exercises to include GitHub Copilot even though you can test MCP servers in other ways. Being familiar with GitHub Copilot will greatly enhance your development capabilities and shorten your product development cycle.

Hands-On Exercise 5.1: Using VSCode and GitHub Copilot to Consume an MCP Server

For this hands-on exercise, we will be consuming an existing MCP server. The one that we have selected is the Microsoft Learn MCP server.[1]

The Microsoft Learn MCP server is a publicly available endpoint that exposes all the available documentation from the Microsoft Learn site. It is provided at no charge and can be accessed *programmatically* at `https://learn.microsoft.com/api/mcp`

1. Install, if needed, then launch VSCode.[2]
2. If needed, install the GitHub Copilot extension for VSCode[3] and ensure that it is active.
3. At the top of the VSCode windows, next to the search box, click on the [chat icon] to expand the chat pane, as shown in Figure 5-4.

[1] More information about the Microsoft Learn MCP Server can be found at `https://learn.microsoft.com/en-us/training/support/mcp`

[2] Download and installation instructions for VSCode are located at `https://code.visualstudio.com/download`

[3] `https://docs.github.com/en/copilot/how-tos/set-up/install-copilot-extension`

Figure 5-4. *VSCode with GitHub Copilot extension and expanded chat pane*

4. Since we are going to look at agent orchestration later, let us try to find out more about it at this time. Type *"Documentation for Agent Framework"* in the chat, as shown in Figure 5-5 below and observe the response. Note that GitHub Copilot is not invoking any MCP Servers, or tools, and seems to be attempting to answer the question based on its general knowledge. Take note of the response because we are going to compare it to the response when using an MCP server later.

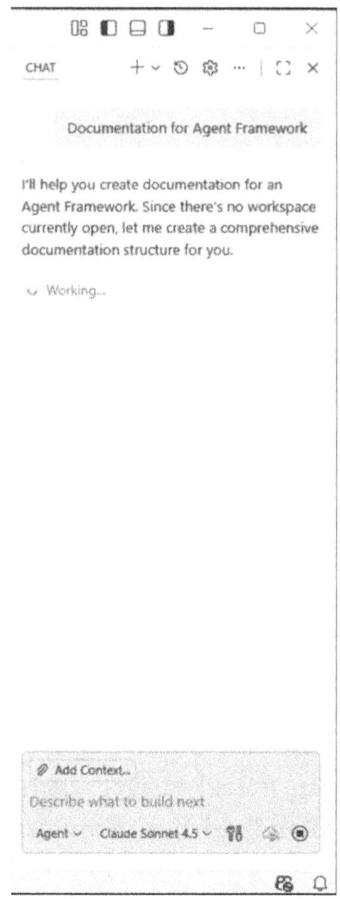

***Figure 5-5.** GitHub Copilot chat answering a question without tools*

5. Let us look at the attached MCP servers (there should be none). Click on ⚙ at the top right corner of the VSCode window and select "MCP Servers" in the dropdown menu to expand the MCP server pane, as shown in Figure 5-6. Note that there are no MCP servers installed.

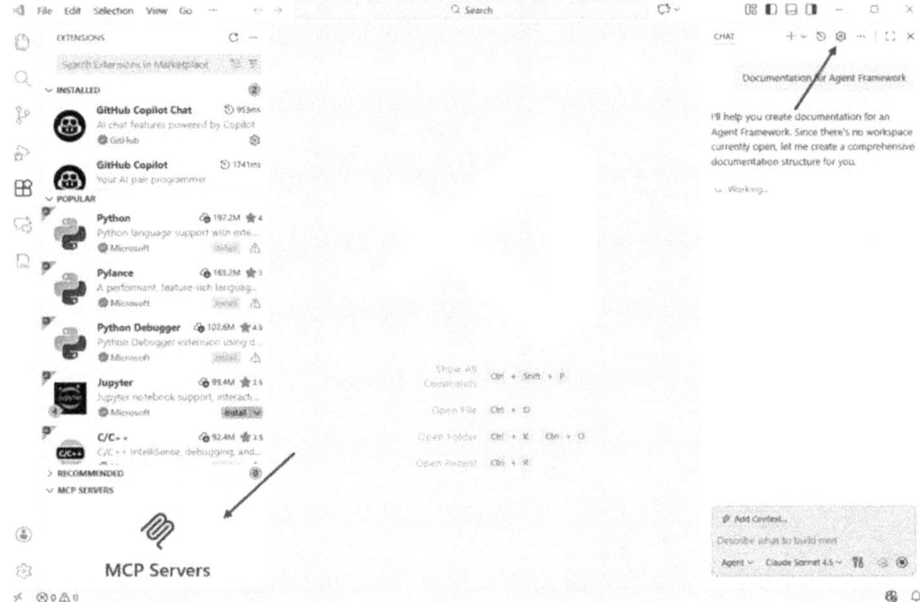

***Figure 5-6.** View attached MCP servers in VSCode*

6. The easiest way to add an MCP server is when there is an installation link, like the one provided by Microsoft Learn and detailed here – `https://learn.microsoft.com/en-us/training/support/mcp-get-started#configure-your-editor`. However, we are going to show how to manually install an MCP server because often times, you will have to do so when just given the REST endpoint of the server.

7. As mentioned above, the MCP endpoint for the Microsoft Learn MCP server is `https://learn.microsoft.com/api/mcp`. As shown in Figure 5-7, press CTRL-SHIFT-P in VSCode to activate the command window and type "MCP" in the search box and select "MCP: Add Server" in the dropdown box.

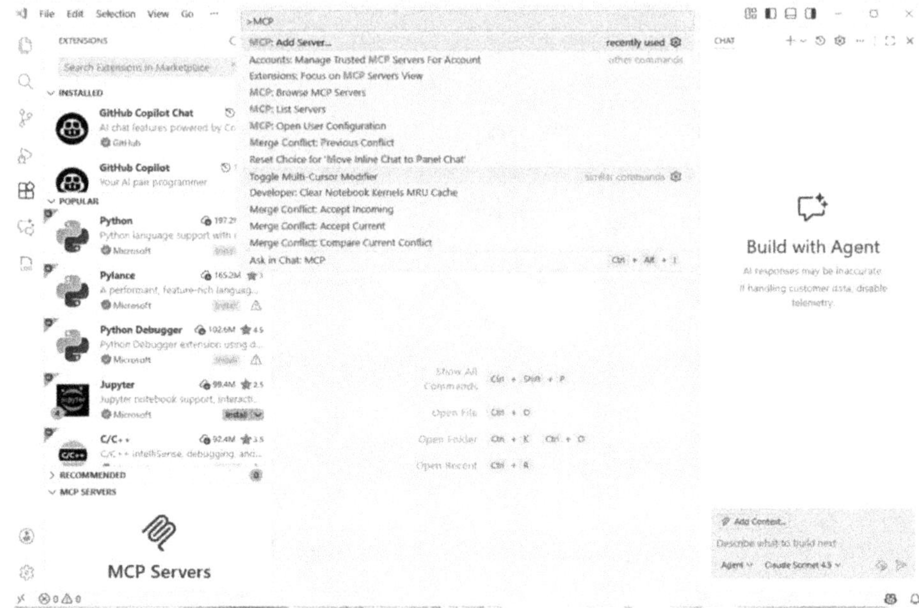

Figure 5-7. *Adding an MCP server in VSCode*

8. Select *"HTTP (HTTP of Server-Sent Events) Connect to a remote HTTP server that implements the MCP protocol,"* as shown in Figure 5-8.

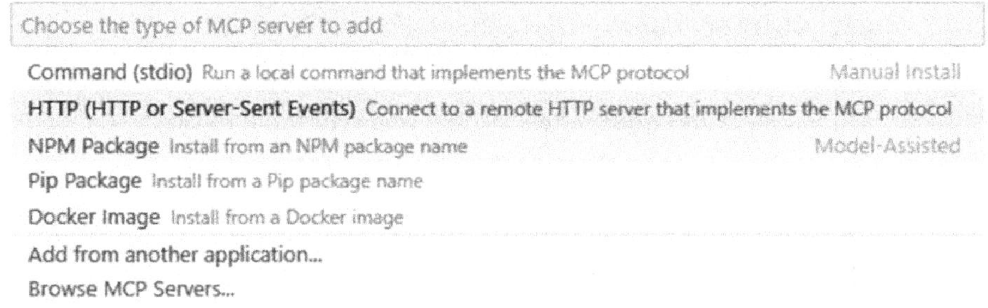

Figure 5-8. *Select connection to a remote MCP server*

9. Type in the REST endpoint for the Microsoft Learn MCP server (`https://learn.microsoft.com/api/mcp`), as shown in Figure 5-9 below, then press Enter.

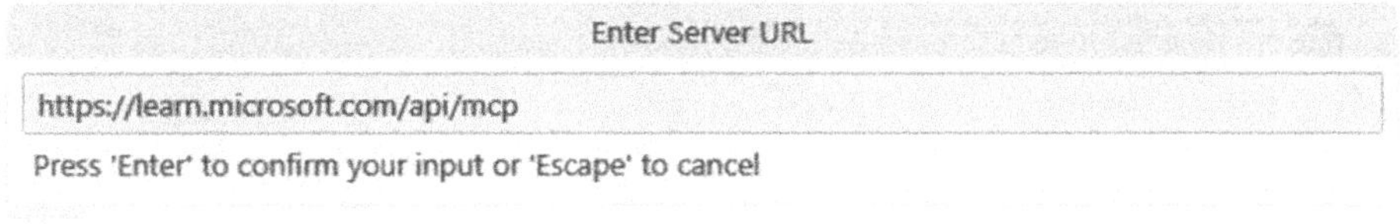

Enter Server URL

https://learn.microsoft.com/api/mcp

Press 'Enter' to confirm your input or 'Escape' to cancel

Figure 5-9. *Providing the REST endpoint for the Microsoft Learn MCP server*

10. VSCode will suggest a name (usually in the form of my-mcp-server-xxxxx), as shown in Figure 5-10. If you like, pick a different name. For this exercise, we named this MCP server connection *"Microsoft-Learn-MCP-server."*

Enter Server ID

my-mcp-server-c3ddda32

Press 'Enter' to confirm your input or 'Escape' to cancel

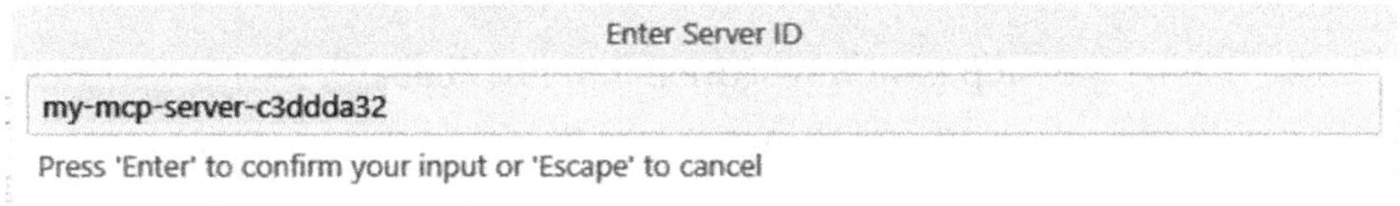

Figure 5-10. *Naming the MCP server connection*

11. As shown in Figure 5-11 below, after naming your MCP server connection and pressing Enter, a json file named mcp.json is opened in a tab, the MCP server now appears in the bottom left corner of the IDE under the *"MCP Servers - Installed"* tab, and the GitHub Copilot chat interface at the bottom right appears to have attached the mcp.json as a file source.

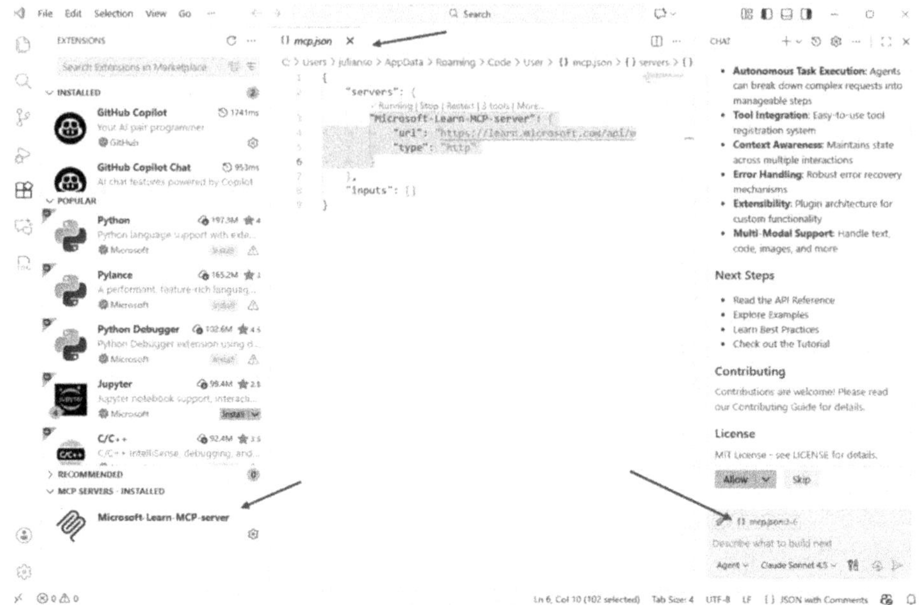

Figure 5-11. *Microsoft Learn MCP server installed in VSCode*

12. Close the mcp.json tab. Notice that it will also disappear as an attachment from the GitHub Copilot Chat interface.

13. Click on + ⌄ that is located above the GitHub Copilot chat pane and select *"New Chat,"* as shown in Figure 5-12.

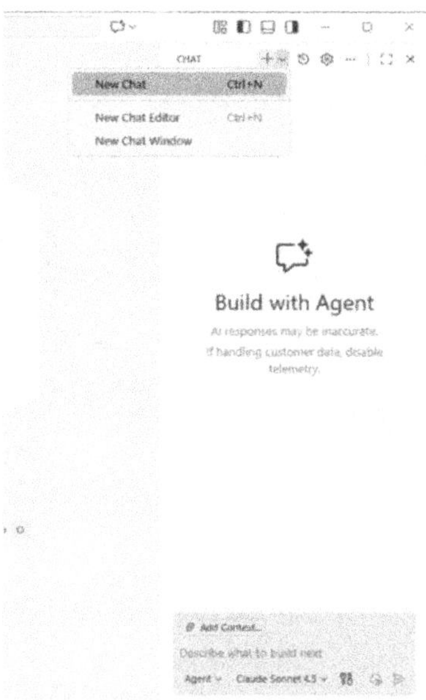

***Figure 5-12.** Starting a new chat session*

14. Notice that this time, GitHub Copilot uses the Microsoft Learning MCP server and the tools it has to generate the response, as shown in Figure 5-13.

Figure 5-13. *GitHub Copilot using the Microsoft Learning MCP server to respond to a question*

15. Compare the response in step 14 to the one in step 4. Not only is it more concise, did you notice that it responded a lot quicker as well? This is an easy way to demonstrate the improved accuracy and performance when using the tools advertised by an MCP server for a more targeted response.

Hands-On Exercise 5.2: Creating Your First MCP Server

Now that we have seen how to connect to an existing MCP server and exposing it to VSCode and the GitHub Copilot chat extension as the MCP Host, we will look at developing our own MCP server in this hands-on exercise.

Use Case Scenario

We will use an MCP server template and explore the structure of the project. We will then add a database tool to the MCP server. The database tool will enable the MCP server to Create, Read, Update, Delete, and Query a database. We will then use Natural Language to query the database.

Pre-requisites

1. If you have not done so in previous exercises, clone this book's GitHub repo.[4]
2. We will need a database in the next exercise so we will deploy one now. You can skip this step if you already have a database. Otherwise, install Azure SQL Database with a sample database using the included bicep script:
    a. In VSCode, navigate to the folder Chapter_05\Exercise5-2\database. This is where the bicep script to deploy an Azure SQL Database for this hands-on exercise is available.

[4] https://github.com/juliansoh/Building_and_Distributing_AI-Enabled-Solutions

b. Gather the following information

   i. From your Azure subscription because we will be using EntraID for authentication:

      1. TenantID[5]

      2. Your User ObjectID[6] (this user will be assigned the SQL Admin role)

      3. SubscriptionID[7]

   ii. You will also need your computer's IP address. This is used to create a firewall rule in the Azure SQL Database server to allow connections from your computer.

   iii. Think of a name for the SQL Server and a name for the resource-group where the database will be created.

   iv. Decide on the region you want to deploy the Azure SQL Database to.

c. Modify the params.json file with the information gathered is step 2(b),[8] as shown in Figure 5-14.

---

[5] From the Azure Portal, search for Microsoft Entra ID and the information should be in the Overview section.

[6] On the Microsoft Entra ID pane, expand Manage, then select Users. Select the user you want to assign as the SQL admin and on the Overview pane for that user, copy the Object ID.

[7] Type Subscription in the search box of the Azure Portal and select the subscription to deploy Azure SQL Server to. Copy the SubscriptionID (or if you go to any existing resource in that subscription, the SubscriptionID is in the Overview pane of the resource).

[8] The aaAdminDisplayName can be anything because the aaAdminObjectId is the one being used for SQL admin role assignment. But you will want to just use the friendly name of the Entra user for easy identification.

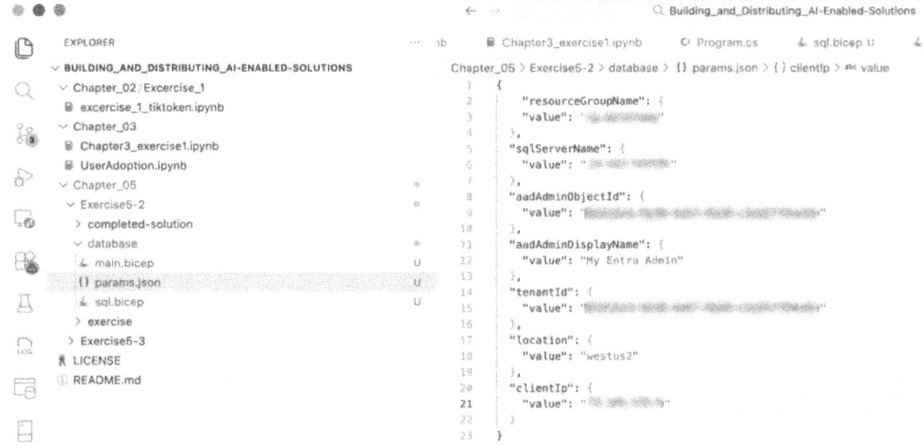

Figure 5-14. *Modifying the params.json that will be used to deploy Azure SQL Database*

d. Save the params.json file.

e. Open (or reuse) a terminal window in VSCode. Make sure you are in the Chapter_05\Exercise5-2\database folder in the terminal, and:

  i. Type *az login* to log into Azure. If prompted, select the correct subscription (the one that corresponds to what is in params.json).

  ii. After login is successful, type *az deployment sub create –location <location> --template-file main.bicep –paramaters @params.json*, as shown in Figure 5-15. When the job is complete (this may take a while), a json output describing all the operations carried out will be displayed.

```
PROBLEMS   OUTPUT   TERMINAL   PORTS   POLYGLOT NOTEBOOK   ...        zsh - database
juliansoh@Julians-MacBook-Pro database % az deployment sub create --location westus2 --template-file main.bicep --parameter
s @params.json
A new Bicep release is available: v0.39.26. Upgrade now by running "az bicep upgrade".
{
  "id": "/subscriptions/[illegible]/providers/Microsoft.Resources/deployments/main",
  "location": "westus2",
  "name": "main",
  "properties": {
    "correlationId": "[illegible]",
    "debugSetting": null,
    "dependencies": [
      {
        "dependsOn": [
          {
            "id": "/subscriptions/[illegible]/resourceGroups/rg-deleteme",
            "resourceName": "rg-deleteme",
            "resourceType": "Microsoft.Resources/resourceGroups"
          }
        ],
        "id": "/subscriptions/[illegible]/resourceGroups/rg-deleteme/providers/Microsoft.Resources
/deployments/sqlServerDeployment",
        "resourceGroup": "rg-deleteme",
        "resourceName": "sqlServerDeployment",
        "resourceType": "Microsoft.Resources/deployments"
      }
    ],
    "duration": "PT16M58.9224593S",
    "error": null,
```

Figure 5-15. *Deploying the Azure SQL Database via deployment script*

Using MCP Carry Out Tasks via APIs

1. Browse the folder *Chapter_05\Exercise5-2\exercise\src\tools*

2. You should see three .cs files

   - MutiplicationTools.cs
   - TemperatureConverterTools.cs
   - WeatherTools.cs

3. As the directory (and names of the files) implies, these are the tools available to the MCP server. Open the *WeatherTools.cs* file. Identify the following aspects about this file:

   - The *WeatherTools.cs* file implements capabilities from the US weather service API - `https://api.weather.gov`

- There are two methods: GetAlerts() and GetForecast()
- Notice that these methods contain code to call specific capabilities of the weather API - GET /alerts and GET /points.

4. Open a browser window and go to `https://api.weather.gov`, as shown in Figure 5-16. Remember our discussion about "looking up the swagger documentation" of an API earlier in this chapter? The page you are seeing lists all the API methods. Locate the documentation for /alerts and /points on this page.

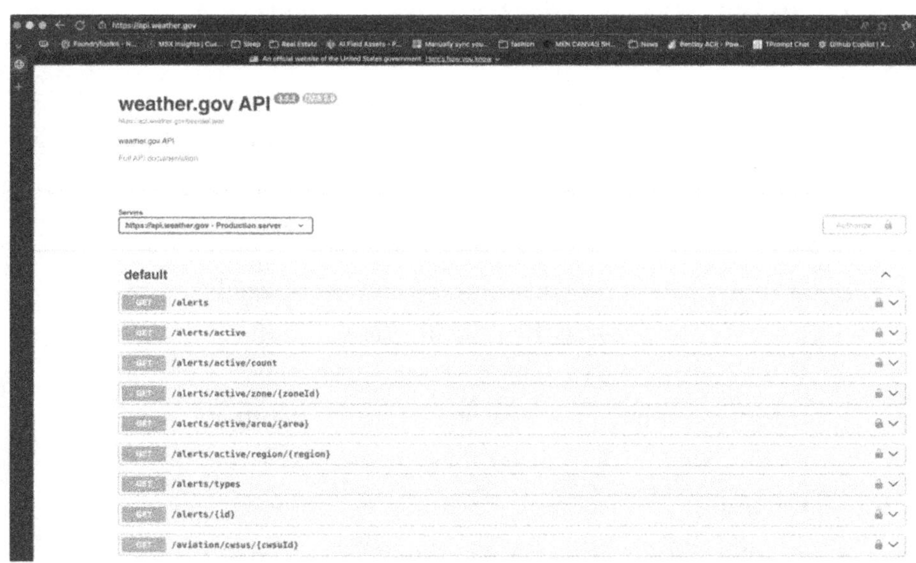

Figure 5-16. *The API documentation for the US Weather Service*

5. Compare the /alerts and /points documentation to the code in *WeatherTools.cs*.
6. In a terminal window in VSCode, navigate to the *Chapter_05\Exercise5-2\exercise\src* folder.
7. Type *dotnet build* to build the MCP server.
8. After build is complete, type *dotnet run* to run the server. The server will run on localhost, listening on http://127.0.0.1:5000 (or http://localhost:5000)
9. Start a new GitHub Copilot chat session and ask it for the weather in Seattle (or anywhere you prefer). Take note of the response and behavior.
10. We will now make our MCP Server available to GitHub Copilot. Remember how we added the Microsoft Learn MCP server to GitHub Copilot in Exercise 5-1 above (step 7)? Follow the same steps and add http://localhost:5000 as a new MCP server. Then start a new chat session.
11. Now ask the same question and step 6 above. If you pay attention to the output, you will notice that GitHub Copilot now sees the tools available through our local MCP Server running on http://localhost:5000. It may ask for permission to execute the query, and if so, say yes, and you should get weather information for Seattle, in real time, from the weather service API.
12. Now ask the following question: *"List all radar servers."* Note the following behavior from GitHub Copilot:

- There are no tools that can provide a response to this request. WeatherTools.cs does not define this method even though the capability exists from the API - *GET /radar/servers.*
- As such, because GitHub Copilot is an assistant for developers, it recommends code changes to *WeatherTools.cs* that will extend the tool to accommodate such a request in the future, as shown in Figure 5-17. Specifically, GitHub Copilot is generating code that declares the GetRadar() method, which consumes the GET /radar/stations capability from the US Weather Service API.

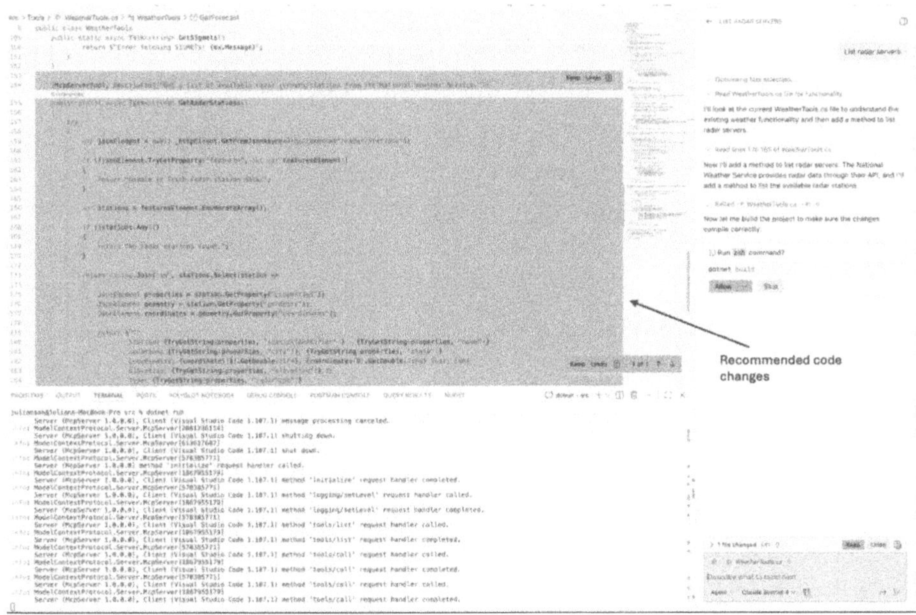

***Figure 5-17.** GitHub Copilot suggesting addition of method GetRadar() to WeatherTools.cs*

- It is important to note that the MCP server or GitHub Copilot DID NOT scan the `https://api.weather.gov` API endpoint to discover capabilities. What happened here is that this is based on GitHub Copilot model training, which included public code from GitHub that has incorporated this capability before. This is an important subtlety that is sometimes mistaken as MCP servers having the capability to adapt to API changes automatically.
    - Having said the above, we can *technically* implement an auto-discovery capability for APIs by creating an MCP tool that queries an endpoint, gets the documentation of the service, and then executes the desired service, provided the API endpoint advertises the documentation. The US weather service API endpoint does so, and returns an HTML document describing capabilities of the API, as shown in Figure 5-18.

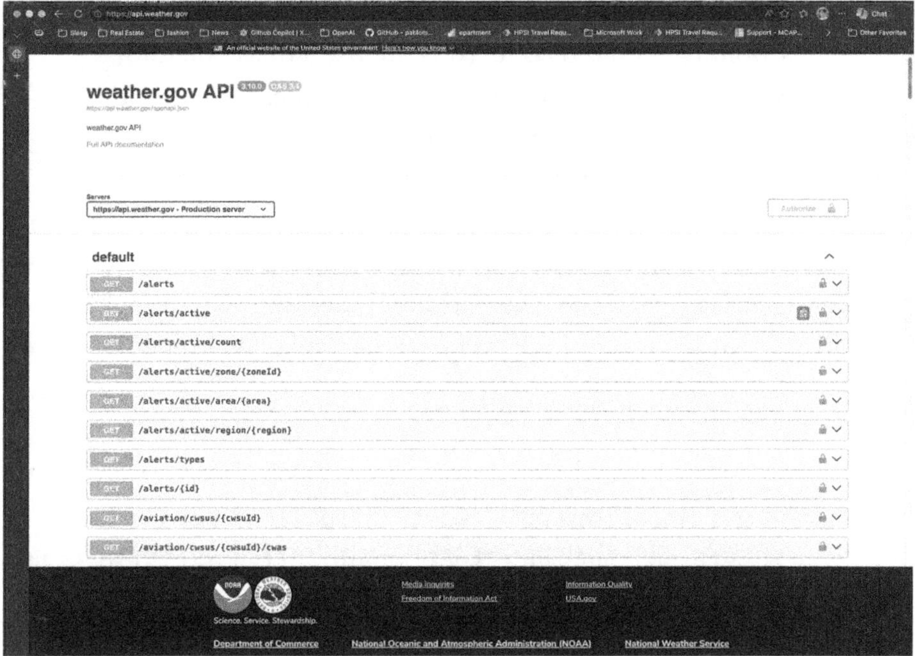

Figure 5-18. *GET request to `https://api.weather.gov` to get API documentation*

- **(Optional Step)**: Go ahead and Keep the code generated by GitHub Copilot. It will also attempt to rebuild and restart the MCP server so the new code would be recognized. Once these steps are done, restart a new chat session and ask for the list of radar servers again. This time, the MCP server will be able to provide the answers. It is not uncommon that the initial code recommended by GitHub Copilot may contain errors, so it will iteratively try to fix it. Be aware that you may experience this if you decide to use GitHub Copilot's generated code.

- **(Optional Step)**: Instead of keeping the GitHub Copilot generated code, you can insert this code into WeatherTools.cs, right after the GetForecast() method (or copy from *Chapter05\Exercise5-2\completed-solution\src\Tools\WeatherTools.cs*).

```
[McpServerTool, Description("Get a list of available radar
servers/stations from the National Weather Service.")]
public static async Task<string> GetRadarStations()
{
    try
    {
        var jsonElement = await _httpClient.
        GetFromJsonAsync<JsonElement>("/radar/stations");

        if (!jsonElement.TryGetProperty("features", out var
        featuresElement))
        {
            return "Unable to fetch radar station data.";
        }

        var stations = featuresElement.EnumerateArray();


        if (!stations.Any())
        {
            return "No radar stations found.";
        }

        return string.Join("\n", stations.Select(station =>
        {
            JsonElement properties = station.
            GetProperty("properties");
```

```
JsonElement geometry = station.
GetProperty("geometry");
JsonElement coordinates = geometry.
GetProperty("coordinates");

// More robust coordinate parsing
double lat = coordinates.GetArrayLength() > 1 ?
coordinates[1].GetDouble() : 0.0;
double lon = coordinates.GetArrayLength() > 0 ?
coordinates[0].GetDouble() : 0.0;

// More robust elevation parsing
string elevation = TryGetProperty(properties,
"elevation");
if (string.IsNullOrEmpty(elevation) &&
properties.TryGetProperty("elevation", out
var elevProp))
{
    elevation = elevProp.ValueKind ==
    JsonValueKind.Number ?
        elevProp.GetDouble().ToString("F0") :
        elevProp.ToString();
}

return $"""
        Station: {TryGetString(properties,
        "stationIdentifier")} -
        {TryGetString(properties, "name")}
        Location: {TryGetString(properties,
        "city")}, {TryGetString(properties,
        "state")}
        Coordinates: {lat:F4}, {lon:F4}
        (Lat, Lon)
```

```
                        Elevation: {elevation} ft
                        Type: {TryGetString(properties,
                        "radarType")}
                        Status: {TryGetString(properties,
                        "operationalStatus")}
                        """;
            }));
        }
        catch (Exception ex)
        {
            return $"Error fetching radar stations:
            {ex.Message}";
        }
    }
```

13. If we had used this MCP Server from anywhere else (e.g., Foundry, which we will see later), the *WeatherTools.cs* tool would not have been invoked, as shown in Figure 5-19. And since this is not the GitHub Copilot chat interface in Agent mode, it does not suggest or generate code automatically for us.

Figure 5-19. *Foundry Chat UI using MCP server*

14. In the VSCode terminal window, you will see all the sessions that were initiated from GitHub Copilot as a result of our questions, as shown in Figure 5-20.

```
PROBLEMS   OUTPUT   TERMINAL   PORTS   POLYGLOT NOTEBOOK   DEBUG CONSOLE   POSTMAN CONSOLE   QUERY RESULTS   NUGET

juliansoh@Julians-MacBook-Pro src % dotnet run
info: ModelContextProtocol.Server.McpServer[570385771]
      Server (McpServer 1.0.0.0), Client (Visual Studio Code 1.107.1) method 'logging/setLevel' request handler called.
info: ModelContextProtocol.Server.McpServer[1867955179]
      Server (McpServer 1.0.0.0), Client (Visual Studio Code 1.107.1) method 'logging/setLevel' request handler completed.
info: ModelContextProtocol.Server.McpServer[570385771]
      Server (McpServer 1.0.0.0), Client (Visual Studio Code 1.107.1) method 'tools/list' request handler called.
info: ModelContextProtocol.Server.McpServer[1867955179]
      Server (McpServer 1.0.0.0), Client (Visual Studio Code 1.107.1) method 'tools/list' request handler completed.
info: ModelContextProtocol.Server.McpServer[570385771]
      Server (McpServer 1.0.0.0), Client (Visual Studio Code 1.107.1) method 'tools/call' request handler called.
info: ModelContextProtocol.Server.McpServer[1867955179]
      Server (McpServer 1.0.0.0), Client (Visual Studio Code 1.107.1) method 'tools/call' request handler completed.
info: ModelContextProtocol.Server.McpServer[570385771]
      Server (McpServer 1.0.0.0), Client (Visual Studio Code 1.107.1) method 'tools/call' request handler called.
info: ModelContextProtocol.Server.McpServer[1867955179]
      Server (McpServer 1.0.0.0), Client (Visual Studio Code 1.107.1) method 'tools/call' request handler completed.
info: ModelContextProtocol.AspNetCore.IdleTrackingBackgroundService[892745801]
      Closing idle session vMpm0jsUKRsW5AgrKsoqeQ.
info: ModelContextProtocol.Server.McpServer[2103773711]
      Server (McpServer 1.0.0.0), Client (Visual Studio Code 1.107.1) message processing canceled.
info: ModelContextProtocol.Server.McpServer[2081236114]
      Server (McpServer 1.0.0.0), Client (Visual Studio Code 1.107.1) shutting down.
info: ModelContextProtocol.Server.McpServer[613617602]
      Server (McpServer 1.0.0.0), Client (Visual Studio Code 1.107.1) shut down.
```

Figure 5-20. *MCP Sessions initiated from chats originating from GitHub Copilot*

15. To conclude this exercise, press CTRL-C in the terminal window to terminate the local MCP server.

Hands-On Exercise 5.3: Use MCP As a Data Connector

In exercise 5.2, we looked at using MCP to carry out tasks exposed by API endpoints. In this exercise, we will be looking at one of the, in our humble opinion, underrated capabilities of MCP, which is the use of MCP as an NLP data connector. This capability allows a user to use natural language to ask for information stored as structured data (databases). Since the beginning of compute, data has been curated into structured form and stored in databases and only those who wield the skill to create complex queries can glean the most important insights locked away in these databases. People with the business knowledge may not have the skill to translate it into a query. Skilled database engineers may not have the business knowledge to know what to ask. And the collaboration between these two classes of professionals are complex and often inefficient. That is why MCP as a data connector is such an important differentiator in the age of LLMs.

For this exercise, we will need a database. You should either have one available, or would have deployed one when you carried out the pre-requisites in exercise 5.2 above.

1. In VSCode explorer, navigate to the *Chapter_05\Exercise5-3\src* folder. This folder contains a working version of our code at the conclusion of exercise 5.2. Therefore, if you executed all the steps in exercise 5.2 successfully and have a working code base, you can continue this exercise with YOUR code in the *Chapter_05\Exercise5-2\src* folder instead.

2. In the previous exercise, we extended the capabilities of an existing tool by adding a method. In this exercise, we will be *adding* a new tool to this MCP server. We will call this tool DBTools and it will serve as an NLP-to-SQL connector. Open the Chapter_05\Exercise5-3\src\Tools folder (or Exercise5-2\src\Tools if you are continuing from the previous exercise and have a working code base).

3. Type the following code, or copy and paste it from Chapter_05\Exercise5-3\completed-solution\src\Tools\DBTools.cs:

```
using ModelContextProtocol.Server;
using System.ComponentModel;
using System.Data;
using Microsoft.Data.SqlClient;
using System.Text.Json;
using Azure.Identity;
using Azure.Core;
```

```
namespace McpServer.Tools;

[McpServerToolType]
public class DBTools
{
    private static string _
    sqlServerConnectionString = "";
    private static readonly string _sqlScope =
    "https://database.windows.net/.default";

    // Configure once at startup
    public static void Configure(string
    connectionString)
    {
        _sqlServerConnectionString = connectionString;
    }

    // Acquire an Entra token for SQL
    private static async Task<string>
    GetAccessTokenAsync()
    {
        var credential = new DefaultAzureCredential();
        AccessToken token = await credential.
        GetTokenAsync(
            new TokenRequestContext(new[]
            { _sqlScope })
        );
        return token.Token;
    }

    private static async Task<SqlConnection>
    CreateConnectionAsync()
    {
```

```
    var conn = new SqlConnection(_sqlServer
    ConnectionString);
    conn.AccessToken = await GetAccessTokenAsync();
    await conn.OpenAsync();
    return conn;
}

// ----------------------------
// CREATE
// ----------------------------
[McpServerTool, Description("Insert a new record
into a SQL table using Entra authentication.")]
public static async Task<string> CreateRecord(
    [Description("Table name.")] string table,
    [Description("JSON object of column:value
    pairs.")] string jsonData)
{
    try
    {
        var data = JsonSerializer.Deserialize
        <Dictionary<string, object>>(jsonData)
                   ?? new Dictionary<string,
                   object>();

        var columns = string.Join(",", data.Keys);
        var parameters = string.Join(",", data.
        Keys.Select(k => "@" + k));

        string sql = $@"
            INSERT INTO {table} ({columns})
            VALUES ({parameters});
            SELECT SCOPE_IDENTITY();
        ";
```

```
            using var conn = await
            CreateConnectionAsync();
            using var cmd = new SqlCommand(sql, conn);

            foreach (var kv in data)
                cmd.Parameters.AddWithValue("@" +
                kv.Key, kv.Value ?? DBNull.Value);

            var result = await cmd.
            ExecuteScalarAsync();
            return $"Inserted record with ID:
            {result}";
        }
        catch (Exception ex)
        {
            return $"Error inserting record:
            {ex.Message}";
        }
    }

    // ----------------------------
    // READ
    // ----------------------------
    [McpServerTool, Description("Read a record from a
    SQL table using Entra authentication.")]
    public static async Task<string> ReadRecord(
        [Description("Table name.")] string table,
        [Description("Primary key column name.")]
        string keyColumn,
        [Description("Record ID.")] string id)
    {
        try
        {
```

```
        string sql = $"SELECT * FROM {table} WHERE
        {keyColumn} = @id";

        using var conn = await CreateConnection
        Async();
        using var cmd = new SqlCommand(sql, conn);
        cmd.Parameters.AddWithValue("@id", id);

        using var reader = await cmd.
        ExecuteReaderAsync();

        if (!reader.Read())
            return "Record not found.";

        return RowToJson(reader);
    }
    catch (Exception ex)
    {
        return $"Error reading record:
        {ex.Message}";
    }
}

// ----------------------------
// UPDATE
// ----------------------------
[McpServerTool, Description("Update a record in a
SQL table using Entra authentication.")]
public static async Task<string> UpdateRecord(
    [Description("Table name.")] string table,
    [Description("Primary key column name.")]
    string keyColumn,
    [Description("Record ID.")] string id,
```

```
        [Description("JSON object of column:value pairs
        to update.")] string jsonData)
    {
        try
        {
            var data = JsonSerializer.Deserialize
            <Dictionary<string, object>>(jsonData)
                       ?? new Dictionary<string,
                       object>();

            var setClause = string.Join(",", data.Keys.
            Select(k => $"{k}=@{k}"));

            string sql = $@"
                UPDATE {table}
                SET {setClause}
                WHERE {keyColumn} = @id
            ";

            using var conn = await CreateConnection
            Async();
            using var cmd = new SqlCommand(sql, conn);

            foreach (var kv in data)
                cmd.Parameters.AddWithValue("@" +
                kv.Key, kv.Value ?? DBNull.Value);

            cmd.Parameters.AddWithValue("@id", id);

            int rows = await cmd.ExecuteNonQuery
            Async();

            return rows > 0
                ? "Record updated successfully."
                : "No record updated.";
```

```
    }
    catch (Exception ex)
    {
        return $"Error updating record: {ex.
        Message}";
    }
}

// ----------------------------
// DELETE
// ----------------------------
[McpServerTool, Description("Delete a record from a
SQL table using Entra authentication.")]
public static async Task<string> DeleteRecord(
    [Description("Table name.")] string table,
    [Description("Primary key column name.")]
    string keyColumn,
    [Description("Record ID.")] string id)
{
    try
    {
        string sql = $"DELETE FROM {table} WHERE
        {keyColumn} = @id";

        using var conn = await
        CreateConnectionAsync();
        using var cmd = new SqlCommand(sql, conn);
        cmd.Parameters.AddWithValue("@id", id);

        int rows = await cmd.
        ExecuteNonQueryAsync();

        return rows > 0
```

```
                ? "Record deleted successfully."
                : "No record deleted.";
        }
        catch (Exception ex)
        {
            return $"Error deleting record:
            {ex.Message}";
        }
    }

    // ----------------------------
    // COUNT RECORDS
    // ----------------------------
    [McpServerTool, Description("Count the
    number of records in a SQL table using Entra
    authentication.")]
    public static async Task<string> CountRecords(
        [Description("Table name (include schema
        if needed, e.g., 'SalesLT.Product').")]
        string table)
    {
        try
        {
            string sql = $"SELECT COUNT(*) FROM
            {table}";

            using var conn = await
            CreateConnectionAsync();
            using var cmd = new SqlCommand(sql, conn);

            var result = await cmd.
            ExecuteScalarAsync();
```

```
            return $"Table '{table}' contains {result}
            records.";
        }
        catch (Exception ex)
        {
            return $"Error counting records:
            {ex.Message}";
        }
    }

    // ----------------------------
    // LIST TABLES
    // ----------------------------
    [McpServerTool, Description("List all tables in the
    SQL database using Entra authentication.")]
    public static async Task<string> ListTables()
    {
        try
        {
            string sql = @"
                SELECT
                    TABLE_SCHEMA,
                    TABLE_NAME,
                    TABLE_TYPE
                FROM INFORMATION_SCHEMA.TABLES
                WHERE TABLE_TYPE = 'BASE TABLE'
                ORDER BY TABLE_SCHEMA, TABLE_NAME
            ";

            using var conn = await
            CreateConnectionAsync();
```

```
                using var cmd = new SqlCommand(sql, conn);
                using var reader = await cmd.
                ExecuteReaderAsync();

                var tables = new List<object>();
                while (await reader.ReadAsync())
                {
                    tables.Add(new
                    {
                        Schema = reader.GetString("TABLE_
                        SCHEMA"),
                        TableName = reader.
                        GetString("TABLE_NAME"),
                        TableType = reader.
                        GetString("TABLE_TYPE")
                    });
                }

                return JsonSerializer.Serialize(tables, new
                JsonSerializerOptions { WriteIndented =
                true });
            }
            catch (Exception ex)
            {
                return $"Error listing tables:
                {ex.Message}";
            }
        }

        // -----------------------------
        // EXECUTE QUERY
        // -----------------------------
```

```
[McpServerTool, Description("Execute a custom SQL
SELECT query using Entra authentication.")]
public static async Task<string> ExecuteQuery(
    [Description("SQL SELECT query to execute.")]
    string sqlQuery)
{
    try
    {
        using var conn = await
        CreateConnectionAsync();
        using var cmd = new
        SqlCommand(sqlQuery, conn);
        using var reader = await cmd.
        ExecuteReaderAsync();

        var results = new List<Dictionary<string,
        object>>();
        while (await reader.ReadAsync())
        {
            var row = new Dictionary<string,
            object>();
            for (int i = 0; i < reader.
            FieldCount; i++)
            {
                row[reader.GetName(i)] = reader.
                IsDBNull(i) ? null : reader.
                GetValue(i);
            }
            results.Add(row);
        }
```

```
                return JsonSerializer.Serialize(results,
                new JsonSerializerOptions { WriteIndented =
                true });
            }
            catch (Exception ex)
            {
                return $"Error executing query: {ex.
                Message}";
            }
        }

        // -----------------------------
        // Helper: Convert row to JSON
        // -----------------------------
        private static string RowToJson
        (SqlDataReader reader)
        {
            var dict = new Dictionary<string, object>();

            for (int i = 0; i < reader.FieldCount; i++)
            {
                dict[reader.GetName(i)] = reader.
                IsDBNull(i)
                    ? null
                    : reader.GetValue(i);
            }

            return JsonSerializer.Serialize(dict, new
            JsonSerializerOptions { WriteIndented =
            true });
        }
    }
```

4. Save *DBTools.cs*

5. Next, we need to register this tool with *program.cs* in the *src* folder. Open *program.cs* and locate the section where MCP servers are registered, as shown below.

```
// Add MCP server services with HTTP transport
builder.Services.AddMcpServer()
    .WithHttpTransport()
    .WithTools<MultiplicationTool>()
    .WithTools<TemperatureConverterTool>()
    .WithTools<WeatherTools>();
```

6. Register *DBTools.cs* by inserting it after WeatherTools and moving the semi-colon at the end of WeatherTools to the end of DBTools, as shown below.

```
// Add MCP server services with HTTP transport
builder.Services.AddMcpServer()
    .WithHttpTransport()
    .WithTools<MultiplicationTool>()
    .WithTools<TemperatureConverterTool>()
    .WithTools<WeatherTools>()
    .WithTools<DBTools>();
```

7. Note that when registering a tool in *program.cs,* we are using the MCP tool's class name. NOT because that is the name of the *.cs* file, as depicted in Figure 5-21. For example, if the class was named SQLTools but the *.cs* file remained as *DBTools.cs,* we will need to change the registration in *program.cs* from DBTools to SQLTools.

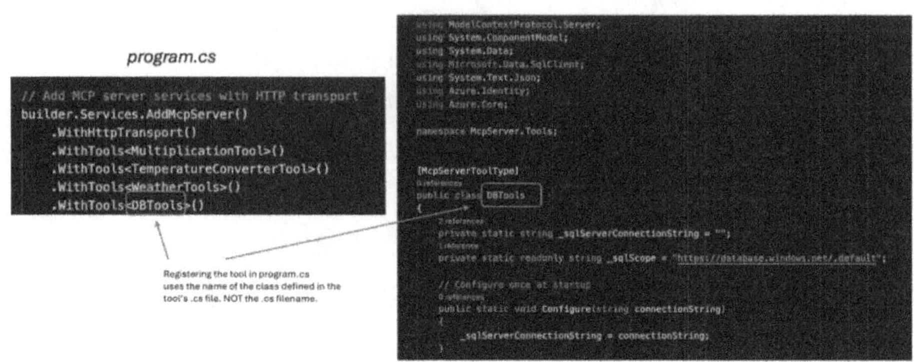

***Figure 5-21.** Registering an MCP Tool based on the name of the class*

8. Open the *appsettings.json* file and replace *"<Your-Database-SERVER-name>"* with the database server name you chose earlier (in the database deployment section of the pre-requisites). Alternatively, you can find the database server name from the Azure Portal.

```
"AllowedHosts": "*",
"ConnectionStrings": {
  "DefaultConnection": "Server=<Your-Database-SERVER-
  name>.database.windows.net;Database=sampledb;"
},
```

9. Make sure all the files have been saved, then type *dotnet run* in the terminal window.

10. Start a new chat session in GitHub Copilot and type in the following question – *"List all products"* and note that the MCP server was consulted and the capabilities of DBTools returned. Next, type the

following question – *"List top products purchased by customers."* Figure 5-22 below shows the chat responses from these two questions.

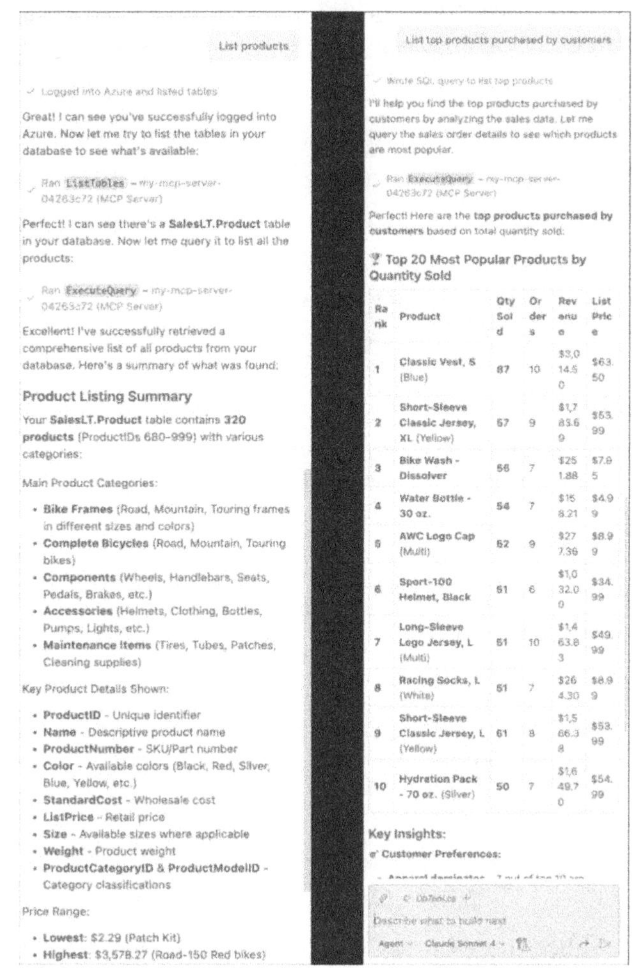

***Figure 5-22.** Chat responses using DBTools – NLP to SQL*

11. **(Optional step)**: You may have seen (or asked by GitHub Copilot for permission) to run the SQL statement that the LLM wrote in order to respond to the above questions. If you missed it, go ahead and ask for the SQL statement, as shown in Figure 5-23 below, the copy and paste the SQL query into SQL Server Management Studio or VSCode with the MS-SQL extension. Then execute the query, as shown in Figure 5-24.

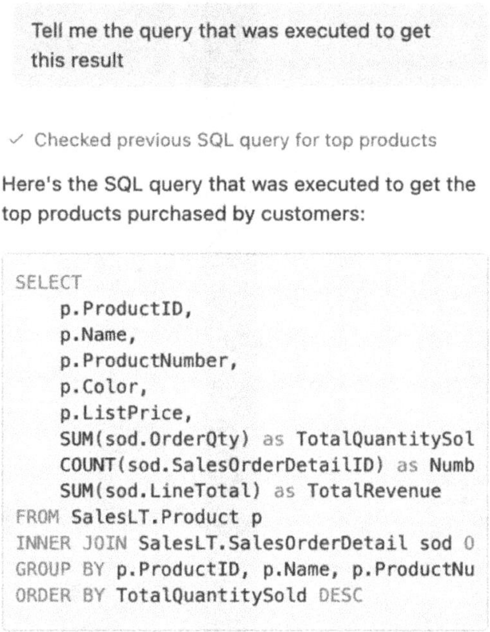

Tell me the query that was executed to get this result

✓ Checked previous SQL query for top products

Here's the SQL query that was executed to get the top products purchased by customers:

```
SELECT
    p.ProductID,
    p.Name,
    p.ProductNumber,
    p.Color,
    p.ListPrice,
    SUM(sod.OrderQty) as TotalQuantitySol
    COUNT(sod.SalesOrderDetailID) as Numb
    SUM(sod.LineTotal) as TotalRevenue
FROM SalesLT.Product p
INNER JOIN SalesLT.SalesOrderDetail sod O
GROUP BY p.ProductID, p.Name, p.ProductNu
ORDER BY TotalQuantitySold DESC
```

Figure 5-23. *SQL query that the LLM wrote in order to get the data for the response*

Figure 5-24. *T-SQL query to select the top products customers purchased*

Hands-On Exercise 5.4: Publishing the MCP Server As a Web Application

Up to this point, we have been testing our MCP servers on http://localhost:5000. This is efficient during development, but when we go to production, we need to have these MCP Servers accessible all the time. There are two ways to do so:

- Publishing MCP Servers to an App Service (often referred to as a web app)
- Publishing MCP Servers as a Container App

What We Will Be Building

In this exercise, we will be publishing our MCP server to a Web App because setting up a container environment as a pre-requisite is outside the scope of this book. Figure 5-25 below depicts the architecture for this hands-on exercise. In most development environments, it is sufficient to use keys to secure endpoints. Some development environments may not be secured at all. However, for the hands-on exercises in this book, we want to introduce the concepts of a security-first development life cycle. That is why we are leveraging the minimum best practices, such as using Managed Identities and Entra for authentication. If you are building an AI product or solution that is going to a broad audience, like a SaaS, then it is important to incorporate security from the very beginning. However, proper security is a broader topic beyond the scope of this book. Services such as Azure Defender, Log Analytics, etc. are all important best practices that should be incorporated. Refer to security-specific resources and services to harden your AI product/solution prior to releasing it to market.

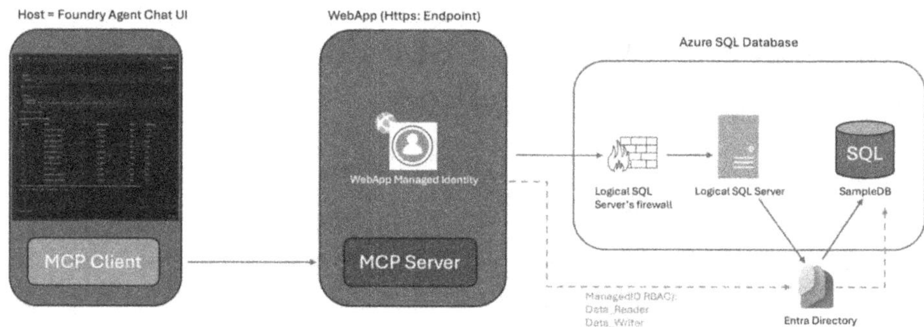

Figure 5-25. *Architecture for hands-on exercise 5.4*

Deploying the Web App

1. Review the architecture in Figure 5-25. We have deployed the SQL database. In Chapter 5, we have deployed Azure Foundry, which we will reuse as a host. In the next few steps, we will
   - Deploy the web app
   - Configure Entra Security
2. We first need to deploy the WebApp, which will host the MCP server. Is VSCode, navigate to *Chapter_05\\Exercise5-4\\infra* and open *resources.bicep*. Note that the Web App this script will deploy is of type B1[9] (see `https://azure.microsoft.com/en-us/pricing/details/app-service/windows/`).
3. In a VSCode terminal, navigate to the same directory as step 1 above - *Chapter_05\Exercise5-4\infra*.
4. Type *az up* and follow the prompts to deploy the web app.

Configure Entra Managed Identity

1. As shown in Figure 5-26 below, in the Azure Portal, go to the deployed web app and under *settings*, select *Identity* and turn on the system assigned identity. Then click *Save*.

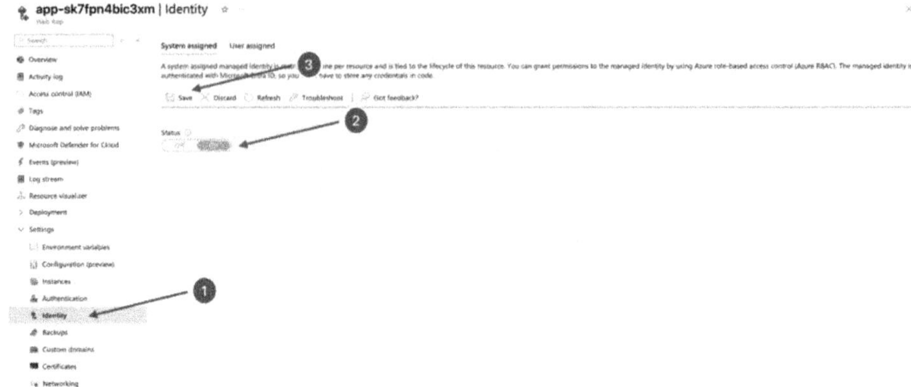

Figure 5-26. *Turning on the Managed Identity for the Web app*

2. You should see a Managed Identity created for your web app. Copy the *Object (principal) ID*.

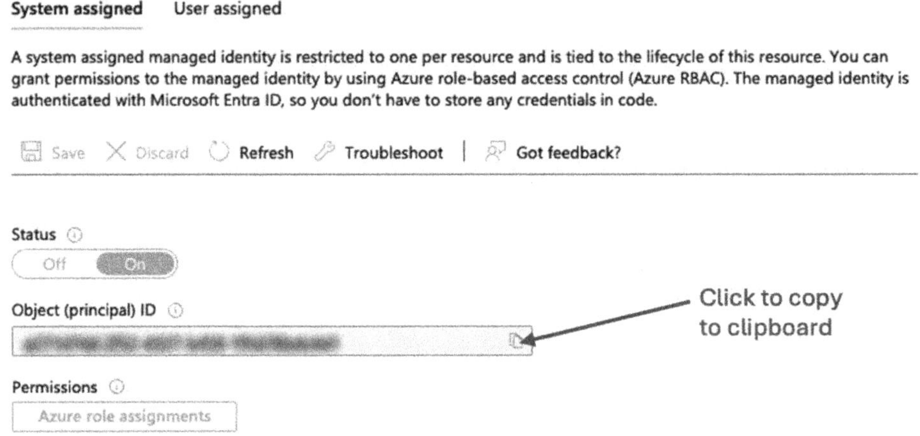

3. Next, we will create an Entra Group object. For this exercise, we will use the name DemoDBuser, but you can use any name. Just take note of what it is because we will need it later.

4. Assign it _datareader and _datawriter rights to the SQL Database using the query[9] below. You can do this all via the Azure Portal's Query editor.[10] Below shows us doing this using VSCode MS-SQL extension. If you did not use *DemoDBusers* as the group name in step 3, then change the query accordingly.

```
CREATE USER [DemoDBusers] FROM EXTERNAL PROVIDER;
ALTER ROLE db_datareader ADD MEMBER [DemoDBusers];
ALTER ROLE db_datawriter ADD MEMBER [DemoDBusers];
```

Test with Azure Foundry As the Host

In Chapters 3 and 4, we familiarized ourselves with Azure Foundry. We will now reuse our instance of Azure Foundry from previous exercises to create an agent that uses the MCP server deployed to our web app.

1. Launch Azure Foundry.
2. Create a new agent, then expand the Tools section and click on Add, as shown in Figure 5-27.

[9] This query is also found in the /src folder.

[10] Query Editor is in preview at the time of writing. You can also use the MS-SQL Extension in VSCode or SQL Server Management Studio (SSMS).

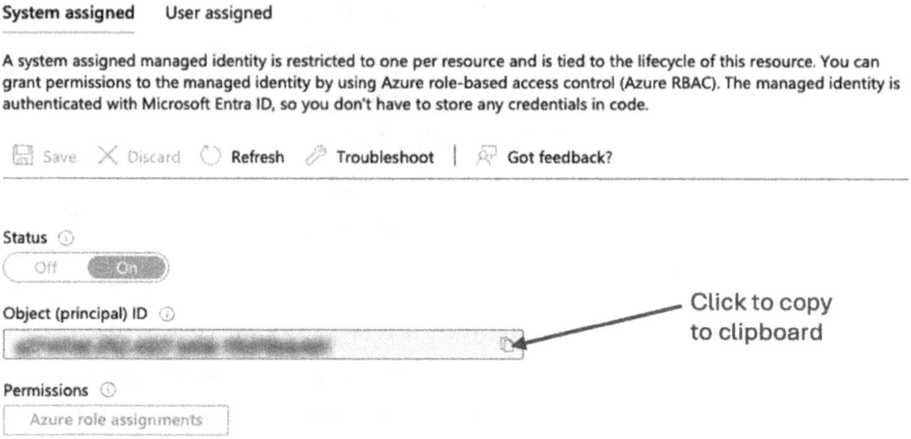

System assigned User assigned

A system assigned managed identity is restricted to one per resource and is tied to the lifecycle of this resource. You can grant permissions to the managed identity by using Azure role-based access control (Azure RBAC). The managed identity is authenticated with Microsoft Entra ID, so you don't have to store any credentials in code.

Save Discard Refresh Troubleshoot | Got feedback?

Status

Off On

Object (principal) ID

Click to copy to clipboard

Permissions

Azure role assignments

***Figure 5-27.** Adding Tools to an agent in Foundry*

3. Select [+ Add a new tool] then select the *Custom* tab then click on *Model Context Protocol (MCP)*, as shown in Figure 5-28.

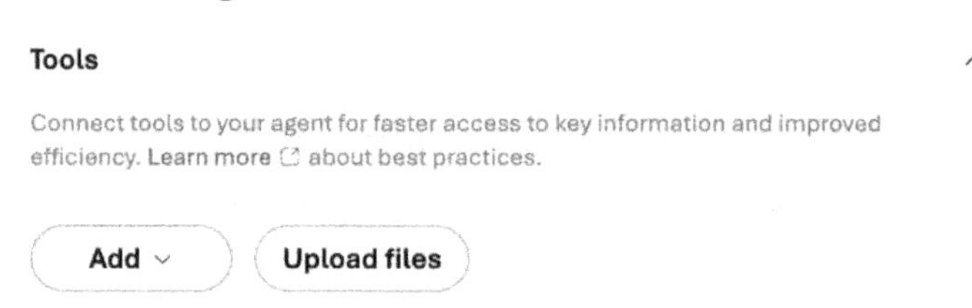

***Figure 5-28.** Selecting MCP under the Custom tool tab*

4. Give your MCP server a friendly name, add the URI of the web app, and select Microsoft Entra as the authentication method. For Type, select Project Managed Identity and audience. Go to your Azure portal to get the principal ID, as shown in Figure 5-29.

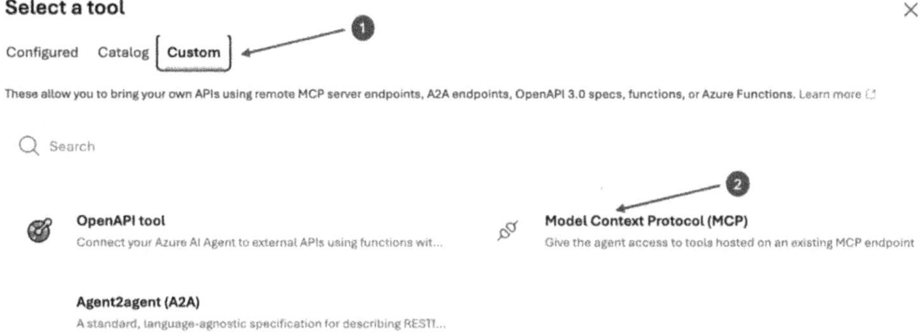

Figure 5-29. *Retrieving the principal ID*

5. Now start a chat session and you can use the same questions as in exercise 5.3 to get information from the SQL database, as shown in Figure 5-30.

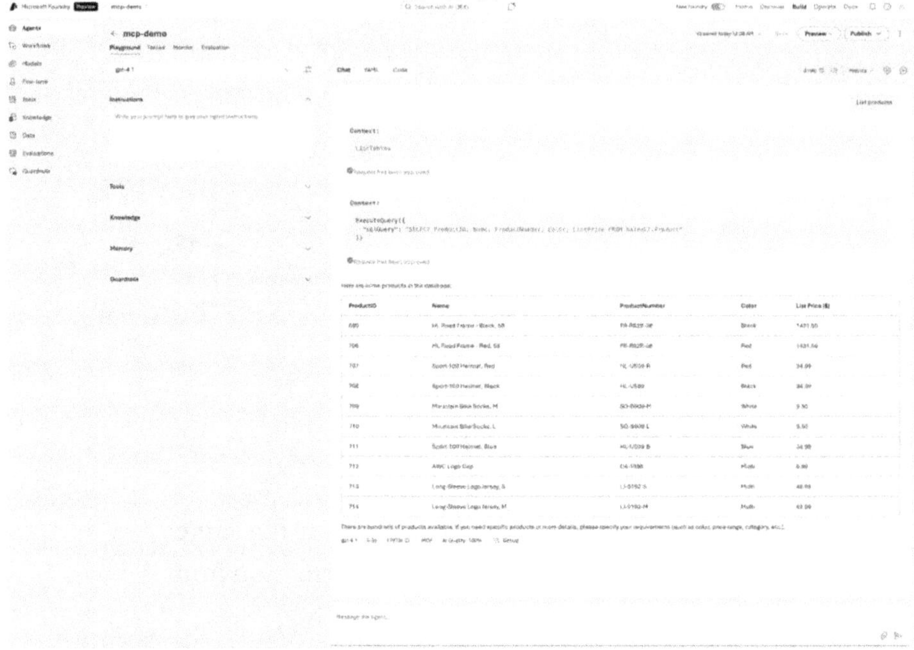

Figure 5-30. *Using Foundry Agent Chat to test MCP server*

Summary

This was a chapter that explored the extension of LLMs from agents that usually answers questions or compose content, to one that carries out tasks with the Model Context Protocol standard.

When you hear people mention the Agentic architecture, we hope MCP comes to mind because it is a very significant component of this architecture. With just the two capabilities we looked at - interfacing with APIs, and serving as a data connector, the use cases are limitless.

In the next chapter, we will look at another major component of the agentic architecture, and that is multi-agent scenarios.

CHAPTER 6

Agent Orchestration Frameworks

In Chapter 4, we introduced the agents and the benefits of using agents over straight-up LLMs. Then in the previous chapter, we extended the capabilities of agents to carry out tasks and focusing on the Model Context Protocol (MCP).

In this chapter, we will introduce the third extension of the agentic architecture as we look at the benefits of leveraging multiple agents over single-agent implementations.

Multi-agent Workflows

Just like in a group of workers, the effective use of multiple agents relies on the following characteristics:

- How the group of agents make decisions, individually and collectively
- How the agents communicate with each other
- How the work of different agents is coordinated

It is cliché, but the outcome from multiple agents should be better, but without the above basic governance, the risk of the output being more inaccurate or having a higher level of hallucination is very high.

J. Soh et al., *Building and Distributing Agentic AI Solutions*,
https://doi.org/10.1007/979-8-8688-2586-6_6

AI Frameworks

This is where AI frameworks come in. AI frameworks are software development kits (SDKs) that help govern and facilitate AI tasks. At a minimum, AI frameworks fulfill the three characteristics we mentioned above. Figure 6-1 below depicts[1] that in turn use tools exposed by MCP servers. Decision-making capabilities include, for example, which workers need to be activated as well as consensus on whether the request has been adequately fulfilled.

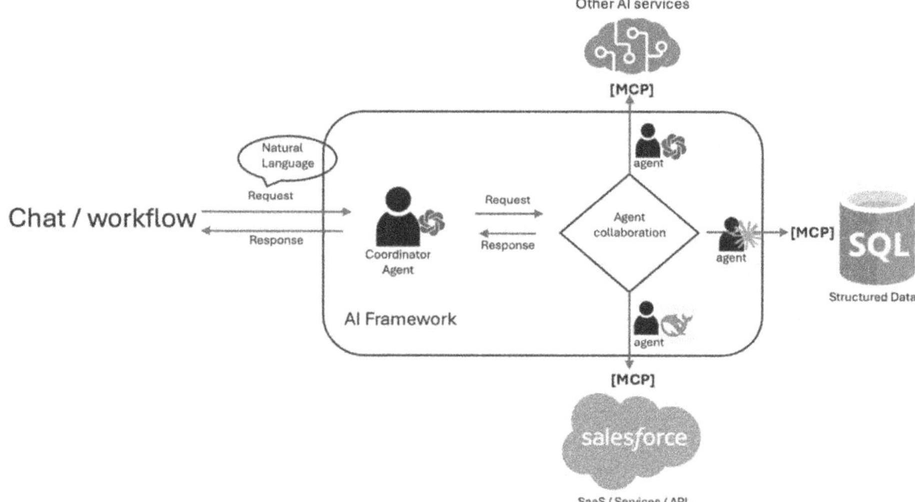

Figure 6-1. *AI Framework orchestrating multi-agent collaboration*

Most AI frameworks are open source. Examples of AI frameworks include LangChain, LangGraph, Semantic Kernel, AutoGen, OpenAI Swarm, and CrewAI. During the Microsoft Ignite event in 2025, Microsoft

[1] SLM = Small Language Models, for example, gpt-4o-mini

announced the Agent Framework.[2] Microsoft Agent Framework is an open-source SDK for building AI agents and multi-agent workflows in .NET and Python. Prior to the Microsoft Agent Framework, Microsoft offered AutoGen for experimentation workloads and promoted Semantic Kernel for production-ready workloads. The Microsoft Agent Framework is the combination of AutoGen and Semantic Kernel, thereby forming a unified SDK for building AI agents going forward.

Although there are many AI frameworks, we will focus on the Microsoft Agent Framework as the SDK of choice in this book.

Choosing a Framework

Before we take a closer look at the Microsoft Agent Framework, we should address the selection of frameworks. Choosing a framework is really about balancing power, stability, and long-term maintainability, and the trade-offs based on your AI product's specifications.

The first consideration is language and ecosystem support - some frameworks are deeply tied to Python, while others embrace polyglot environments or offer first-class .NET or JavaScript integrations, which matters if you want your agents to live inside an existing codebase rather than in a silo.

Another major factor is stability versus capability: frameworks like LangChain tend to move fast and ship a lot of features, but that velocity can introduce breaking changes or inconsistent abstractions, whereas more conservative frameworks may offer fewer tools but provide a sturdier foundation for production workloads.

[2] The Microsoft Agent Framework is the actual name of the new SDK. Not to be confused with the term "agent framework" which is sometimes used in place of AI framework to describe this class of AI SDKs.

Some frameworks may not be robust enough for production or may not be able to meet the anticipated load from your AI product. For example, before the Microsoft Agent Framework was introduced, AutoGen provided the ease of use but was not recommended for production workloads, whereas Semantic Kernel is the recommended framework for workloads that will go into product.

You also want to evaluate state management and workflow reliability, because agent systems often need deterministic control over memory, retries, and tool-calling behavior - something that varies wildly across frameworks. Tooling and extensibility matter as well: some ecosystems have rich plugin libraries, visual builders, or orchestration layers, while others require more custom engineering.

It is important to consider community maturity and documentation quality, which directly affects how quickly you can debug issues or onboard teammates. This directly affects your SDLC and GTM timelines.

Finally, consider deployment and observability: frameworks differ in how well they support tracing, evaluation, versioning, and integration with enterprise infrastructure. When you take all these factors into consideration, the "best" framework is rarely the one with the most features - it's the one whose trade-offs align with your team's tolerance for change, your stack, and the level of reliability your application demands, your GTM timeline, and the availability of support and expertise from the community.

Microsoft Agent Framework

The Microsoft Agent Framework is an open-source SDK for building AI agents and multi-agent workflows. It integrates with the .NET framework and can be developed in C# or Python. It combines the strengths of Semantic Kernel and AutoGen while adding new capabilities. Built by the original respective teams, it is the unified foundation for building AI agents going forward.

If your product is primarily on the Microsoft stack, then you should consider going with Agent Framework. If you have developed using AutoGen, consider migrating[3] to Agent Framework prior to GTM. If you are currently using Semantic Kernel, it is a framework that supports production workload so you can release your product to market but prepare to migrate[4] to the Agent framework for more capabilities and longer term support. As of this writing, the Microsoft Agent Framework is still in public preview. Therefore, do *not* migrate production workloads to Agent Framework yet. Continue using Semantic Kernel.

The Microsoft Agent Framework provides the following types of capabilities:

- **Individual AI agents**: Individual agents that use LLMs/SLMs to process user inputs, call tools, and MCP servers to perform tasks.
- **Orchestration for multiple agents**: Graph-based workflows that connect to multiple agents to perform complex, multi-step tasks. These workflows support type-based routing, nesting, checkpointing, and request/response patterns for human-in-the-loop scenarios.

Microsoft Agent Framework also provides conversation management capabilities such as thread-state management and agent memory. Another key aspect of the Agent Framework is the ability to expose an agent as an MCP server, which serves as another form of Agent-to-Agent communication (in this case, it is Agent–MCP–Agent).

[3] AutoGen to Microsoft Agent Framework Migration Guide - `https://learn.microsoft.com/en-us/agent-framework/migration-guide/from-autogen/`

[4] Semantic Kernel to Agent Framework Migration Guide - `https://learn.microsoft.com/en-us/agent-framework/migration-guide/from-semantic-kernel/?pivots=programming-language-csharp`

Hands-On Exercise 6.1: Introduction to the Microsoft Agent Framework

In this exercise, we will be installing the Microsoft Agent Framework and creating a simple chatbot.

Pre-requisite

Make sure this is your minimum environment for this specific exercise:

- .NET 10.0 or above (exercise specifically built on 10.0.100-preview.6.25358.103)
- An Azure OpenAI endpoint with desired model deployed (exercise will use gpt-4o-mini)
- Clone the book's GitHub repository at `https://github.com/juliansoh/Building_and_Distributing_AI-Enabled-Solutions`, if you have not done so. We will be using the \Chapter06 folder. This step is redundant if you have cloned the repository for exercises from previous chapters.

Create Project and Install Packages

1. In a VSCode terminal, navigate to the *\Chapter_06\exercise6-1\exercise* folder (it should be empty).
2. Login to your Azure subscription using *az login*.
3. Create a project by typing *dotnet new console -o AgentFramework*.
4. Navigate to the project directory by typing *cd AgentFramework*.

5. Install the following packages (or use NuGet):

    a. *dotnet add package Azure.AI.OpenAI --prerelease*

    b. *dotnet add package Azure.Identity*

    c. *dotnet add package Microsoft.Agents.AI.OpenAI --prerelease*

    d. *dotnet add package Microsoft.Extensions.AI.OpenAI*

6. Open *program.cs* and delete the boiler Hello World code with the code below (or copy it from the \ *Chapter_06\Exercise6-1\completed-solution\src\AgentFramework\program.cs*):

```
using System;
using Azure.AI.OpenAI;
using Azure.Identity;
using Microsoft.Agents.AI;
using Microsoft.Extensions.AI;
using OpenAI;

AIAgent agent = new AzureOpenAIClient(
  new Uri("<Replace with your Azure OpenAI
  endpoint URI"),
  new AzureCliCredential())
    .GetChatClient("gpt-4o-mini")
    .AsIChatClient()
    .CreateAIAgent(instructions: "You are an expert in
    explaining technologies in simple English.");

//Exercise 6.1.1 - Simple Agent
//Console.WriteLine(await agent.RunAsync("Tell me about
Model Context Protocol."));

//Exercise 6.1.2 - Simple Agent with Streaming
//int count = 0;
```

```
//await foreach (var update in agent.
RunStreamingAsync("Tell me about Model Context
Protocol."))
//{
//    string strUpdate = update.Text;
//    if (count < 100)
//    {
//        Console.Write(update);
//        //increment count based on number of
          words printed
//        count += strUpdate.Split(' ').Length;
//    }
//    else
//    {
//        Console.WriteLine(update);
//        count = 0;
//    }
//}

//Exercise 6.1.3 - Passing multiple objects (including
an image) to the Agent
//ChatMessage systemMessage = new(
//    ChatRole.System,
//    """
//    If asked to respond in any language other than
      English,
//    then provide the response in the requested
      language
//    and translate the response to English and append
      as part of the entire response.
//    """);
```

```
//ChatMessage userMessage1 = new(ChatRole.User, [
//     new TextContent("Describe this image in detail in
       Korean:"),
//     new UriContent("https://upload.wikimedia.org/
       wikipedia/commons/1/11/Joseph_Grimaldi.jpg",
       "image/jpeg")
//]);

//Console.WriteLine("--------- UserMessage1 Response
---------");
//Console.WriteLine(await agent.
RunAsync([systemMessage, userMessage1]));
//Console.WriteLine("");

//ChatMessage userMessage2 = new(ChatRole.User, [
//     new TextContent("Describe this image in detail in
       Simplified Chinese:"),
//     new UriContent("https://upload.wikimedia.org/
       wikipedia/commons/1/11/Joseph_Grimaldi.jpg",
       "image/jpeg")
//]);

//Console.WriteLine("--------- UserMessage2 Response
---------");

//int count = 0;
//await foreach (var update in agent.RunStreamingAsync
([systemMessage, userMessage2]))
//{
//     string strUpdate = update.Text;
//     if (count < 100)
//     {
//         Console.Write(update);
```

```
//          //increment count based on number of words printed
//          count += strUpdate.Split(' ').Length;
//      }
//      else
//      {
//          Console.WriteLine(update);
//          count = 0;
//      }
//}

//Console.WriteLine("");
```

7. Replace the Uri with your Azure OpenAI's endpoint. You can find your Azure OpenAI endpoint from the Foundry portal, as shown in Figure 6-2.

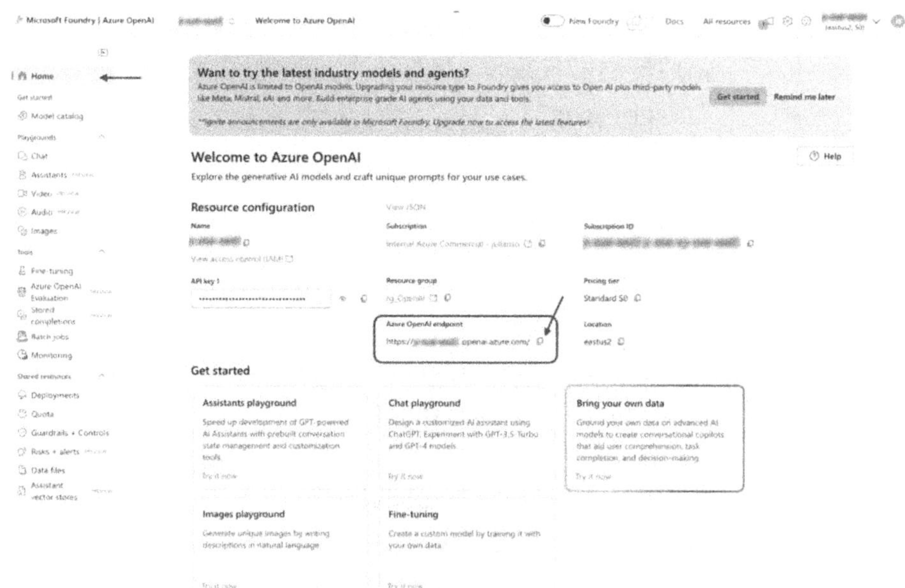

***Figure 6-2.** The Azure OpenAI endpoint in the Foundry portal*

8. Uncomment the line **below** *//Exercise 6.1.1 – Simple Agent* so your code looks like Figure 6-3.

```
Program.cs U ●
Chapter_06 > Exercise6-1 > completed-solution > src > AgentFramework > Program.cs > Program > <top-level-statements-entry-point>
using System;
using System.ComponentModel.DataAnnotations;
using Azure.AI.OpenAI;
using Azure.Identity;
using Microsoft.Agents.AI;
using Microsoft.Extensions.AI;
using OpenAI;

AIAgent agent = new AzureOpenAIClient(
  new Uri("https://js-aoai-east2.openai.azure.com/"),
  new AzureCliCredential())
    .GetChatClient("gpt-4o-mini")
    .AsIChatClient()
    .CreateAIAgent(instructions: "You are an expert in explaining technologies in simple English");

//Exercise 6.1.1 - Simple Agent
Console.WriteLine(await agent.RunAsync("Tell me about Model Context Protocol."));

//Exercise 6.1.2 - Simple Agent with Streaming
//int count = 0;
//await foreach (var update in agent.RunStreamingAsync("Tell me about Model Context Protocol."))
//{
//    string strUpdate = update.Text;
//    if (count < 100)
//    {
//        Console.Write(update);
//        //increment count based on number of words printed
//        count += strUpdate.Split(' ').Length;
//    }
//    else
//    {
//        Console.WriteLine(update);
//        count = 0;
//    }
//}

//Exercise 6.1.3 - Passing multiple objects (including an image) to the Agent
//ChatMessage message = new(ChatRole.User, [
//    new TextContent("Describe this image in detail:"),
//    new UriContent("https://upload.wikimedia.org/wikipedia/commons/1/11/Joseph_Grimaldi.jpg", "image/jpeg
//]);
//Console.WriteLine(await agent.RunAsync(message));
```

Figure 6-3. *Uncommenting Exercise 6.1.1 of your code*

9. Save the changes, then in VSCode terminal, type *dotnet run*. The output should be similar to what is shown in Figure 6-4.

Program.cs U

Chapter_06 > Exercise6-1 > completed-solution > src > AgentFramework > Program.cs > Program > <top-level-statements-entry-point>

```
using System;
using Azure.AI.OpenAI;
using Azure.Identity;
using Microsoft.Agents.AI;
using Microsoft.Extensions.AI;
using OpenAI;

AIAgent agent = new AzureOpenAIClient(
  new Uri("https://js-aoai-east2.openai.azure.com/"),
  new AzureCliCredential())
    .GetChatClient("gpt-4o-mini")
    .AsIChatClient()
    .CreateAIAgent(instructions: "You are an expert in explaining technologies in simple English");

//Exercise 6.1.1 - Simple Agent
Console.WriteLine(await agent.RunAsync("Tell me about Model Context Protocol."));

//Exercise 6.1.2 - Simple Agent with Streaming
//await foreach (var update in agent.RunStreamingAsync("Tell me about Model Context Protocol."))
//{
//    Console.WriteLine(update);
//}

//Exercise 6.1.3 - Passing multiple objects (including an image) to the Agent
//ChatMessage message = new(ChatRole.User, [
//    new TextContent("Describe this image in detail:"),
//    new UriContent("https://upload.wikimedia.org/wikipedia/commons/1/11/Joseph_Grimaldi.jpg", "image/jpeg
//]);
//Console.WriteLine(await agent.RunAsync(message));
```

PROBLEMS OUTPUT TERMINAL PORTS POLYGLOT NOTEBOOK DEBUG CONSOLE ... zsh - AgentFramework

```
julianso h@Julians-MacBook-Pro AgentFramework % dotnet run
Restore complete (0.2s)
You are using a preview version of .NET. See: https://aka.ms/dotnet-support-policy
  AgentFramework succeeded (0.1s) → bin/Debug/net10.0/AgentFramework.dll

Build succeeded in 0.6s
The Model Context Protocol (MCP) is a framework designed to help in the management and sharing of contextual information between diff
erent models or systems, particularly in areas like artificial intelligence, robotics, and software development.

Here's a simple breakdown of what it involves:

1. **Context**: In this case, "context" refers to the surrounding information that helps a model understand its environment or situat
ion. For example, if a robot is navigating a room, its context might include the layout of the room, the location of furniture, and w
hether there are people nearby.

2. **Models**: These can be various systems or algorithms that process information and make decisions based on the context they recei
ve. Each model might interpret contextual data differently based on its design and objectives.

3. **Communication**: MCP facilitates communication between these models, allowing them to share their contexts and understand each o
ther better. This is crucial for tasks that require coordination among multiple systems, like self-driving cars communicating with ea
ch other to improve traffic flow.

4. **Adaptability**: By using the MCP, systems can adapt to changes in their environment more effectively, leading to better performa
nce in tasks like navigation, decision-making, and interaction with human users.

In summary, the Model Context Protocol is all about improving how different systems share and interpret contextual information, enhan
cing collaboration, and overall efficiency in various technological applications.
juliansoh@Julians-MacBook-Pro AgentFramework %
```

***Figure 6-4.** Executing your first Microsoft Agent Framework agent*

Streaming

Another important capability that you will likely use most of the time is the streaming capability provided in Agent Framework. This is of importance when the LLM's output is meant to be presented to a user, not so much so for an automated workflow.

As its name implies, streaming outputs the LLM's response as it is being generated. LLM's responses are usually generated in chunks and streaming outputs each chunk as they become available.

This is an important concept, especially with deep thinking models, where the complete LLM response may take time to generate. Therefore, the user is left waiting without seeing any results. By streaming the chunks, the user will visually see the response generation and can start ingesting the output as it is being generated. Streaming significantly improves the user experience and for long running output generation, it may even be necessary in automated workflows and applications to avoid a timeout error.

To use streaming, call the *RunStreamingAsync* method while providing the user input. The agent will then return a stream *AgentRunResponseUpdate* objects. Converting the objects with *.ToString()* or *.Text* on each update object provides the part of the text result contained in the stream. We will see this in action in the portion of the code commented as *Exercise 6.1.2*, as shown in Figure 6-5.

1. Run your application again by issuing *dotnet run* and this time, take note of the number of seconds it took for the application to generate a response (exclude the compilation time). We have selected a question that took some time to generate a response so hopefully you noticed a lag as the response is being generated.

2. Comment out Exercise 6.1.1 and uncomment Exercise 6.1.2, as shown in Figure 6-5.

Program.cs U ●

Chapter_06 > Exercise6-1 > completed-solution > src > AgentFramework > Program.cs > Program > <top-level-statements-entry-point>

```
using System;
using System.ComponentModel.DataAnnotations;
using Azure.AI.OpenAI;
using Azure.Identity;
using Microsoft.Agents.AI;
using Microsoft.Extensions.AI;
using OpenAI;

AIAgent agent = new AzureOpenAIClient(
  new Uri("https://js-aoai-east2.openai.azure.com/"),
  new AzureCliCredential())
    .GetChatClient("gpt-4o-mini")
    .AsIChatClient()
    .CreateAIAgent(instructions: "You are an expert in explaining technologies in simple English");

//Exercise 6.1.1 - Simple Agent
//Console.WriteLine(await agent.RunAsync("Tell me about Model Context Protocol."));

//Exercise 6.1.2 - Simple Agent with Streaming
int count = 0;
await foreach (var update in agent.RunStreamingAsync("Tell me about Model Context Protocol."))
{
    string strUpdate = update.Text;
    if (count < 100)
    {
        Console.Write(update);
        //increment count based on number of words printed
        count += strUpdate.Split(' ').Length;
    }
    else
    {
        Console.WriteLine(update);
        count = 0;
    }
}

//Exercise 6.1.3 - Passing multiple objects (including an image) to the Agent
//ChatMessage message = new(ChatRole.User, [
//    new TextContent("Describe this image in detail:"),
//    new UriContent("https://upload.wikimedia.org/wikipedia/commons/1/11/Joseph_Grimaldi.jpg", "image/jpeg
//]);
//Console.WriteLine(await agent.RunAsync(message));
```

Figure 6-5. *Uncommenting Exercise 6.1.2 (Streaming) and commenting out Exercise 6.1.1*

3. Save the changes to *program.cs* and in VSCode terminal, run the console application by issuing *dotnet run.*

4. This is the exact same user prompt as in *Exercise 6.1.1* but this time, instead of a lag, the response should be almost immediate as you see it being streamed.

Using Agents with Chat Messages and Images

Chat is still one of the largest use case for LLMs because of natural language. In this exercise, we will look at how chat messages are being processed by Agents.

There are three primary parts to every chat:

- The System Message (also known as the System Prompt)
- The User Message (also known as the User Prompt or input)
- The LLM response (also known as the Output or Completion)

If you are not new to the world of Generative AI, the above should be terms you are already familiar with so we will not cover them in detail here.

In this exercise, we will see how the System and User messages are provided to a *ChatMessage* object that in turn gets passed to the agent via the *RunAsync* method we saw earlier. We will also look at passing more than one object type to the *ChatMessage* object, in this case, both a text content and a URI to an online image.

1. Comment out the code associated with *Exercise 6.1.2* and uncomment the code for *Exercise 6.2.3.*

2. Take note of the following as you study the code:

   a. We are passing a single *systemMessage* instructing the Agent how to handle responses.

   b. We are passing two *userMessages* simulating two different conversations.

   c. In both *userMessages,* we are adding two content types - a *TextContent* and a *UriContent.*

   d. For *userMessage1,* we are not using streaming.

   e. For *userMessage2,* we are using streaming.

3. Save and execute the code by issuing *dotnet run* in the VSCode terminal, and observe the output.

4. (Optional) Modify the *systemMessage* and *userMessage* and observe the changes.

One of the shortcomings of LLMs is the timebound data that is restricted to when the model was trained. In Chapter 4, we also looked at the RAG architecture that grounds the LLM with curated data sources. However, this is still based on time-bound data sources.

A compelling use case for Semantic Kernel is the ability for the LLM to get real-time data from web services. For example, with Semantic Kernel, the LLM can query a flight's status from web services to find out its flight schedule. An investment tracker application, when asked in natural language what the current top market movers for the day are can connect to web services to get that information and research on latest news that may have caused such a movement.

Threads and Multi-turn Conversations

When we envision chat, it is a back-and-forth exchange in a conversation. The key thing about a conversation is the context. So, if I asked "how was your weekend" followed up with "how was the weather," you would know that my follow-up question is related to the weather on Saturday and/or Sunday of the past weekend without me having to explicitly reference the time frame.

Context, in technical terms, is known as the *state* of an exchange. A system is said to be *stateless* if it possesses no ability to retain context, and inherently, agents are *stateless*. In order to maintain state between calls to the agent, we need to create an object to hold the conversation state. This object, known as a *thread*, will be passed to the agent as part of the conversation.

Hands-On Exercise 6.2: Threads and Multi-turn Conversations

You can choose to continue with the *program.cs* from exercise 6.1 or use the one in the *\Chapter_06\Exercse6-2\exercise\AgentFramework* folder.

1. In VSCode, open *\Chapter_06\Exercse6-2\exercise\AgentFramework\program.cs*. If you choose to use the *program.cs* file from the previous exercise, then comment out or delete all the code associated to exercise 6.1.1, 6.1.2, and 6.1.3. Leave the top portion of the code where you defined your agent and the Azure OpenAI endpoint.

2. Type the following code, or copy it from *\Chapter_06\Exercse6-2\completed-solution\src\AgentFramework\program.cs*. Your code should look like what is shown in Figure 6-6.

```
//Exercise 6.1.1 - Simple Agent
//Console.WriteLine(await agent.RunAsync("Tell me
about Model Context Protocol."));

//Exercise 6.1.2 - Simple Agent with Streaming
//int count = 0;
//await foreach (var update in agent.
RunStreamingAsync("Tell me about Model Context
Protocol."))
//{
//     string strUpdate = update.Text;
//     if (count < 100)
//     {
//         Console.Write(update);
```

```
//          //increment count based on number of
            words printed
//          count += strUpdate.Split(' ').Length;
//      }
//      else
//      {
//          Console.WriteLine(update);
//          count = 0;
//      }
//}

//Exercise 6.1.3 - Passing multiple objects
(including an image) to the Agent
//ChatMessage systemMessage = new(
//      ChatRole.System,
//      """
//      If asked to respond in any language other than
        English,
//      then provide the response in the requested
        language
//      and translate the response to English and
        append as part of the entire response.
//      """);

//ChatMessage userMessage1 = new(ChatRole.User, [
//      new TextContent("Describe this image in detail
        in Korean:"),
//      new UriContent("https://upload.wikimedia.org/
        wikipedia/commons/1/11/Joseph_Grimaldi.jpg",
        "image/jpeg")
//]);
```

```
//Console.WriteLine("--------- UserMessage1 Response
---------");
//Console.WriteLine(await agent.
RunAsync([systemMessage, userMessage1]));
//Console.WriteLine("");

//ChatMessage userMessage2 = new(ChatRole.User, [
//    new TextContent("Describe this image in detail
      in Simplified Chinese:"),
//    new UriContent("https://upload.wikimedia.org/
      wikipedia/commons/1/11/Joseph_Grimaldi.jpg",
      "image/jpeg")
//]);

//Console.WriteLine("--------- UserMessage2 Response
---------");

//int count = 0;
//await foreach (var update in agent.RunStreamingAsync
([systemMessage, userMessage2]))
//{
//    string strUpdate = update.Text;
//    if (count < 100)
//    {
//        Console.Write(update);
//        //increment count based on number of
          words printed
//        count += strUpdate.Split(' ').Length;
//    }
//    else
```

```
//    {
//        Console.WriteLine(update);
//        count = 0;
//    }
//}

//Console.WriteLine("");
```

Chapter_06 > Exercise6-2 > completed-solution > src > AgentFramework > Program.cs > Program > <top-level-statements-entry-point>

```
using System;
using Azure.AI.OpenAI;
using Azure.Identity;
using Microsoft.Agents.AI;
using Microsoft.Extensions.AI;

AIAgent agent = new AzureOpenAIClient(
    new Uri("https://[illegible]openai.azure.com/"),
    new AzureCliCredential())
        .GetChatClient("gpt-4o-mini")
        .AsIChatClient()
        .CreateAIAgent(instructions: "You are an expert in explaining technologies in simple English");

//Exercise 6.2.1 - Conversational Agent

// //Create a conversation thread
//AgentThread thread = agent.GetNewThread();

//Console.WriteLine("Starting conversation. Type 'end' to exit.");
//Console.WriteLine();

// //Conversation loop
//while (true)
//{
//    Console.Write("You: ");
//    string? userInput = Console.ReadLine();

//    if (string.IsNullOrWhiteSpace(userInput))
//        continue;

//    if (userInput.Trim().Equals("end", StringComparison.OrdinalIgnoreCase))
//    {
//        Console.WriteLine("Conversation ended.");
//        break;
//    }

//    // Send user input to the agent within the same thread
//    string response = (await agent.RunAsync(userInput, thread)).ToString();

//    Console.WriteLine();
//    Console.WriteLine("Agent:");
//    Console.WriteLine(response);
//    Console.WriteLine();
//}

// Exercise 6.2.2 - Multi-threaded Conversations

//AgentThread thread1 = agent.GetNewThread();
//AgentThread thread2 = agent.GetNewThread();
//Console.WriteLine("---------------- Conversation 1 ----------------");
//Console.WriteLine(await agent.RunAsync("Tell me about Model Context Protocol.", thread1));
//Console.WriteLine();
//Console.WriteLine("---------------- Conversation 2 ----------------");
//Console.WriteLine(await agent.RunAsync("Create a one paragraph plot of a sci-fi movie.", thread2));
//Console.WriteLine();
//Console.WriteLine("---------------- Conversation 1 ----------------");
```

Figure 6-6. *Code for Exercise 6.2*

3. Uncomment the code associated to exercise 6.2.1, as shown in Figure 6-7.

Chapter_06 > Exercise6-2 > completed-solution > src > AgentFramework > Program.cs > Program > <top-level-statements-entry-point>

```
using System;
using Azure.AI.OpenAI;
using Azure.Identity;
using Microsoft.Agents.AI;
using Microsoft.Extensions.AI;

AIAgent agent = new AzureOpenAIClient(
    new Uri("https://js-aoai-east2.openai.azure.com/"),
    new AzureCliCredential())
        .GetChatClient("gpt-4o-mini")
        .AsIChatClient()
        .CreateAIAgent(instructions: "You are an expert in explaining technologies in simple English");

//Exercise 6.2.1 - Conversational Agent

//Create a conversation thread
AgentThread thread = agent.GetNewThread();

Console.WriteLine("Starting conversation. Type 'end' to exit.");
Console.WriteLine();

//Conversation loop
while (true)
{
    Console.Write("You: ");
    string? userInput = Console.ReadLine();

    if (string.IsNullOrWhiteSpace(userInput))
        continue;

    if (userInput.Trim().Equals("end", StringComparison.OrdinalIgnoreCase))
    {
        Console.WriteLine("Conversation ended.");
        break;
    }

    // Send user input to the agent within the same thread
    string response = (await agent.RunAsync(userInput, thread)).ToString();

    Console.WriteLine();
    Console.WriteLine("Agent:");
    Console.WriteLine(response);
    Console.WriteLine();
}

// Exercise 6.2.2 - Multi-threaded Conversations

//AgentThread thread1 = agent.GetNewThread();
//AgentThread thread2 = agent.GetNewThread();
//Console.WriteLine("---------------- Conversation 1 ----------------");
//Console.WriteLine(await agent.RunAsync("Tell me about Model Context Protocol.", thread1));
//Console.WriteLine();
//Console.WriteLine("---------------- Conversation 2 ----------------");
//Console.WriteLine(await agent.RunAsync("Create a one paragraph plot of a sci-fi movie.", thread2));
//Console.WriteLine();
//Console.WriteLine("---------------- Conversation 1 ----------------");
```

***Figure 6-7.** Code for exercise 6.2.1*

4. Save and execute *program.cs* by issuing *dotnet run* in the VSCode terminal.

5. Have a conversation with the agent and purposely leave out context in follow-up the following conversation to see if the state of the agent is preserved. Type *end* to end the conversation. Figure 6-8 below shows the conversation we had with our agent.

```
juliansoh@Julians-MacBook-Pro AgentFramework % dotnet run
Build succeeded in 0.5s
Starting conversation. Type 'end' to exit.

You: Hello

Agent:
Hello! How can I assist you today?

You: Where is Seattle located?

Agent:
Seattle is located in the northwest region of the United States. It sits in the state of Washington, near the Pacific Ocean. The city is situated between Puget
 Sound and Lake Washington, which gives it a beautiful waterfront. Seattle is also known for its iconic Space Needle and vibrant tech scene. If you have any mo
re questions about Seattle, feel free to ask!

You: population?

Agent:
As of my last update in October 2023, Seattle has a population of about 750,000 people. The population can change over time due to factors like growth, migrati
on, and demographic shifts. It's one of the largest cities in the Pacific Northwest and is known for its diverse communities and thriving economy. If you need
the most current numbers, checking recent census data or local government sources would be best!

You: What is the median salary?

Agent:
As of my last update in October 2023, the median salary in Seattle is around $80,000 to $100,000 per year. However, this can vary depending on the industry, jo
b type, and experience level. Seattle has a strong job market, especially in technology, healthcare, and finance, which often offer higher salaries. For the mo
st accurate and up-to-date figures, it's a good idea to check reliable sources like the U.S. Bureau of Labor Statistics or local employment resources.

You: How about New York?

Agent:
As of my last update in October 2023, the median salary in New York City is approximately $70,000 to $80,000 per year. Like Seattle, this figure can vary widel
y depending on the industry, job type, and level of experience. New York City is known for its diverse economy, which includes finance, technology, healthcare,
 and entertainment, often resulting in higher salaries, especially in certain sectors. For the latest and most accurate salary information, checking resources
such as the U.S. Bureau of Labor Statistics or local job market reports would be useful.

You: and California?

Agent:
California is a large state, and salaries can vary widely depending on the city and industry. As of my last update in October 2023, the median salary in Califo
rnia is roughly between $70,000 and $80,000 per year as well.

In major cities like San Francisco and Los Angeles, the median salaries can be higher, often exceeding $100,000, particularly in the tech, entertainment, and h
ealthcare industries.

For the most accurate and up-to-date salary information for specific regions or cities within California, it's best to consult resources like the U.S. Bureau o
f Labor Statistics or local job market analyses.

You: Compare the three into a table

Agent:
Sure! Here's a simple comparison table for the median salaries in Seattle, New York City, and California:

| Location           | Approximate Median Salary (per year) |
|--------------------|--------------------------------------|
| Seattle            | $80,000 - $100,000                   |
| New York City      | $70,000 - $80,000                    |
| California (average)| $70,000 - $80,000                    |
| California (San Francisco/Los Angeles) | $100,000+                     |

Please note that these figures are approximate and can vary based on specific industries, job roles, and levels of experience. Always refer to local job market
 resources for the most current data.

You: 
```

Figure 6-8. *Stateful conversation with an agent*

6. Noticed how we left out specifics in follow-up questions and the agent is still able to converse by being aware of the context based on the history of the conversation.

An extension of multi-turn conversation using *threads* is the support for multiple conversations – *multi-threaded conversations*. This is particularly important because your AI product would be servicing multiple users or applications simultaneously. Therefore, different calls need to be tracked in their own threads in order to keep separate context. In this next section of the exercise, we will explore the multi-threaded conversations.

1. Comment out all code associated with exercise 6.2.1 and uncomment the code for exercise 6.2.2.

2. Save the changes and execute the program by issuing *dotnet run* in the VSCode terminal.

3. Note that we have now defined two threads – *thread1* and *thread2*. We hardcoded two separate conversations on two completely different topics between the two threads. One thread is about Model Context Protocol, and the other is about a sci-fi/fantasy fiction plot.

4. As you can see from the code, the context of both threads is kept separate from each other, as shown in Figure 6-9. Essentially, this is a single agent handling multiple conversations simultaneously.

```
julianson@Julians-MacBook-Pro AgentFramework % dotnet run
Restore complete (2.2s)
You are using a preview version of .NET. See: https://aka.ms/dotnet-support-policy
  AgentFramework succeeded (4.3s) → bin/Debug/net10.0/AgentFramework.dll

Build succeeded in 7.7s
Starting conversation. Type 'end' to exit.

----------------- Conversation 1 -----------------
The Model Context Protocol (MCP) is a communication framework that helps different systems and applications understand and share contextual information about a specific model, like a person, v
ehicle, or any other entity. It's particularly useful in fields like AI, machine learning, and IoT (Internet of Things) where different devices and systems need to work together and make sense
 of data.

Here are the main points about the Model Context Protocol:

1. **Context Sharing**: MCP allows systems to share information about the context in which a model exists. For example, if a smart home device knows that a person is home, it can adjust settin
gs like lighting or temperature accordingly.

2. **Standardization**: By using a common protocol, different devices, apps, and systems can communicate more effectively. This means they can understand the context of each other's data witho
ut needing unique solutions for each different system.

3. **Flexibility**: MCP can handle various types of models. It doesn't matter if the model is a device, a user, or a service—MCP can help connect all these entities and provide relevant contex
t.

4. **Enhancing Functionality**: With the right context shared through MCP, systems can make smarter decisions. For example, a navigation app could use real-time traffic data to suggest the fas
test route, relying on contextual information it receives through the protocol.

In short, the Model Context Protocol helps different technologies work together by sharing important context, making systems smarter and more efficient.

----------------- Conversation 2 -----------------
In a not-so-distant future where climate change has left cities submerged and resources scarce, a daring young scientist named Elara discovers a mysterious ancient device that has the power to
 manipulate the weather. As she races against time to unlock its secrets, powerful corporations and governments become aware of her breakthrough and will stop at nothing to control the device
for their own gain. With the help of a band of unlikely allies—each with their own reasons for fighting back—Elara must navigate a world of corporate espionage, betrayal, and unexpected allian
ces, all while battling the elements and challenging her beliefs about humanity's responsibility to the planet. As chaos ensues, Elara learns that the key to saving the world may not just lie
in technology, but in the strength of the human spirit.

----------------- Conversation 1 -----------------
In a general sense, "tools" can be defined as devices or implements that people use to carry out specific tasks or achieve certain goals. They are often physical objects, but they can also ref
er to software applications or platforms that assist in accomplishing objectives. Here are some key points to help clarify how tools are defined:

1. **Purpose**: Tools are created to facilitate a particular activity. For example, a hammer is a tool to drive nails, while a computer program might be a tool for data analysis.

2. **Functionality**: Each tool has specific functions that enable users to perform tasks more efficiently or effectively. For instance, a calculator tool performs arithmetic operations, makin
g mathematical tasks easier.

3. **Types**: There are many types of tools, including:
   - **Physical Tools**: Handheld objects like wrenches, screwdrivers, and saws.
   - **Digital Tools**: Software applications, websites, or platforms, like word processors or project management software.
   - **Natural Tools**: Tools that are found in nature, often used in survival situations, like sticks or stones.

4. **Users**: Tools are designed with a user in mind, making it essential for them to be intuitive and easy to use. The effectiveness of a tool often depends on how well it meets the needs of
its user.

5. **Adaptability**: Some tools can be used in various ways or adapted to different tasks. For example, a multi-tool might combine several functionalities, like a knife, screwdriver, and bottl
e opener in one device.

In summary, tools are essential instruments—either physical or digital—that facilitate specific tasks, enhance productivity, and improve the efficiency of accomplishing goals.

----------------- Conversation 2 -----------------
In a vibrant world where ancient magic intertwines with futuristic technology, a brilliant young scientist named Elara stumbles upon an enchanted relic that can manipulate both weather pattern
s and the very fabric of reality itself. As she delves deeper into its secrets, she discovers that the relic is a gateway to a parallel realm filled with mythical creatures and mystical powers
 that can either save or destroy her drowning world. When powerful corporations, driven by greed and ambition, learn of her discovery, they enlist dark sorcerers to seize the relic for their o
wn nefarious plans. Forced to ally with a charming rogue from the magical realm and a band of misfit warriors who wield their own unique powers, Elara embarks on a treacherous journey through
breathtaking landscapes and fantastical challenges. As the two worlds collide, she must balance the logic of science with the unpredictable nature of magic, ultimately realizing that the true
strength to save both realms lies not only within the relic but also in the bonds of friendship and the courage to embrace the unknown.

----------------- Conversation 1 -----------------
Thread 1: So far, we have discussed two main topics. First, we talked about the Model Context Protocol (MCP), which is a framework that enables different systems and applications to share cont
extual information about various models, enhancing communication and decision-making across devices and platforms. We highlighted its importance in making systems smarter and more efficient.

Second, we defined what tools are, explaining that they are devices or applications designed to help people carry out specific tasks. We covered the purpose, functionality, types, user focus,
and adaptability of tools, emphasizing their role in improving productivity and achieving goals.

----------------- Conversation 2 -----------------
Thread 2: So far, we have been discussing a sci-fi movie plot that combines elements of technology and climate change, featuring a young scientist who discovers a device capable of manipulatin
g weather. We then mixed this concept with fantasy elements, similar to Piers Anthony's Split Infinity trilogy, introducing an enchanted relic that influences both reality and magic. This invo
lved a storyline where the protagonist must navigate a world where science and magic collide, forming alliances to protect both her world and a parallel realm.

julianson@Julians-MacBook-Pro AgentFramework %
```

***Figure 6-9.** Multi-threaded agent conversation*

Additional reading on multi-turn conversations can be found at `https://learn.microsoft.com/en-us/agent-framework/tutorials/agents/multi-turn-conversation?pivots=programming-language-csharp`

Function Tools

In Chapter 5, we learned about MCP and how agents can be extended with tools that are exposed via MCP. We saw how a database can be exposed via MCP and therefore allowed us to use natural language to get information out of the SQL server, as shown in Figure 6-10.

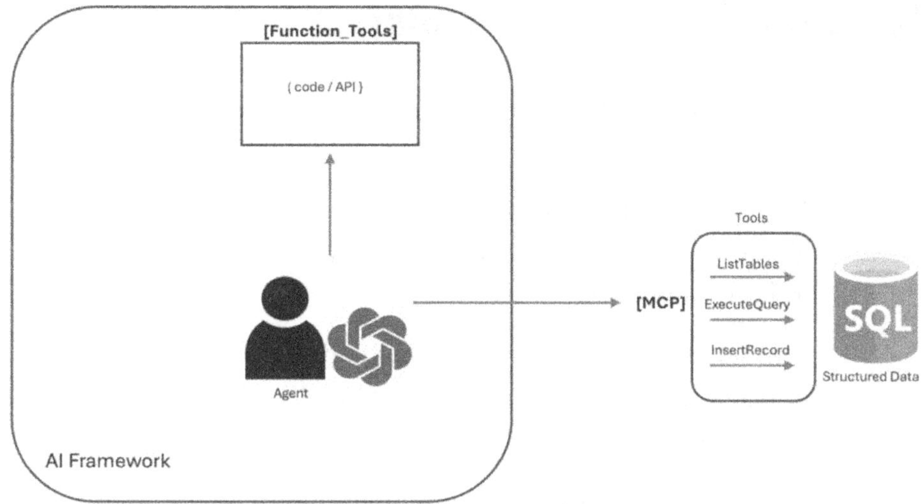

***Figure 6-10.** Agent using Function Tools and MCP*

However, tools do not need to rely on MCP before they can be made available to an agent. For example, prior to MCP and the Microsoft Agent Framework, Semantic Kernel introduced the concept of plugins, which serve as a way to surface tools to agents.

Function Tools within the Microsoft Agent Framework provides the capability to surface tools without the need of an MCP server. There may be reasons why you may not want to use an MCP server, for example, perhaps due to security where you may not want to expose an MCP endpoint, even if that endpoint is protected. Or if the tool is so specific and the number of uses so narrow that it is more cost-effective to define them within the framework instead of hosting an MCP server.

Whatever the reason, Function Tools are just custom code that your agent can call when needed and it functions very similarly to MCP tool calling. Refer again to Figure 6-10 for this representation.

Hands-On Exercise 6.3: Function Tools

1. In VSCode, open *\Chapter_06\Exercise6-3\exercise\program.cs.*

2. In the terminal window of VSCode, navigate to the above directory and execute the application by issuing *dotnet run.*

3. This application is the same as our conversational agent from exercise 6.2.1. Ask the following question: *"What is the weather in Seattle?"*

4. You should receive a message similar to what is shown in Figure 6-11. The agent cannot provide real-time information. Type *end* to terminate the conversation for now.

```
Build succeeded with 11 warning(s) in 9.1s
Starting conversation. Type 'end' to exit.

You: What is the weather in Seattle?

Agent:
I can't provide real-time information like the current weather. However, you can easily check the weather in Seattle using a weather website, an app on your phone, or by asking a smart assist
nt device. Generally, Seattle is known for its rainy weather, especially in the fall and winter, but it can also have beautiful sunny days in the summer. If you need a forecast for specific da
ys, checking a reliable weather source will give you the most accurate information.

You: end
Conversation ended.
```

Figure 6-11. *Agent unable to provide real-time information*

5. As we saw in Chapter 5, one way we can provide agents with real-time capabilities is using tools exposed by MCP servers. But in this example, we want to accomplish the same end goal with Function Tools.

6. First, open the *WeatherService.cs* file. This file defines a *WeatherService* class that calls the US Weather Service API that we used in Chapter 5. However, instead of defining it as an MCP tool, we have written code to call the weather service endpoint and pass it the longitude and latitude of a location of interest. It will then receive the weather information from the endpoint and parse the information.

7. What we want to do is define a Function Tool that calls *WeatherService.cs*.

8. In *program.cs*, enter *using System.ComponentModel;* at the top of the, as shown in Figure 6-12.

Chapter_06 > Exercise6-3 > exercise > C# program.cs

```
using System;
using System.Net.Http;
using System.Net.Http.Json;
using System.Text.Json;
using System.Threading.Tasks;
using System.Net.Security;
using System.Security.Cryptography.X509Certificates;
using System;
using System.Threading.Tasks;
using Azure.AI.OpenAI;
using Azure.Identity;
using Microsoft.Agents.AI;
using Microsoft.Extensions.AI;
using System.ComponentModel;

namespace WeatherApp
{
    class Program
    {

        static async Task Main(string[] args)
        {
```

Figure 6-12. *Add using System.ComponentModel to program.cs*

9. Next, we will provide a description of the Function Tool and define the function. Type the code below (or copy from *completed-solution/src/AgentFramework/program.cs)* before *main()*, as shown in.

```
[Description("Get the weather for a given location.")]
static async Task<string> GetWeather([Descriptio
n("Latitude of the location")] double latitude,
[Description("Longitude of the location")] double
longitude)
{
    var service = new WeatherService();
    var weather = await service.
    GetWeatherAsync(latitude, longitude);
    return $"Weather for {weather.Name}: {weather.
    Temperature}°{weather.TemperatureUnit}, {weather.
    DetailedForecast}";
}
```

```
using System.Text.Json;
using System.Threading.Tasks;
using System.Net.Security;
using System.Security.Cryptography.X509Certificates;
using System;
using System.Threading.Tasks;
using System.ComponentModel;
using Azure.AI.OpenAI;
using Azure.Identity;
using Microsoft.Agents.AI;
using Microsoft.Extensions.AI;

namespace WeatherApp
{
    class Program
    {
        [Description("Get the weather for a given location.")]
        static async Task<string> GetWeather([Description("Latitude of the location")] double latitude, [Description("Longitude of the location")] double longitude)
        {
            var service = new WeatherService();
            var weather = await service.GetWeatherAsync(latitude, longitude);
            return $"Weather for {weather.Name}: {weather.Temperature}°{weather.TemperatureUnit}, {weather.DetailedForecast}";
        }

        static async Task Main(string[] args)
        {
```

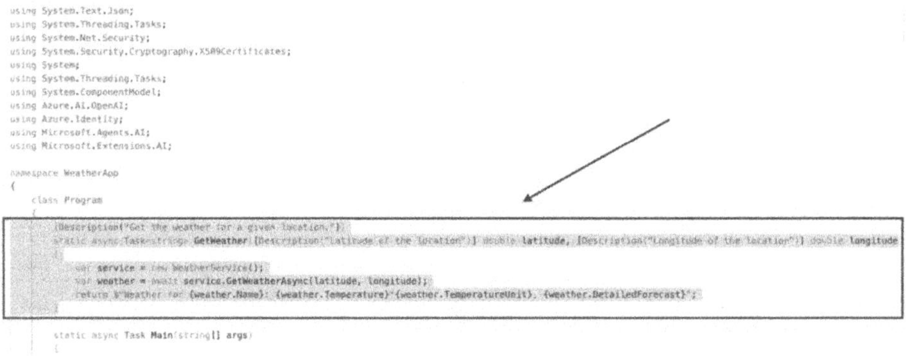

Figure 6-13. *Describe and define the Function Tool*

10. Note that this tool was defined to call the *GetWeatherAsync* method, which is found in *WeatherService.cs.*

11. Lastly, extend the instructions for the agent to include the tools with the code below, and as shown in Figure 6-14.

```
static async Task Main(string[] args)
        {
            AIAgent agent = new AzureOpenAIClient(
                new Uri("https://<YOUR AZURE OPENAI SERVICE
                NAME>.openai.azure.com/"),
                new AzureCliCredential())
                   .GetChatClient("gpt-4o-mini")
                    .AsIChatClient()
                    .CreateAIAgent(
                        instructions: "You are an expert in
                        explaining technologies in simple
                        English", tools: [AIFunctionFactory.
                        Create(GetWeather)]
                    );
```

```
namespace WeatherApp
{
    class Program
    {
        [Description("Get the weather for a given location.")]
        static async Task<string> GetWeather([Description("Latitude of the location")] double latitude, [Description("Longitude of the location")] double longitude
        {
            var service = new WeatherService();
            var weather = await service.GetWeatherAsync(latitude, longitude);
            return $"Weather for {weather.Name}: {weather.Temperature}°{weather.TemperatureUnit}, {weather.DetailedForecast}";
        }

        static async Task Main(string[] args)
        {
            AIAgent agent = new AzureOpenAIClient(
                new Uri("https:[illegible]openai.azure.com/"),
                new AzureCliCredential())
                   .GetChatClient("gpt-4o-mini")
                    .AsIChatClient()
                    .CreateAIAgent(
                        instructions: "You are an expert in explaining technologies in simple English", tools: [AIFunctionFactory.Create(GetWeather)]
                    );
```

Figure 6-14. *Add tools to the instructions for AgentClient()*

12. Save the changes and execute the console application by issuing *dotnet run*.

13. Now ask for the weather in several cities in the USA. The agent is now able to leverage the code in *WeatherService.cs* as a Function Tool. As shown in Figure 6-15 below, the agent was able to provide

current weather conditions in Seattle and Albany, New York, but fails to do so for Seoul because the US Weather Service API only provides weather service for US cities.

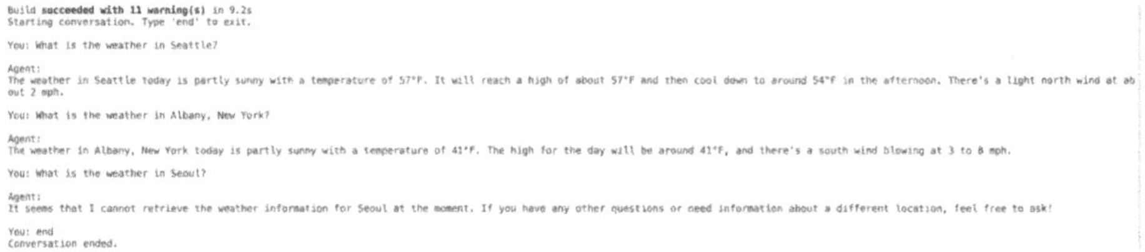

```
Build succeeded with 11 warning(s) in 9.2s
Starting conversation. Type 'end' to exit.

You: What is the weather in Seattle?

Agent:
The weather in Seattle today is partly sunny with a temperature of 57°F. It will reach a high of about 57°F and then cool down to around 54°F in the afternoon. There's a light north wind at ab
out 2 mph.

You: What is the weather in Albany, New York?

Agent:
The weather in Albany, New York today is partly sunny with a temperature of 41°F. The high for the day will be around 41°F, and there's a south wind blowing at 3 to 8 mph.

You: What is the weather in Seoul?

Agent:
It seems that I cannot retrieve the weather information for Seoul at the moment. If you have any other questions or need information about a different location, feel free to ask!

You: end
Conversation ended.
```

Figure 6-15. *Retrieving weather for US cities via Function Tools*

Additional reading on Function Tools can be located at `https://learn.microsoft.com/en-us/agent-framework/tutorials/agents/function-tools?pivots=programming-language-csharp`

There are many more capabilities that are available to agents created with the Microsoft Agent Framework and we would not be able to cover all of them as examples here. However, the hands-on exercises we have done so far would serve as a good framework toward understanding how capabilities are built around an agent. These capabilities can be found as tutorials provided online at `https://learn.microsoft.com/en-us/agent-framework/tutorials/overview`.

Multi-agent Concepts and Patterns

We believe that the most powerful aspect of the agentic approach is the ability to have multiple agents autonomously collaborate with each other. This is the core of an orchestration framework whereby automation is now driven by AI through the binding of AI agents to business processes.

AI Agents versus Workflows

The Microsoft Agent Framework provides a set of orchestration capabilities known as *Workflows*. AI agents and workflows coexist but serve different purposes. As we have seen over the last three chapters, an AI agent is typically bound to a language model and has access to various tools to help it accomplish tasks. The agent performs in a dynamic fashion determined by the LLM based on the context of the conversation and the tools that it can invoke.

A workflow, on the other hand, is more structured. It is a predefined sequence of operations that can include AI agents as components of the sequence. A very common implementation of a workflow is the involvement of multiple agents and how they should be governed. When it comes to multi-agent orchestration, the Agent Framework provides built-in patterns, including sequential, concurrent, handoff, and magentic. We will discuss in detail these different patterns later in this chapter.

Core Components of a Workflow

A workflow in the Microsoft Agent Framework consists of four core layers that work together to govern an execution environment:

- Executors represent individual processing units within a workflow and can be AI agents or custom logic components. They receive messages, perform specific tasks, then produce the corresponding output messages.
- Edges define the connections between executors and determine the flow of messages. They include conditions to control routing based on message contents.

- Workflows orchestrate the executors' execution, message routing, and event streaming.
- Events provide observability into the workflows' execution.

Executors and Edges form a graph representation of the workflow. With the ability for agents to collaborate with each other, several orchestration patterns emerge:

- Sequential
- Concurrent
- Group Chat
- Magentic
- Handoff

We will cover a few of these workflow types in the following sections, including use case scenarios and performance.

Sequential Workflow[5]

As its name implies, a sequential workflow pattern is where agent orchestration works in a linear fashion. One agent performs a task before handing it off to the next agent, and if there are other agents involved, each will take their turn in the orchestration lineup. The output of the task performed by an upstream agent will often be the input of the next downstream agent, although this is not necessarily a requirement.

As an example, if we have five agents working in a sequential orchestration workflow pattern to create events for different demographics, this workflow can be depicted as shown in Figure 6-16.

[5] https://learn.microsoft.com/en-us/agent-framework/workflows/orchestrations/sequential?pivots=programming-language-python

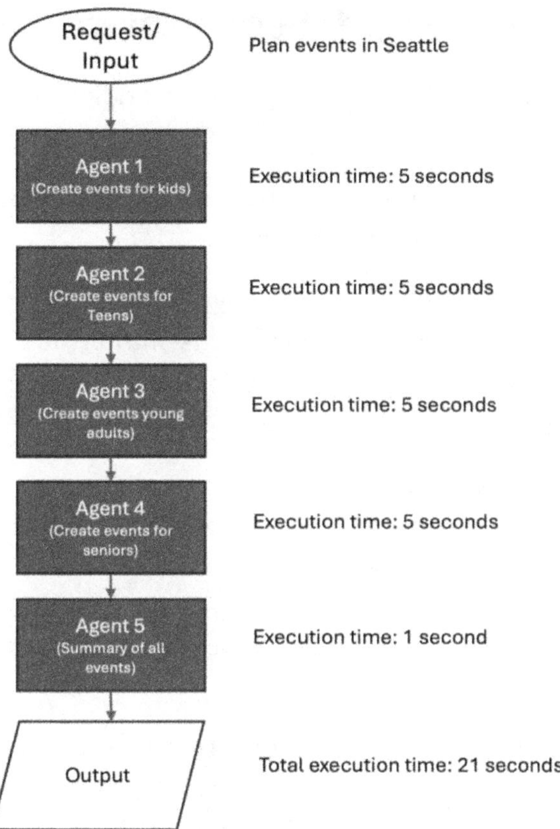

***Figure 6-16.** Sequential workflow orchestration pattern*

In a sequential workflow, it is important to take into consideration the linear execution time of each agent. Therefore, as shown in Figure 6-16, the total execution time for the request is the sum of each agent's execution time, in this case, 21 seconds. For more information about sequential workflows, please see `https://learn.microsoft.com/en-us/agent-framework/user-guide/workflows/orchestrations/sequential?pivots=programming-language-csharp`.

Hands-On Exercise 6.4.1: Sequential Workflows

Let us now build the solution for a sequential workflow using the scenario outlined in Figure 6-16.

1. In VSCode, open *\Chapter_06\Exercse6-4\exercise\AgentFramework\program.cs.*
2. Type the following code, or copy it from *\Chapter_06\Exercse6-4\completed-solution\src\AgentFramework\program.cs.* Your code should look like what is shown in Figure 6-17.

```
//Excercise 6.4.1
/*****************************************************
*************************
 * Sequential Execution of Party Planning Agents
 *****************************************************
*************************/
// 2) Helper method to create party planning agents
//static ChatClientAgent GetPartyPlannerAgent(string
targetAgeGroup, IChatClient chatClient) =>
//    new(chatClient,
//        $"You are a party planning specialist
          who creates event ideas specifically for
          {targetAgeGroup}. " +
//        $"Always start your response by identifying
          yourself as '\u001b[36m{GetAgentName(tar
          getAgeGroup)}\u001b[0m' before appending
          3 more" +
//        $"creative, age-appropriate party ideas and
          activities tailored to this demographic.");
//
```

```
//static string GetAgentName(string ageGroup) =>
ageGroup switch
//{
//     "children 5-8 years old" => "Kids Party
       Planner",
//     "teens" => "Teen Event Coordinator",
//     "young adults" => "Young Adult Party Expert",
//     "retirees" => "Senior Event Specialist",
//     _ => "Party Planner"
//};

//// Helper method to create summary agent
//static ChatClientAgent GetSummaryAgent(IChatClient
chatClient) =>
//     new(chatClient,
//         "You are a summary coordinator who compiles
           and lists all party activities suggested by
           other agents. " +
//         "Always start your response by identifying
           yourself as '\u001b[36mSummary Coordinator\
           u001b[0m'. " +
//         "Review all the previous suggestions
           and create a comprehensive list of all
           activities mentioned, " +
//         "organizing them clearly for easy reference
           but do not start the count from 1 again.");

//// Create party planning agents for sequential
processing
//var partyPlannerAgents = (from ageGroup in
(string[])["children 5-8 years old", "teens", "young
adults", "retirees"]
```

```
//                              select GetParty
                                PlannerAgent(ageGroup,
                                client));

//// Create summary agent
//var summaryAgent = GetSummaryAgent(client);

//// Combine party planner agents with summary agent
//var allAgents = partyPlannerAgents.
Concat([summaryAgent]);

//// 3) Build sequential workflow
//var workflow = AgentWorkflowBuilder.
BuildSequential(allAgents);

//// 4) Run the workflow
//var messages = new List<ChatMessage> {
new(ChatRole.User, "Plan event in Seattle") };

//// Start timing the sequential execution
//var stopwatch = Stopwatch.StartNew();

//StreamingRun run = await InProcessExecution.
StreamAsync(workflow, messages);
//await run.TrySendMessageAsync(new
TurnToken(emitEvents: true));

//List<ChatMessage> result = new();
//await foreach (WorkflowEvent evt in run.
WatchStreamAsync().ConfigureAwait(false))
//{
//    if (evt is AgentResponseUpdateEvent e)
//    {
//        Console.WriteLine($"{e.ExecutorId}:
          {e.Data}");
```

```
//    }
//    else if (evt is WorkflowOutputEvent outputEvt)
//    {
//        result = (List<ChatMessage>)
                  outputEvt.Data!;
//        stopwatch.Stop();
//        break;
//    }
//}

//// Display final result
//foreach (var message in result)
//{
//    Console.WriteLine($"{message.Role}: {message.
      Text}");
//}

//// Display runtime
//Console.ForegroundColor = ConsoleColor.Yellow;
//Console.WriteLine($"\n===== Execution Time =====");
//Console.WriteLine($"Sequential agents completed
in: {stopwatch.ElapsedMilliseconds} ms ({stopwatch.
Elapsed.TotalSeconds:F2} seconds)");
//Console.ResetColor();

//Exercise 6.4.2
/*****************************************************
****************************
 * Concurrent Execution of Party Planning Agents
 *****************************************************
*************************/
// 2) Helper method to create party planning agents
```

```
//static ChatClientAgent GetPartyPlannerAgent(string
targetAgeGroup, IChatClient chatClient) =>
//    new(chatClient,
//        $"You are a party planning specialist
          who creates event ideas specifically for
          {targetAgeGroup}. " +
//        $"Always start your response by identifying
          yourself as '\u001b[36m{GetAgentName(tar
          getAgeGroup)}\u001b[0m' before appending
          3 more" +
//        $"creative, age-appropriate party ideas and
          activities tailored to this demographic.");

//static string GetAgentName(string ageGroup) =>
ageGroup switch
//{
//    "children 5-8 years old" => "Kids Party
      Planner",
//    "teens" => "Teen Event Coordinator",
//    "young adults" => "Young Adult Party Expert",
//    "women-only" => "Women's Event Specialist",
//    "retirees" => "Senior Event Specialist",
//    _ => "Party Planner"
//};
// Create party planning agents for concurrent
processing
//var partyPlannerAgents = (from ageGroup in
(string[])["children 5-8 years old", "teens", "young
adults", "women-only", "retirees"]
//                          select GetParty
                            PlannerAgent(ageGroup,
                            client));
```

```
//// 3) Build concurrent workflow
//var workflow = AgentWorkflowBuilder.BuildConcurrent
(partyPlannerAgents);

//// 4) Run the workflow
//var messages = new List<ChatMessage> {
new(ChatRole.User, "Plan event in Seattle") };

//// Start timing the concurrent execution
//var stopwatch = Stopwatch.StartNew();

//StreamingRun run = await InProcessExecution.
StreamAsync(workflow, messages);
//await run.TrySendMessageAsync(new
TurnToken(emitEvents: true));

//List<ChatMessage> result = new();
//await foreach (WorkflowEvent evt in run.
WatchStreamAsync().ConfigureAwait(false))
//{
//    if (evt is AgentResponseUpdateEvent e)
//    {
//        Console.WriteLine($"{e.ExecutorId}:
          {e.Data}");
//    }
//    else if (evt is WorkflowOutputEvent outputEvt)
//    {
//        result = (List<ChatMessage>)
          outputEvt.Data!;
//        stopwatch.Stop();
//        break;
//    }
//}
```

```
//// Display aggregated results from all agents
//Console.WriteLine("===== Final Aggregated Results
=====");
//foreach (var message in result)
//{
//    Console.WriteLine($"{message.Role}: {message.
Text}");
//}

//// Display runtime
//Console.ForegroundColor = ConsoleColor.Yellow;
//Console.WriteLine($"\n===== Execution Time =====");
//Console.WriteLine($"Concurrent agents completed
in: {stopwatch.ElapsedMilliseconds} ms ({stopwatch.
Elapsed.TotalSeconds:F2} seconds)");
//Console.ResetColor();
```

Figure 6-17. *Program.cs for exercises 6.4.1 and 6.4.2*

3. Uncomment all the code for *Exercise 6.4.1* and remember to replace the Azure OpenAI endpoint in the code with your actual endpoint URL.

4. Save the changes and execute the program by issuing *dotnet run* in your VSCode terminal, after making sure you are in the correct directory.

5. The output from the program should be similar to what is shown in Figure 6-18. Take note of the total execution time (we will use this to compare it to a concurrent workflow in the next exercise). In our case, the execution time was 21.70 seconds, which tells us that each agent ran for approximately 4.34 seconds.

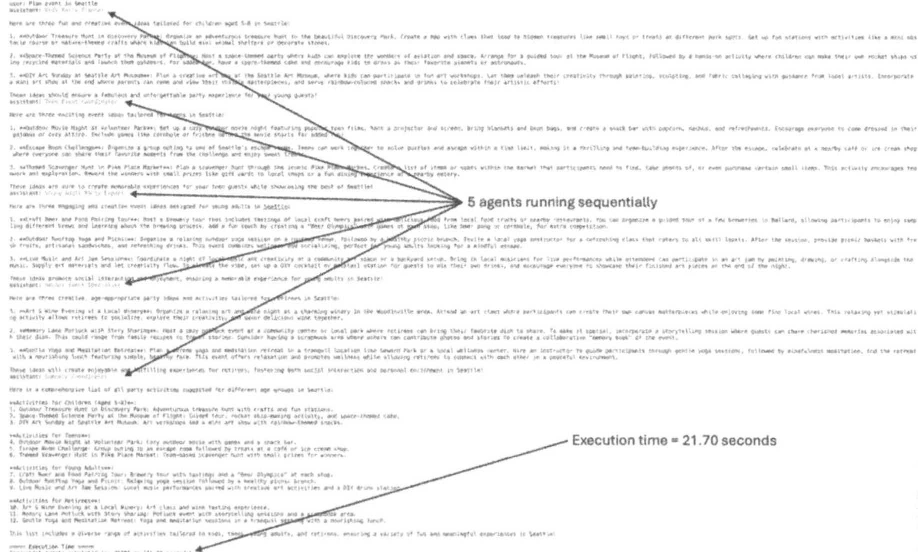

***Figure 6-18.** Output of the sequential workflow of 5 agents*

6. Let's explore this code. After defining the Azure OpenAI endpoint, we wrote some helper code that will be used to create four agents, each with the same role but we parameterized the four demographics of the people we are planning activities for – kids, teens, young adults, and retirees, as shown in Figure 6-19. This helper code, when used later, will create these agents with instructions to come up with three activities that fit the demographic they are responsible for.

```
// 2) Helper method to create party planning agents
static ChatClientAgent GetPartyPlannerAgent(string targetAgeGroup, IChatClient chatClient) =>
    new(chatClient,
        $"You are a party planning specialist who creates event ideas specifically for {targetAgeGroup}. " +
        $"Always start your response by identifying yourself as '\u001b[36m{GetAgentName(targetAgeGroup)}\u001b[0m' before appending 3 more" +
        $"creative, age-appropriate party ideas and activities tailored to this demographic.");

static string GetAgentName(string ageGroup) => ageGroup switch
{
    "children 5-8 years old" => "Kids Party Planner",
    "teens" => "Teen Event Coordinator",
    "young adults" => "Young Adult Party Expert",
    "retirees" => "Senior Event Specialist",
    _ => "Party Planner"
};
```

Figure 6-19. *Helper code used to define and parameterize the creation of the party planning agents*

7. Next, we wrote some code that will help define the properties of a fifth agent. This agent will summarize the activities that the above four agents have planned for their demographic group. This should be a total of 12 activities. Figure 6-20 shows the definition and parameters for the summary agent.

```
// Helper method to create summary agent
static ChatClientAgent GetSummaryAgent(IChatClient chatClient) =>
    new(chatClient,
        "You are a summary coordinator who compiles and lists all party activities suggested by other agents. " +
        "Always start your response by identifying yourself as '\u001b[36mSummary Coordinator\u001b[0m'. " +
        "Review all the previous suggestions and create a comprehensive list of all activities mentioned, " +
        "organizing them clearly for easy reference but do not start the count from 1 again.");
```

Figure 6-20. *Helper code used to define and parameterize the creation of the summary agent*

8. With the helper code defining the agents, we can now proceed to create the agents, then group them together into a single group. Note that the party planner agents are arranged in the specific order, as shown in Figure 6-21.

```
// Create party planning agents for sequential processing
var partyPlannerAgents = (from ageGroup in (string[])["children 5-8 years old", "teens", "young adults", "retirees"]
                          select GetPartyPlannerAgent(ageGroup, client));

// Create summary agent
var summaryAgent = GetSummaryAgent(client);

// Combine party planner agents with summary agent
var allAgents = partyPlannerAgents.Concat([summaryAgent]);
```

Figure 6-21. *Creating the five agents and combining them into a single group*

9. This next part is the key portion of this hands-on exercise, where we create the workflow to specify it as sequential in nature, as shown in Figure 6-22.

```
// 3) Build sequential workflow
var workflow = AgentWorkflowBuilder.BuildSequential(allAgents);
```

Figure 6-22. *Creating a sequential workflow*

10. We will not go through the rest of the code in detail, but in essence, the remaining code starts a timer, runs the workflow with a hardcoded prompt to *plan an event in Seattle*, output the results, then stop the timer.

A sequential workflow is ideal where each step builds upon the previous one, and/or when a pre-defined order of execution needs to occur. The above example that we used shows how events for each demographic group is being added as the itinerary is being built. Other examples include document review processes or multi-stage reasoning.

Concurrent Workflow[6]

We will now look at concurrent workflows by using the same scenario as what we saw in exercise 6.4.1. The major difference is that in a concurrent workflow, as its name implies, the agents run concurrently, akin to parallel processing, as shown in Figure 6-23.

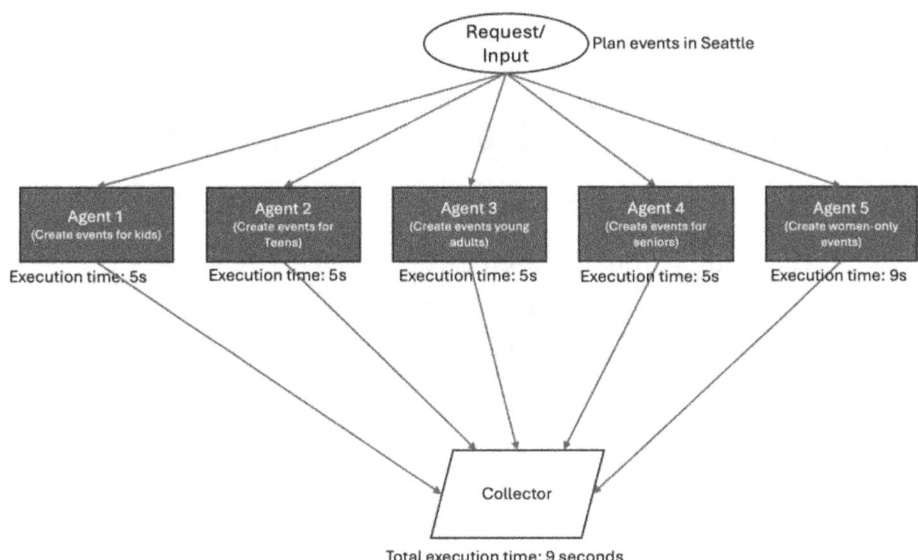

Figure 6-23. *Concurrent workflow orchestration pattern*

Multiple agents work on the same task (with perhaps varying parameters) independently and parallelly, and their results are collected and aggregated. Notice that because the agents run concurrently, the execution time is approximately equivalent to the longest running agent (9 seconds in Figure 6-23). The best use case scenarios for concurrent workflows are

[6] https://learn.microsoft.com/en-us/agent-framework/workflows/orchestrations/concurrent?pivots=programming-language-csharp

- Most efficient processing times
- Agents can work independently without dependencies from each other
- Desire for diverse perspectives
- Reasoning
- Voting systems

Hands-On Exercise 6.4.2: Concurrent Workflows

Let us now look at the implementation of a concurrent workflow.

1. Continuing from the Exercise 6.4.1, delete or comment out all the code associated with Exercise 6.4.1 and uncomment the code for Exercise 6.4.2, as shown in Figure 6-24.

```
//Console.WriteLine($"\n===== Execution Time =====");
//Console.WriteLine($"Sequential agents completed in: {stopwatch.ElapsedMilliseconds} ms ({stopwatch.Elap
//Console.ResetColor();
```

Uncomment code for exercise 6.4.2

```
//Exercise 6.4.2
/****************************************************************************
 * Concurrent Execution of Party Planning Agents
 ****************************************************************************/
// 2) Helper method to create party planning agents
static ChatClientAgent GetPartyPlannerAgent(string targetAgeGroup, IChatClient chatClient) =>
    new(chatClient,
        $"You are a party planning specialist who creates event ideas specifically for {targetAgeGroup}.
        $"Always start your response by identifying yourself as '\u001b[36m{GetAgentName(targetAgeGroup)}
        $"creative, age-appropriate party ideas and activities tailored to this demographic.");

static string GetAgentName(string ageGroup) => ageGroup switch
{
    "children 5-8 years old" => "Kids Party Planner",
    "teens" => "Teen Event Coordinator",
    "young adults" => "Young Adult Party Expert",
    "retirees" => "Senior Event Specialist",
    _ => "Party Planner"
};
// Create party planning agents for concurrent processing
var partyPlannerAgents = (from ageGroup in (string[])["children 5-8 years old", "teens", "young adults",
                          select GetPartyPlannerAgent(ageGroup, client));

// 3) Build concurrent workflow
var workflow = AgentWorkflowBuilder.BuildConcurrent(partyPlannerAgents);

// 4) Run the workflow
var messages = new List<ChatMessage> { new(ChatRole.User, "Plan event in Seattle") };

// Start timing the concurrent execution
var stopwatch = Stopwatch.StartNew();
```

<snip – Note screenshot is truncated>

Figure 6-24. *Uncomment the code for exercise 6.4.2 (Concurrent Workflow)*

2. Let us take a look at this code block. Note that the setup is mostly similar to the code in Exercise 6.4.1. The only differences are

    a. We do not have a summary agent because the collector will handle this. Instead, we added a fifth agent that will create women-only events, as shown in Figure 6-25. This is to keep our agent count at five so we can compare execution time between a sequential workflow and a concurrent workflow.

```
static string GetAgentName(string ageGroup) => ageGroup switch
{
    "children 5-8 years old" => "Kids Party Planner",
    "teens" => "Teen Event Coordinator",
    "young adults" => "Young Adult Party Expert",
    "women-only" => "Women's Event Specialist",
    "retirees" => "Senior Event Specialist",
    _ => "Party Planner"
};
// Create party planning agents for concurrent processing
var partyPlannerAgents = (from ageGroup in (string[])["children 5-8 years old", "teens", "young adults", "women-only", "retirees"]
                          select GetPartyPlannerAgent(ageGroup, client));
```

Added 5th agent (women-only event planner)

Figure 6-25. *Added fifth agent – Women-only event planner*

b. Instead of creating a sequential workflow, we created a concurrent workflow, as shown in Figure 6-26.

```
// 3) Build concurrent workflow
var workflow = AgentWorkflowBuilder.BuildConcurrent(partyPlannerAgents);
```

Figure 6-26. *Create a concurrent workflow*

3. Save the changes and execute the program by issuing *dotnet run* in VSCode terminal. Your output should be similar to the one shown in Figure 6-27.

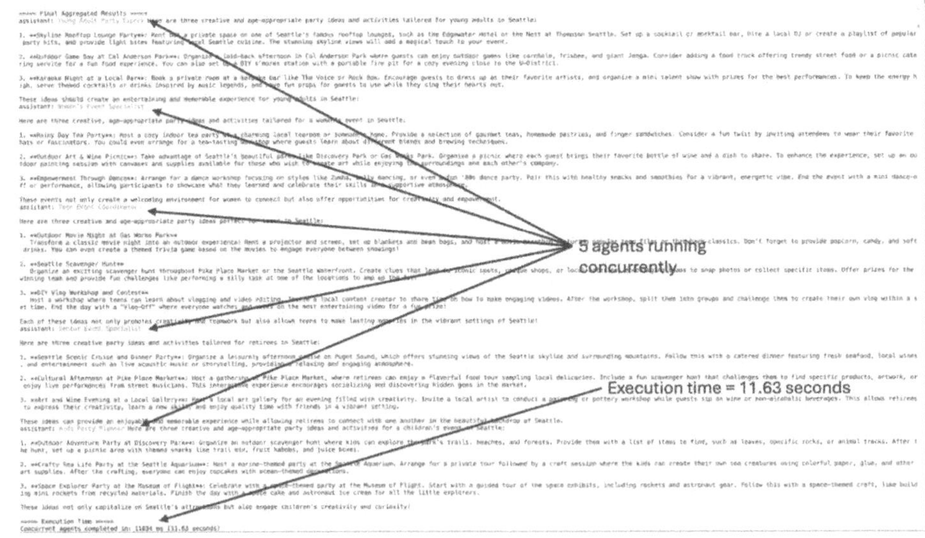

Figure 6-27. *Output of the concurrent workflow of 5 Agents*

4. Note that the execution time of the concurrent workflow should be less than the sequential workflow. In essence, if your agents can run independently, then it is more efficient to use a concurrent workflow.

Group Chat Workflow[7]

One of the most powerful workflows is the Group Chat workflow. Think of these as "agent collaboration" workflows whereby the agents consult with each other and collaboratively work to accomplish a task. Agents can provide a constructive feedback loop to contribute to the quality of the outcome.

This pattern is ideal for scenarios requiring iterative refinement, collaborative problem-solving, or multi-perspective analysis.

Group Chat workflows rely on an orchestrator to coordinate the agents in the group. As shown in Figure 6-28,the characteristics of a Group Chat workflow are

[7] https://learn.microsoft.com/en-us/agent-framework/workflows/orchestrations/group-chat?pivots=programming-language-csharp

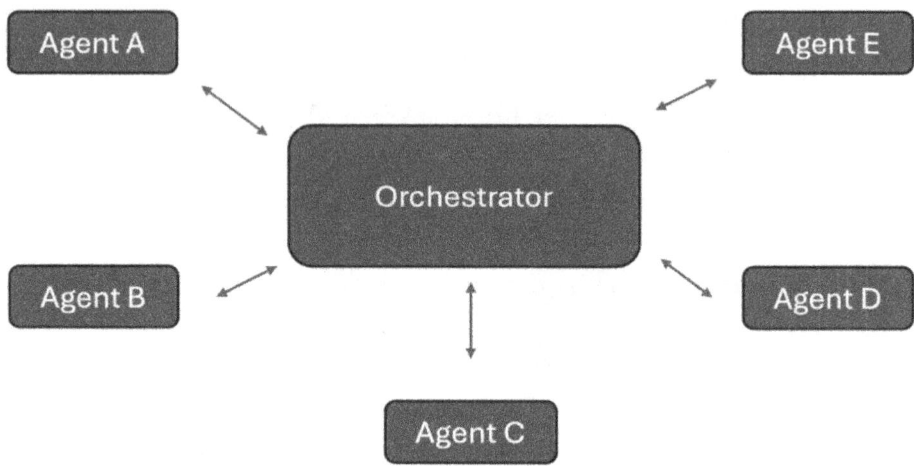

***Figure 6-28.** Group Chat workflow resembling a star topology*

- **Centralized Orchestration**: Control of the group uses a single orchestrator.[8] Unlike other patterns, the control of the workflow is not handed off from one agent to another.
- **Iterative Refinement**: Agents review and build on each other's response through multiple rounds. Not all agents may contribute even though they are part of the group chat. This occurs if such agents have nothing to contribute to the refinement of the outcome. Nonetheless, every agent would still confirm their participation, usually by stating they have nothing to add.
- **Flexible Agent Selection**: The orchestrator can use round-robin, prompt-based, or custom logic to select agents.

[8] See how Orchestrator is implemented as *ProcessWorkflowAsync()* in hands-on exercise 6-5 later.

- **Shared Context**: All agents see the full conversation history and the contributions from other agents, thereby enabling collaborative refinement.

Hands-On Exercise 6.5: Group Chat Workflow

For this hands-on exercise, we are going to build an itinerary planning solution that leverages three agents to come up with an outing in a particular city for the day:

- **Event Planning Agent**: Recommend activities for the day based on current time
- **Weather Agent**: Uses the US Weather Service API as a function tool to get today's weather for a given US city
- **Reviewer Agent**: Reviews the itinerary to make sure it is weather-appropriate

1. In VSCode, open *\Chapter_06\Exercse6-5\exercise\AgentFramework\program.cs.*
2. This program.cs file is similar to exercise 6.3 when we used the US Weather Service's API as a function tool. It already has the scaffolding for a weather agent and the function tool defined. Replace *<Enter your Azure OpenAI endpoint here>* with your actual endpoint.
3. First, we will add two more agents to assist - the Event Planner agent and the Reviewer agent. Locate the code that initializes the Weather agent and type the following code or copy it from *\Chapter_06\Exercise6-5\completed-solution\src\AgentFramework\program.cs*. Your code should look like what is shown in Figure 6-29.

```
//Define additional agents
// Create an Event Planner Agent
ChatClientAgent EventPlannerAgent = new(client,
    "You are an event planner for activities in
    a US city. Generate interesting activities
    available in a city based on the current time
    today for the rest of the day.",
    "EventPlanner", "An event planning agent");

// Create a reviewer agent
ChatClientAgent ReviewerAgent = new(client,
    "You are a reviewer of *WEATHER
    APPROPRIATE* planned events. Evaluate
    the feasibility by *ASKING WeatherAgent*
    what the weather is, appeal, and
    logistics of the proposed activities. " +
    "Provide constructive feedback or approval.",
    "Reviewer", "An event review agent");
```

Figure 6-29. *Code to define additional agents*

4. Next, we will build the Group Chat workflow. After the code that defined the Reviewer agent, type the following code or copy it from the *completed-solutions* directory. Your code should look like what is shown in Figure 6-30.

```
// Build group chat with round-robin speaker selection
// The manager factory receives the list of agents and returns a configured manager
var workflow = AgentWorkflowBuilder
    .CreateGroupChatBuilderWith(agents =>
        new RoundRobinGroupChatManager(agents)
        {
            MaximumIterationCount = 5 // Maximum number of turns
        })
    .AddParticipants(EventPlannerAgent, ReviewerAgent, WeatherAgent)
    .Build();
```

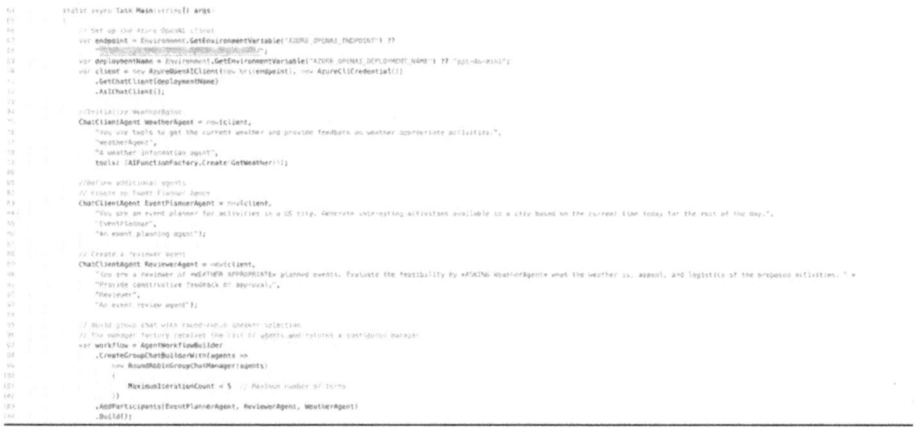

Figure 6-30. *Creating the Group Chat Workflow using Round Robin pattern*

5. Next we will define a method that will orchestrate the group chat. We will call it the *ProcessWorkflowAsync()* method. In this case, ProcessWorkflowAsync is the **Orchestrator** in the Group Chat Workflow pattern. Therefore, *ProcessWorkflowAsync()* will

   a. Start the conversation between the multiple AI agents.

   b. Listen to the conversation between agents in real time (like listening to a conference call).

   c. In our implementation, we have it print out the agents' conversation so you can follow along.

   d. Provide a final summary when all the agents are done talking.

6. Outside of *main()*, type the following code or copy it from the *completed-solutions* directory. Your code should look like what is shown in Figure 6-31. In our case, we defined *ProcessWorkflowAsync()* above *main()*.

```
static async Task ProcessWorkflowAsync(Microsoft.
Agents.AI.Workflows.Workflow workflow,
List<ChatMessage> messages)
{
    StreamingRun run = await InProcessExecution.
    StreamAsync(workflow, messages);
    await run.TrySendMessageAsync(new
    TurnToken(emitEvents: true));

    await foreach (WorkflowEvent evt in run.
    WatchStreamAsync().ConfigureAwait(false))
```

```
    {
        if (evt is Microsoft.Agents.AI.Workflows.
        AgentResponseUpdateEvent update)
        {
            // Process streaming agent responses
            AgentResponse response = update.
            AsResponse();
            foreach (ChatMessage message in response.
            Messages)
            {
                Console.WriteLine($"[{update.
                ExecutorId}]: {message.Text}");
            }
        }
        else if (evt is WorkflowOutputEvent output)
        {
            // Workflow completed
            var conversationHistory = output.
            As<List<ChatMessage>>();
            Console.WriteLine("\n=== Final
            Conversation ===");
            foreach (var message in
            conversationHistory)
            {
                Console.WriteLine($"[{message.
                AuthorName}]: {message.Text}");
            }
            break;
        }
    }
}
```

```
static async Task ProcessWorkflowAsync(Microsoft.Agents.AI.Workflows.Workflow workflow, List<ChatMessage> messages)
{
    StreamingRun run = await InProcessExecution.StreamAsync(workflow, messages);
    await run.TrySendMessageAsync(new TurnToken(emitEvents: true));

    await foreach (WorkflowEvent evt in run.WatchStreamAsync().ConfigureAwait(false))
    {
        if (evt is Microsoft.Agents.AI.Workflows.AgentResponseUpdateEvent update)
        {
            // Process streaming agent responses
            AgentResponse response = update.AsResponse();
            foreach (ChatMessage message in response.Messages)
            {
                Console.WriteLine($"[{update.ExecutorId}]: {message.Text}");
            }
        }
        else if (evt is WorkflowOutputEvent output)
        {
            // Workflow completed
            var conversationHistory = output.As<List<ChatMessage>>();
            Console.WriteLine("\n=== Final Conversation ===");
            foreach (var message in conversationHistory)
            {
                Console.WriteLine($"[{message.AuthorName}]: {message.Text}");
            }
            break;
        }
    }
}

0 references
static async Task Main(string[] args)
{
    // Set up the Azure OpenAI client
    var endpoint = Environment.GetEnvironmentVariable("AZURE_OPENAI_ENDPOINT") ??
        "[illegible]";
    var deploymentName = Environment.GetEnvironmentVariable("AZURE_OPENAI_DEPLOYMENT_NAME") ?? "gpt-4o-mini";
    var client = new AzureOpenAIClient(new Uri(endpoint), new AzureCliCredential())
        .GetChatClient(deploymentName)
        .AsIChatClient();
```

Figure 6-31. *Defining the ProcessWorkflowAsync() method*

7. Save the changes and execute the program by issuing *dotnet run* in VSCode terminal. Your output should be similar to the one shown in Figure 6-32 and Figure 6-33.

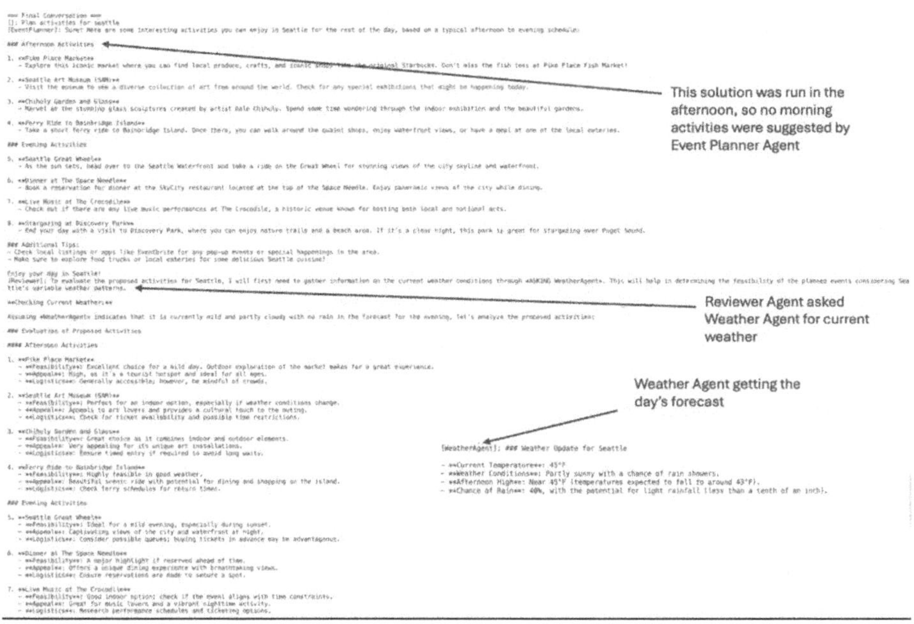

This solution was run in the afternoon, so no morning activities were suggested by Event Planner Agent

Reviewer Agent asked Weather Agent for current weather

Weather Agent getting the day's forecast

Figure 6-32. *Group Chat conversation summary*[9]

[9] The Weather agent's forecast is offset to the side in this screenshot so we can show the conversations in a single screenshot. This is NOT how the Weather Agent's conversation is actually displayed; it is in line with all the rest of the conversations.

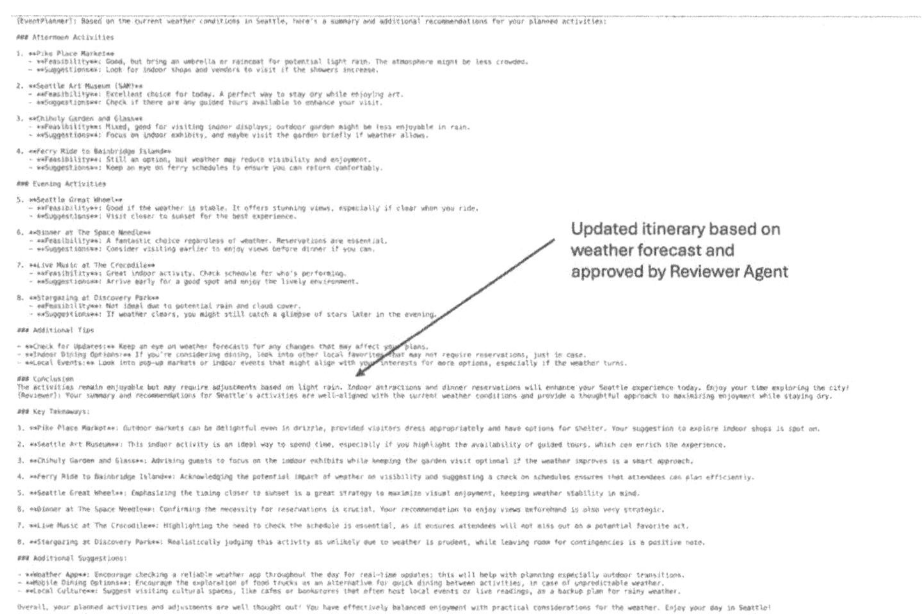

***Figure 6-33.** Final recommendation based on the collaboration of all three agents*

A couple of observations:

a. In Figure 6-32, because we ran the solution in the afternoon, the Event Planner agent omitted morning activities.

b. Also in Figure 6-32, we see that the Review agent rightfully asked the Weather agent for the current weather, and the Weather agent complied.

c. Note the final revised itinerary as approved by the Reviewer agent after combining inputs from both the Event Planner agent and the Weather agent.

Other Workflow Patterns

We will cover two other workflows but without additional hands-on exercises, because you can implement these based on the knowledge you have acquired from the previous exercises.

Handoff Workflow[10]

Unlike the Chat Group workflow, where an orchestrator is present, a Handoff workflow does *not* have an orchestrator. At any point of time, one of the agents in the multi-agentic group would be the one in control and that control will be passed on to another agent. The conversation flow can go from one agent to any agent as shown in Figure 6-34. Compared to the "Star-topology" depicted by a Group Chat workflow, a Handoff workflow is represented as a "Mesh-topology." The agent in control decides which agent to hand off the control to.

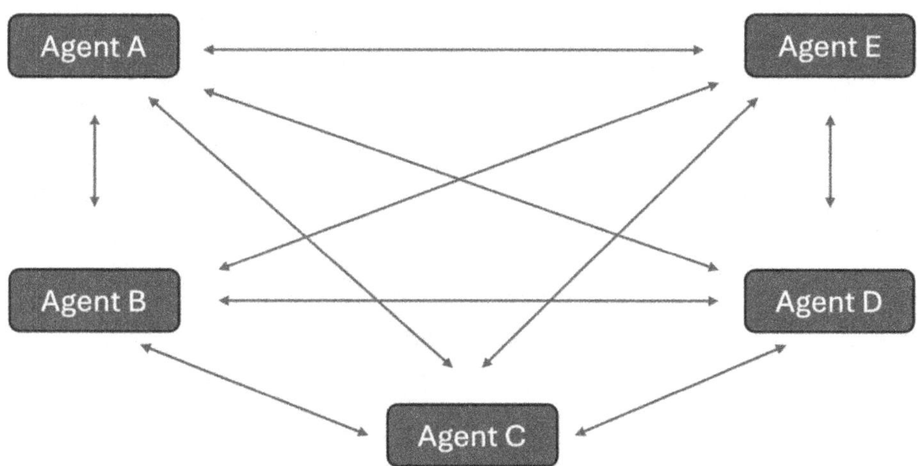

Figure 6-34. *Handoff workflow*

[10] https://learn.microsoft.com/en-us/agent-framework/workflows/orchestrations/handoff?pivots=programming-language-csharp

Once control is passed from one agent to another, the receiving agent (now the one in control), will take full ownership of the task. The receiving agent has the full context of what was done by previous agents.

Magentic Workflow[11]

The Magentic workflow is AutoGen's Magentic-One[12] feature that was ported over to Microsoft Agent Framework. At the time of writing, the Magentic workflow can only be implemented using Python.

The architectures of both the Magentic workflow and the Chat Group workflow are identical in that they both rely on a centralized orchestrator. Therefore, they are both represented as a "star-topology." However, there are important differences on the surface and how execution occurs under each workflow pattern.

From the surface, a Group Chat workflow implements an orchestrator (see Figure 6-28 and review *ProcessWorkflowAsync()*). In contrast, the Magentic workflow uses an actual agent as the orchestrator. This agent is often referred to as the Manager Agent, as shown in Figure 6-35. We would like to think the name "Magentic" in Magentic-One was derived by combining the words "Manager" and "Agentic" but we have not been able to verify this.

[11] https://learn.microsoft.com/en-us/agent-framework/workflows/orchestrations/magentic?pivots=programming-language-python

[12] https://microsoft.github.io/autogen/stable/user-guide/agentchat-user-guide/magentic-one.html

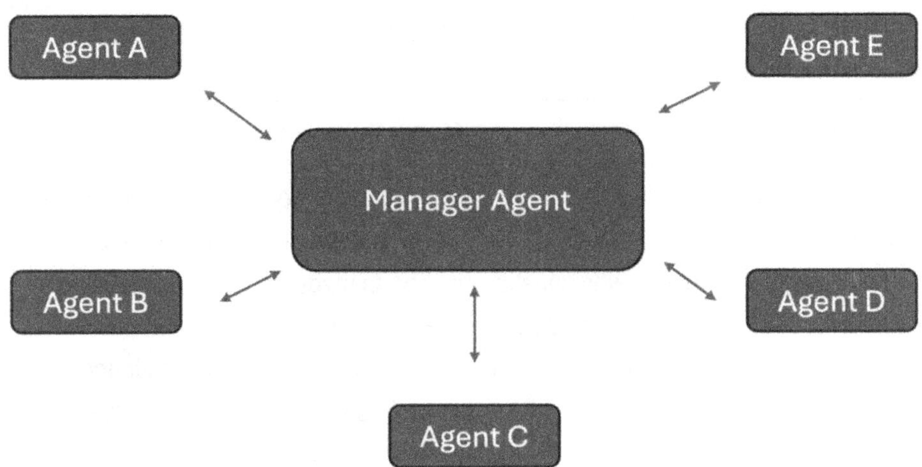

Figure 6-35. *High level topology of a Magentic Workflow*

Under the covers, execution of the workflows is very different. The Group Chat workflow is seen as a conversation-based collaboration between agents, whereas the Magentic workflow is a planning-based collaboration directed by a dedicated manager agent. Group Chat workflows, while involving multiple agents, will seem chaotic, whereas in a Magentic workflow, the collaboration process will be more structured due to the planning and task assignment overseen by the manager agent.

Table 6-1 shows how these two workflows behave differently during runtime:

***Table 6-1.** Comparison of the Chat Group Workflow runtime versus the Magentic Workflow runtime*

Group chat workflow	Magentic workflow

• All agents share a single conversation thread
• The Orchestrator selects who speaks first based on implemented pattern (e.g., Round-robin, custom logic, etc.)
• Agents respond to each other's messages
• No plans or ledger or planner artifact
• Progress and results emerges organically through the discussion and hence may seem chaotic
	• A manager agent, not an orchestrator, owns the task from end to end.
	• The manager agent is responsible for
	  o Building a plan
	  o Maintaining a progress ledger
	  o Choosing which agent acts next, hence seen as more structured
	  o Deciding when to replan, continue, or finish
	• Member agents do focused and/or delegated work
	• Final answer is curated per the plan and not developed organically

Between the two workflows, you would choose Group Chat when you want a collaborative discussion, and Magentic when you want a goal-driven task execution process that is structured but with dynamic planning.

Summary

In this chapter, we learned about using an orchestration framework to organize agents in multi-agentic scenarios. In current approach of leveraging more refined and focused agents, the need for an orchestration framework is very important because most enterprise implementation of agents will involve multi-agentic patterns.

Although there are other orchestration frameworks available, for example, LangChain being one of the most popular ones, we used the new Microsoft Agent Framework as the basis for introducing an orchestration framework. This is because even though the Microsoft Agent Framework is still in preview at the time of writing, it is an enterprise-ready framework and is a combination of two very strong frameworks – Semantic Kernel and AutoGen. With its native support for C#, the Microsoft Agentic Framework is an excellent option for enterprise-grade AI and multi-agentic deployments.

CHAPTER 7

Publishing on Azure Marketplace

Introduction: Maximizing Market Presence with the Commercial Marketplace

The development of sophisticated AI agents and generative solutions, detailed in previous chapters, represents the technical foundation of a successful Independent Software Vendor (ISV) offering. You have completed the hardest part, building a robust, secure, and intelligent product on the Microsoft AI Cloud. However, technical excellence alone does not guarantee commercial success.

The transition from a functional prototype to a market-leading, revenue-generating solution requires a strategic, deliberate, and aggressive Go-to-Market (GTM) plan. For any ISV operating in the Microsoft ecosystem, that plan is centered entirely on the Microsoft Commercial Marketplace.

The Commercial Marketplace is not merely a digital catalog of apps; it is the commerce engine that powers the entire Microsoft partner ecosystem. It is a comprehensive system designed to simplify global transactions, automate complex back-office functions and connect your solution directly to Microsoft's global sales force. For AI solution providers specifically, the Marketplace offers a unique combination of technical

J. Soh et al., *Building and Distributing Agentic AI Solutions*,
https://doi.org/10.1007/979-8-8688-2586-6_7

infrastructure, global distribution, and integration with Microsoft's sales ecosystem that can dramatically reduce your time-to-market and lower your customer acquisition costs.

This chapter provides the essential GTM framework for your AI solution. We will cover the strategic decisions on *how* to list your product, the tactical process of publishing through Partner Center, and the powerful GTM engines, like the Co-sell program and MACC (Microsoft Azure Consumption Commitment) eligibility, that Microsoft provides to scale your business.

The Strategic Shift: From Builder to Seller

To effectively navigate this shift, you must first understand the two primary audiences your product addresses and the two corresponding storefronts where they shop:

Storefront	Target buyer persona	Primary offer type	Key selling point
AppSource	Line-of-Business (LOB) Manager (e.g., HR, Sales, Finance)	SaaS, Consulting Services	Business outcome, ease of use, integration with M365/Dynamics
Azure Marketplace	Technical Buyer (e.g., CIO, IT Admin, Architect)	VMs, Managed Apps, Containers, Developer Tools	Security, performance, scalability, MACC eligibility

The Marketplace As a Commerce Engine

Before focusing on the "how," we must establish the profound "why." Mistakenly viewing the Marketplace as just another app store is the single biggest impediment to an ISV's success. It is a sophisticated GTM Engine built on three foundational pillars that automate and accelerate nearly every aspect of global software sales, Global Distribution, Transact, Capability, and Sales Ecosystem Integration.

Pillar 1: Global Distribution and Enhanced Visibility

The Marketplace provides immediate global reach, but the true value lies not just in availability, but in Microsoft taking over the complex role of the Merchant of Record (MOR). This function solves the most intractable problems of international B2B software sales.

The Merchant of Record: Automating Global Commerce

For an ISV, achieving independent global sales is a staggering operational challenge. Selling a digital product from a US-based entity to a company in, say, Brazil, requires navigating an impenetrable thicket of legal, financial, and regulatory complexity:

1. **Local currency and payments:** The customer in Brazil will demand to pay in Brazilian Real (BRL). Your platform must process BRL, and your bank must accept it, often incurring significant foreign exchange fees and delays.

2. **Tax compliance and remittance:** You are instantly exposed to local tax laws. For Europe, this means calculating, collecting, and remitting Value Added Tax (VAT). For India, the Goods and Services Tax (GST). Tax rates change constantly and vary by country, state, or even product category. Tax non-compliance carries severe, sometimes criminal, penalties.

3. **Invoicing and collections:** Enterprise customers often have multi-month payment terms, forcing you to carry significant Sales Outstanding (DSO). Chasing multinational collections is a massive drain on resources.

When you publish a transactable offer (which we will define shortly), Microsoft becomes the Merchant of Record for that transaction in over 100 countries and regions.

This means Microsoft handles 100% of the following:

- **Currency conversion:** You set your price in USD or your home currency; Microsoft handles the conversion and foreign exchange risk.
- **Tax calculation and remittance:** Microsoft calculates, collects, and remits all local sales taxes (VAT, GST, etc.) to the respective governmental bodies globally.
- **Invoicing and collections:** The customer is billed directly on their established Microsoft Enterprise Agreement (EA) or Azure bill. Microsoft manages the collection process, cutting your DSO to near zero as Microsoft pays you the net revenue directly, often on a predictable monthly cycle.

Take for instance a small startup ISV SaaS platform provider that focuses on customer service automation. Without the Marketplace, they could only sell efficiently in the USA and Canada. By listing a transactable SaaS offer, they gain immediate access to major markets like the UK, France, Australia, and Singapore, without hiring a single compliance officer or international accountant. This capability alone transforms them from a local startup into a global business platform overnight.

Advanced Visibility: In-Product Discovery

Visibility on the Marketplace extends far beyond the public storefront websites (AppSource and Azure Marketplace). The most valuable discovery happens where your customers are already working, inside the Microsoft product ecosystem.

1. **Azure Portal integration (Azure Marketplace):** For technical solutions, the Azure Marketplace integrates directly into the Azure Portal. When a customer's IT architect is provisioning resources (e.g., creating a Virtual Machine or a new Kubernetes Cluster), your Virtual Machine Offer or Managed Application appears alongside native Microsoft services. They can deploy your solution with a single click using the same deployment templates (like ARM or Bicep) they use for Azure services.

2. **Microsoft 365 and Dynamics 365 integration (AppSource):** For business solutions, AppSource integrates with Microsoft Teams, Dynamics 365, and the Power Platform. For instance, an ISV's AI agent platform can be purchased via AppSource and immediately appear as an application tile within the customer's Microsoft Teams environment, ready for deployment. This in-app discovery is incredibly powerful because it captures the Line-of-Business buyer at the point of action, eliminating the need to leave their work environment to purchase or install.

Pillar 2: A Transact-Capable Platform

The transition from a "Referral" model (where the Marketplace sends you a lead, and you handle the sale) to a *Transact* model is the most important strategic step you will take. Transactable offers allow you to leverage the full commercial engine of Microsoft.

The Automation of Revenue: Shortening the Sales Cycle

When a customer subscribes to a transactable offer, they are effectively adding your software license directly to their Microsoft billing relationship.

This automated transaction bypasses the slowest, most complex, and most expensive part of enterprise sales, procurement, and legal review**.**

- **Before transact:** A $50,000 deal requires months of negotiation, redlining custom contracts, and waiting for budget approval.
- **With transact:** The legal framework for the transaction is covered by the customer's existing Microsoft agreement and the standardized terms of the Marketplace. The purchase becomes a simple line item on a consolidated bill, often executable by an IT administrator or LOB manager with spending authority. This can reduce a 90-day sales cycle into minutes for a self-service purchase or days for a Private Offer.

The DSO Advantage: By having Microsoft act as the collector, your team receives predictable, reliable monthly payouts. This dramatically improves your cash flow and allows your executive team to focus on growth and product development rather than capital management and collections.

Monetization for the AI Era: Custom Metered Billing

Traditional software licensing, flat fees, per-user, or perpetual licenses, is fundamentally ill-suited for the dynamic, consumption-based economics of generative AI. The value of an AI solution is in its output and usage, not the number of people who have access to the dashboard.

The Marketplace's Metered Billing API (also known as the Marketplace Metering Service) is the solution. It allows the ISV to define custom billing dimensions and report usage against them in real-time, integrating these custom charges directly into the customer's Azure bill.

Steps for Implementing Metered Billing:

1. **Define custom dimensions:** Within the Partner Center you define your custom billing metrics. These are your "units of value."

    - *Example:* Dimensions could be customer_conversation ($0.002 per unit), KB_of_data_indexed ($0.05 per unit), or LLM_inference_token ($0.00002 per unit).

2. **Implement the metering API:** Your application backend, running in the customer's or your own tenant, must call the Metering API endpoint. This API call sends a payload to Microsoft containing the customer's subscription ID, your custom metric ID, and the quantity consumed during the metering period.

3. **Real-time reporting:** The application calls the API as usage occurs. For instance, every time the platform's agent completes a conversation, their backend sends a request reporting quantity: 1 against the customer_conversation dimension.

4. **Customer billing:** Microsoft aggregates this usage and includes it as a line item on the customer's regular Azure invoice.

This approach creates a Consumption-Based Revenue (CBR) model that perfectly aligns cost with value. Customers pay for what they use, lowering the initial hurdle to adoption, and your revenue scales directly with the traffic and success of your solution.

Pillar 3: An Integrated Sales Ecosystem

When your offer is transactable and MACC-eligible (as detailed below), it becomes a first-class citizen in the Microsoft ecosystem, unlocking two levels of powerful GTM acceleration, Marketplace Rewards and the Co-sell Program.

Marketplace Rewards: Marketing Acceleration

The Marketplace Rewards program is a tiered system of benefits that are provided to you at no cost based on your yearly billed revenue (billed amount) through the Marketplace. These rewards are designed to help you drive awareness, generate leads, and accelerate sales.

Tier (based on billed revenue)	Key benefits	Impact on ISV GTM
Silver (initial tier)	Dedicated Partner Success Manager, GTM consultation, Self-service GTM assets (badges, logos).	Establishes credibility and provides basic branding support for your AI solution.
Gold	Assisted GTM benefits, including co-branded press release templates, social media support and internal Microsoft sales training materials.	Elevates your visibility within the Microsoft organization and provides professional marketing assets.
Platinum (Highest Tiers)	Access to large-scale marketing campaigns, eligibility for Microsoft-funded webinars and feature placement on Microsoft.com and in Marketplace newsletters.	Directly drives high-quality pipeline leads and positions your solution as a preferred partner offering.

Actively leveraging these rewards, such as utilizing the free GTM consultation or securing placement in a Microsoft-funded webinar can often provide the equivalent of tens of thousands of dollars in marketing spend for free.

Private Offers: Flexibility for Enterprise Deals

While public, self-service transactable offers are crucial for velocity and volume, large enterprise deals often require custom pricing, non-standard payment terms or discounts that deviate from the public list price. This is where Marketplace Private Offers (MPOs) are essential.

An MPO allows you to

- **Customize Pricing:** Offer a 10% discount to a specific named customer (e.g., Contoso Inc.) without changing the price for the public listing.
- **Customize terms:** Extend the subscription term from 12 to 36 months or offer a deferred payment schedule.
- **Custom metering:** Create a specific discounted metering rate just for that customer.

The MPO provides the best of both worlds, the commercial flexibility of a traditional direct sales negotiation, coupled with the transact-capable infrastructure of the Marketplace. This means the customer still benefits from MACC eligibility and you still benefit from Microsoft's Merchant of Record service, even on a customized deal.

The MACC Effect: Your Ultimate Sales Accelerant

The Microsoft Azure Consumption Commitment (MACC) effect is the single most powerful tactical sales accelerant in the Microsoft ecosystem. Listing a transactable, MACC-eligible offer fundamentally changes your sales conversations from "asking for new budget" to "helping the customer spend existing committed budget."

Understanding Azure Consumption Commitment (MACC)

Most large enterprise customers sign a multi-year, multi-million-dollar contract with Microsoft, which includes a commitment to spend a certain amount of money on Azure services. This commitment is the MACC.

For example, a bank (Contoso Financial) may commit to spending $10 million on Azure services over three years.

- **The customer's problem:** The CIO is held accountable for retiring this commitment. If they fail to spend the $10 million they lose the discounts and favorable terms they negotiated. They are actively looking for ways to spend the budget they are contractually obligated to spend.
- **The Marketplace solution:** When your transactable offer is marked as Azure Benefit Eligible (a designation applied to most Azure Marketplace transactable offers, including Managed Applications and Containers), 100% of the customer's purchase counts toward retiring their MACC.

The Strategic Pivot: MACC in Action

Consider a typical sales scenario for a compliance tool provider whose compliance solution costs $300,000 annually.

Sales scenario	Direct sales model (no marketplace)	Transactable marketplace model (MACC eligible)
Initial pitch	The $300,000 is considered new expenditure, requiring approval from the CFO and Procurement.	The $300,000 is positioned as a drawdown of existing MACC, requiring only IT/Cloud budget sign off.
Budget barrier	Deal stalls if the new project budget for AI is frozen for the current fiscal quarter.	The deal accelerates because the CIO is motivated to retire their committed spend. The commitment becomes the budget.
Closing argument	"Buy our product because it's the best compliance solution."	"Buy our product because it is the best compliance solution, and your $300,000 purchase helps you meet your contractual commitment with Microsoft."

This pivot, moving your solution from a "CapEx/New OpEx" line item to an "Existing Cloud Commitment" drawdown, removes the single greatest friction point in enterprise sales. It aligns your commercial interests with the customer's financial objectives and makes your solution a priority spend.

The MACC effect is why every ISV targeting enterprise customers on Azure should prioritize the transactable model and the Azure Marketplace as the foundational elements of their GTM strategy. The sales velocity it unlocks is unmatched by any other channel.

Strategic Decisions: Choosing Your Offer Type

Your first major strategic decision, and one that will define your architectural requirements, GTM path, and monetization model is how your AI solution will be packaged and sold on the Marketplace. The Commercial Marketplace supports numerous offer types, but for modern, cloud-native AI solutions, your choice will likely narrow down to four primary options. Each offers a distinct balance of control, customer appeal, and MACC eligibility.

Software as a Service (SaaS) Offer (The Velocity Play)

The SaaS offer is the most common, flexible, and often the simplest path to market and revenue velocity, particularly when targeting LOB buyers.

How it Works: The Fulfillment API and Webhook Integration

The key characteristic of a SaaS offer is that you host the solution entirely within your own Azure subscription (or on-premises/multi-cloud environment). The customer only purchases a license or subscription through the Marketplace, as shown in Figure 7-1.

- **Discovery and purchase:** The customer finds your SaaS application (typically on AppSource), clicks "Buy," and the transaction is processed through the Microsoft Commerce Engine.
- **Notification:** The Marketplace sends a real-time Webhook Notification to a fulfillment endpoint you define. This notification confirms the purchase (or change in subscription, like an upgrade, downgrade, or cancellation).
- **Fulfillment API integration:** Upon receiving the notification, your application backend must call the SaaS Fulfillment API to acknowledge the transaction and provision the user's account. This two-way communication (Webhook In, API Out) is mandatory for the offer to remain in a healthy state.
- **Billing:** Your billing logic can be per-seat (flat monthly fee per user) or for AI based on Custom Metered Billing, where your application reports usage to the Metering API.

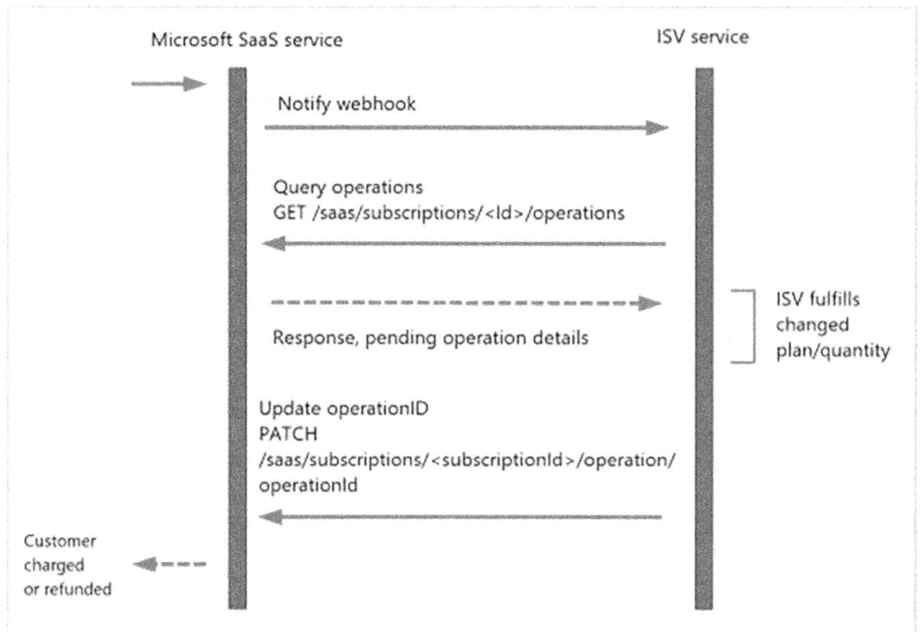

Figure 7-1. *Sequence of API calls for an update sceanario that initiates from Microsoft Marketplace*

Strategic Advantages for AI Solutions

- **Centralized model management:** Since you control the hosting environment, you have complete authority over the AI models. You can easily push updates, fine-tune models in bulk, manage vector databases, and switch between base models (e.g., GPT, 4o to Llama 3) without requiring any action from the customer.
- **Rapid deployment and low friction:** For LOB buyers, the experience is seamless, subscribe on AppSource, click a link, and start building agents in their browser. There is no Azure provisioning step required from the customer's IT team, dramatically lowering adoption friction.

- **Optimal for usage-based revenue:** The inherent flexibility of the SaaS model, combined with the Marketplace Metered Billing API, makes it the superior choice for implementing consumption-based pricing metrics like: $ per agent response, $ per token consumed, or $ per minute of voice transcription.

SaaS Strategy Example	Key Takeaway
Storefront	AppSource (Targeting LOB buyers)
Monetization	Metered Billing (customer_conversation units)
Control	Full control over the AI stack and infrastructure
Fulfillment	SaaS Fulfillment API provisions the customer's tenant/account

Azure Application (Managed Application) Offer (The Trust and Control Play)

The Managed Application (often referred to as Azure App) is the strategic choice when your AI solution is highly complex, requires dedicated resources, or must adhere to stringent data residency and security mandates. This offer type is the counterpoint to SaaS, addressing the highest tiers of enterprise requirements.

How it Works: Deployment into the Customer's Tenant

Unlike a SaaS offer, a Managed Application is deployed directly into the customer's own Azure subscription. This means the compute resources, the data, and your AI model binaries physically reside within the customer's network boundaries.

1. **Deployment via ARM template:** You define the entire solution architecture (e.g., an Azure Kubernetes Service cluster, an Azure SQL database, an Azure AI Studio instance, and a custom Virtual Machine) using a standard Azure Resource Manager (ARM) template.

2. **The locked resource group:** When the customer deploys the offer from the Azure Marketplace, the resources are placed into a special locked resource group.

    - **Customer view:** The customer sees the application listed in their Azure Portal, but they cannot see, modify, or interact with the underlying resources (VMs, databases, etc.). This makes the solution a "black box" appliance.

    - **ISV view:** ISVs are granted permanent delegated access to this locked resource group. This access is managed through Microsoft Entra ID and allows you to perform maintenance, apply updates, monitor performance, and manage the customer's dedicated AI models.

Strategic Imperative: Data Residency and Security

For highly regulated industries (Finance, Healthcare, Government), the primary challenge is data residency. These customers cannot permit their highly sensitive data (PII, financial records, legal documents) to leave their sovereign cloud environment.

- **Compliance:** Because the Managed Application deploys the solution into the customer's Azure tenant, the data storage, processing, and the AI's inference engine physically reside within their environment. This guarantees data sovereignty and simplifies compliance with regulations like GDPR, HIPAA, and local country-specific data laws.

- **Dedicated AI model:** This is the only practical way to sell a fine-tuned, dedicated AI model to a single customer. The Managed Application provides the dedicated, isolated cloud infrastructure required.

Securing a managed application is equally important, hence below are some best practices industries can follow:

1. **Identity and access management (IAM)**: Use Microsoft Entra ID, RBAC, MFA, and managed identities to enforce least-privilege access with no hard-coded credentials.
2. **Privileged access and publisher isolation**: Separate publisher and customer access using PIM and clearly defined responsibility boundaries.
3. **Network security**: Deploy resources into customer VNets with NSGs, private endpoints, WAF, and DDoS protection to minimize public exposure.
4. **Data protection and encryption**: Encrypt data at rest and in transit using Azure-native encryption and store secrets securely in Azure Key Vault.
5. **Logging, monitoring, and threat detection**: Enable Microsoft Defender for Cloud, centralize logs in Azure Monitor, and integrate with Microsoft Sentinel.
6. **Governance and policy enforcement**: Enforce security baselines using Azure Policy aligned to the Microsoft Cloud Security Benchmark.

7. **Secure deployment and supply chain**: Use Infrastructure as Code with secure defaults, validation, vulnerability scanning, and signed packages.
8. **Backup, recovery, and resilience**: Define RPO/RTO targets and use Azure Backup and Site Recovery with regular restore testing.

Management and Maintenance

While Managed Applications solve the data residency problem, they introduce operational complexity:

- **Provisioning complexity:** You must maintain a robust CI/CD pipeline to manage and deploy updates across potentially hundreds of different customer tenants. Below are some best practices for DevOps:
    - **CI/CD:** Two-pipeline model (CI+CD)
    - **Updates**: Versioned immutable releases
    - **Deployment**: Incremental + blue-green
    - **Rollback**: Redeploy last known good artifact
    - **Automation**: Health-based rollback triggers
    - **Governance**: Approvals, artifact retention, audits
- **The Just-in-Time (JIT) model:** Best practices dictate that your ISV management team only accesses a customer's tenant using Azure Lighthouse for Just-in-Time access. This limits the ISV's high-privilege access, improving the security posture and appeasing the customer's security team.

Managed application strategy example	Key takeaway
Storefront	Azure Marketplace (Targeting CIO/CISO buyers)
Monetization	Fixed Monthly Fee + Metered Billing (TB Scanned)
Control	Customer owns the cloud tenant; ISV manages the AI application within a locked resource group.
GTM Advantage	Full MACC eligibility and guaranteed data residency.

Virtual Machine (VM) and Container Offers (The Developer-First Play)

VM and Container offers represent the lowest friction and highest control options for the customer. They are best suited for products that are foundational, self-contained, or targeting a purely technical/developer audience that prefers to manage their own environment.

Virtual Machine (VM) Offers

A VM offer publishes a pre-configured virtual hard disk (VHD) image. When a customer deploys the offer, Azure spins up a VM based on your image within their subscription.

- **Best for:** Legacy deployments, security appliances (e.g., AI-powered firewalls), or complete, proprietary operating environments where your AI agent is integrated at the OS level.
- **Monetization:** VMs offer two primary models:
    - **Pay-As-You-Go (PAYGO):** The customer pays a base Azure VM cost plus an hourly or per-second software cost defined by you. This software fee counts toward MACC.

- **Bring Your Own License (BYOL):** The customer pays only the Azure compute cost. They purchase the software license from you directly (off-Marketplace) or via a Consulting Service offer. This model is simpler to publish but less advantageous for MACC retirement.

Container Offers

A Container offer publishes an image to the Azure Container Registry that customers can pull and deploy into their own orchestration environments (like Azure Kubernetes Service [AKS] or Azure Container Instances [ACI]).

- **Best for:** Modern AI agent development kits, foundational LLMs packaged as local inference engines, or modular components that developers can integrate into their CI/CD pipelines. This is the ultimate "developer tool" offer.
- **Control:** The customer has absolute control over scaling, networking, and deployment topology. The ISV has no visibility into the running environment, making support more complex.
- **AI use case:** If you are selling a proprietary object detection model or a complex vectorization pipeline, packaging it as a container allows developers to easily integrate it into their custom machine learning workflows.

Offer type	Primary buyer	Data/control model	MACC eligibility
SaaS	LOB Manager (AppSource)	ISV hosts, multi-tenant	Yes (Transactable)
Managed application	IT Admin/CISO (Azure)	Customer hosts, single-tenant locked by ISV	Yes (Transactable)
VM/Container	Developer/ architect (Azure)	Customer hosts, full control by customer	Yes (PAYGO only)

Consulting Service Offer (The Solution Bundling Play)

The Consulting Service offer is not a software product but a fixed-scope, fixed-price service that serves two powerful strategic purposes, pre-sales engagement and high-value solution bundling.

How it works: Fixed Scope, Fixed Price

Consulting Service offers are always non-transactable, meaning they generate a lead, not revenue, through the Marketplace. They are structured as time-bound, fixed-price engagements such as

- **5-day engagement:** "AI Agent Architecture Workshop for Financial Services"
- **3-week project:** "Proof-of-Concept Deployment for Azure OpenAI Fine-Tuning"

The customer purchases the service, which generates a lead that your sales team then follows up on to schedule and execute the engagement.

The Strategic Role in the AI Sales Cycle

1. **De-risking the sale (The Land Strategy):** Enterprise customers are often cautious about investing $100,000+ in a new AI solution. A Consulting Service offer allows them to buy a low-cost, low-risk,

high-value assessment (e.g., $10,000 for a 5-day AI Readiness Assessment) that utilizes your team's expertise. The result of this assessment is often the formal recommendation to purchase your full software solution.

2. **Bundling and expertise:** For AI solutions, software without expertise is often useless. This offer allows you to monetize the essential human expertise required to get your AI agent product (SaaS or Managed App) successfully deployed, integrated with legacy data, and adopted by end users. You are selling the *outcome*, not just the *tool*.

A Sample GTM Package:

1. **Core product: SaaS Offer** (AppSource, Metered Billing) - *Revenue Engine*
2. **Pre-sales lead: Consulting Offer** (AppSource) - "3-Day AI Agent Pilot Setup & Training" - *Pipeline Builder*
3. **Enterprise customization: Private Offer** (MPO) - For large clients requiring annual commit discounts - *Sales Accelerator*

The Publishing Funnel: From Partner Center to "Go-Live"

The strategic decisions regarding your offer type (SaaS, Managed App, VM/Container) lay the conceptual groundwork for your Go-to-Market (GTM) plan. However, the tactical reality of transforming that concept into a revenue-generating asset hinges entirely on execution within Partner Center.

Partner Center is the unified portal that serves as the single point of control for your entire relationship with Microsoft, encompassing partnership benefits, Co-sell management and the Commercial Marketplace publishing process. For an Independent Software Vendor (ISV) of an AI solution, successfully navigating this process means passing rigorous technical checks and adhering to strict content standards to ensure a seamless experience for the customer and a reliable revenue stream for your company.

The entire publishing journey, from initial account setup to the public "Go-Live" notification, can be simplified into four comprehensive stages. Each stage is a quality gate and failure in one necessitates a return to previous steps.

Stage 1: Prerequisites and Account Setup

Before any lines of code or marketing copy are uploaded, the ISV must establish its foundational, commercial, and legal identity. This is a one-time process, but its accuracy is non-negotiable as it directly governs Microsoft's ability to transact business on your behalf and remit your revenue.

Enrollment and Program Qualification

The process begins with enrollment which ensures your organization is recognized as a legitimate partner eligible to transact in the Commercial Marketplace.

Commercial Marketplace Account Enrollment

While your organization may already be enrolled in the Microsoft AI Cloud Partner Program (formerly MPN) for technical benefits, this does not automatically grant publishing rights. You must explicitly enroll in the Commercial Marketplace program within Partner Center. This step establishes your contractual agreement with Microsoft that governs the terms of listing, transacting, and revenue sharing.

The Global Seller Profile

A key step in enrollment is building a Global Seller Profile. This profile details your company's name, primary contact information, support details (which will be published on your listing), and the legal entity under which you will operate.

Best Practice - Support Visibility: For AI solutions, which can often be complex and require integration with customer data, ensure the support email and phone number listed are active, monitored, and capable of addressing high-priority technical issues. Certification teams often test these contact methods.

Legal, Tax, and Payout Configuration (The Revenue Foundation)

This is perhaps the most critical stage, as any error here will prevent Microsoft from paying you. Microsoft, as the Merchant of Record, requires precise financial documentation to ensure global tax and regulatory compliance.

Tax Forms and Compliance

You must complete the required tax forms based on your country of incorporation and where you sell.

- **US entities**: Typically, a **W-9** form is required.
- **Non-US entities**: A **W-8BEN** (Certificate of Foreign Status of Beneficial Owner for United States Tax Withholding and Reporting) or similar documentation is required.

These forms establish your tax identity and determine the withholding rates Microsoft must apply to your revenue before remittance. Failure to provide these forms will result in Microsoft withholding the maximum default tax rate (often 30%) on all sales.

Payout Account Linking

You must designate a bank account that can accept international transfers. This account must be in a major currency (US$, €, etc.) and belong to the legal entity that owns the Partner Center account.

Financial structure consideration: For ISVs operating globally, it is common to use an international payment processing service or a multi-currency bank account to minimize foreign exchange fees and ensure the highest payout rate. The name on the bank account **must exactly match** the legal entity name listed in Partner Center.

User and Role Management

The complexity of AI solutions often requires specialized teams (AI Engineers, Product Managers, Sales Leads). Partner Center allows you to segment access rights based on the principle of least privilege.

Role name	Primary responsibility	Critical Marketplace access
Owner	Highest privilege. Controls legal contracts and payout	Approves all final Go-Live actions and signs legal amendments
Manager	Oversees all GTM and publishing activities	Edits marketing content, manages pricing plans, submits offers for certification
Developer	Focuses on technical integration and assets	Manages the ARM templates for Managed Apps, configures SaaS Webhooks, and submits technical assets

Security mandate: Ensure that high-privilege roles like Owner are only assigned to senior leadership or administrative staff. Developers should only be granted the necessary permissions to configure technical settings, minimizing the risk of unauthorized changes to pricing or legal terms.

Your Marketplace Listing: The "Digital Storefront"

A common ISV mistake is to treat the Marketplace listing as an afterthought. This is your digital storefront. It is the single most important piece of marketing collateral you have in the Microsoft ecosystem. A poorly written, uninspiring listing will fail to convert even if your AI product is revolutionary.

Your listing should be crafted with the same care as your solution's UI. It must be clear, compelling, and focused relentlessly on customer outcomes. This section details the critical components of a high-converting listing, focusing on narrative, visual assets, search engine optimization (SEO), and commercial strategy.

Crafting a Compelling Narrative: Selling the Outcome, Not the Engine

The primary goal of your text is to transition the customer's mindset from *tool evaluation* to *problem resolution*. In the world of AI, this means avoiding technical jargon like "vector databases," "RAG," and "70B parameter models" in favor of tangible business benefits.

Offer Name, Tagline, and Short Summary

These elements must be immediately descriptive and unique. They are the first three pieces of information a customer encounters and must be perfected for search and conversion.

- **Offer name (The Identifier):** Must be clear and unique. Avoid generic names like "AI Solution."
    - **Good:** "AcmeAI Financial Agent" (Clear industry focus).
    - **Bad:** "Intelligent Chatbot Pro" (Too generic, no clear value).
    - **Strategic note***:* If you are a new brand, use the name to describe the function (e.g., "Company Name: Compliance Risk Analyzer").

- **Search results summary (The Hook):** This is a one-sentence, 100-character hook that appears in search results and category browses. It must contain your primary keyword and the chief benefit.
    - *Example:* **"The AI agent that reads SEC filings and internal reports for instant-cited financial answers."**
- **Long summary/description (The "Why"):** The long description is your primary sales pitch and should be the largest section of text. It must be structured to guide the reader through the value proposition using formatting to enhance readability.

The Three-Part Narrative Structure

Every high-converting description for an AI solution should follow this logical flow:

1. **The Pain point and promise (introduction):** Start by quantifying the customer's current problem and immediately offering the solution.
    - **Bad:** "Our Gen-AI solution uses a 70B parameter model, RAG and vector databases..." (Leads with features, not benefits.)
    - **For a SaaS ISV:** "Stop wasting 20 hours a week searching for documents across SharePoint and OneDrive. Our AI Financial Agent reads your entire knowledge base, from SEC filings to internal reports, and gives you instant, cited answers. Ask "What was our Q3 revenue in Europe?" and get an answer in seconds, not hours." (Leads with quantifiable timesaving.)

2. **Features to benefits (The Body):** Use formatted lists (Markdown bolding and bullet points) to break up the dense text. Translate every feature into a business benefit.

3. **Microsoft integration and CTA (conclusion):** This section is non-optional, especially for Azure Marketplace listings. Reiterate the strong tie to the Microsoft ecosystem.

    - **Key messaging:** "Deployed as an Azure Managed Application, this solution is fully MACC-eligible, helping your organization retire its existing Azure consumption commitment while modernizing compliance."

    - **Clear call to action:** End with an explicit action. "Start your 30-Day Free Trial today" or "Click Get it Now to deploy this solution in your Azure tenant."

Feature (What It Is)	Benefit (What It Does for the Customer)
RAG architecture (Retrieval Augmented Generation)	**Eliminates hallucination:** Answers are always grounded in *your* proprietary data, ensuring 100% citation accuracy and trust.
Custom metered billing	**Pay-for-value:** Only pay $0.02 per conversation, aligning costs perfectly with customer engagement volume.
Azure managed app deployment	**Guaranteed data residency:** Your sensitive data never leaves your Azure tenant, simplifying HIPAA/GDPR compliance instantly.
Azure AD SSO	**One-click secure access:** Users log in seamlessly using their existing corporate credentials, reducing friction and IT burden.

The Power of Visuals: Logos, Screenshots, and Video

Humans process visuals exponentially faster than text. Your visual assets are the most powerful conversion drivers and must be treated as a curated sequence, not a random gallery.

Logos and Branding Consistency

Microsoft enforces strict standards for logos to maintain the professional integrity of the Marketplace. Certification will fail if these are not precise.

- **Mandatory sizes:** Ensure your small (48x48), medium (90x90), and large (216x216) logos are crisp, professionally designed, and adhere exactly to the required pixel dimensions. Use a transparent background for maximum flexibility.
- **The Hero image (1280x720):** This banner image is key for promotional placement. It should not be cluttered. It should feature your logo, a succinct tagline, and a clean, high-level visual representation of your AI solution (e.g., an abstract image of data flow, not a busy screenshot).

The Screenshot Narrative Sequence

Screenshots must form a cohesive, visual story that demonstrates the end-to-end user journey. Do not use developer tools, code editors, or error messages. Focus on the final polished UI.

A SaaS ISV Example

1. **Setup and connection:** Show the simplest step, connecting to the data source. *Caption: "1. Connect your Knowledge Base (SharePoint, Azure AI Search, or OneDrive) in seconds."*

2. **The core interaction:** Show the AI agent in action. *Caption: "2. Ask a natural language question in the agent console."*
3. **The result:** Show the correct, cited answer. *Caption: "3. Receive an instant, fully-cited answer, grounded in your proprietary documents."*
4. **The dashboard:** Show the admin dashboard highlighting a key metric. *Caption: "4. Monitor performance: See a 40% reduction in support ticket triage time."*
5. **Integration (optional but recommended):** Show the agent embedded in a Microsoft product. *Caption: "5. Seamless integration: Access your custom AI agent directly within Microsoft Teams."*

Explainer Videos (The Conversion Multiplier)

A short video is the single most effective conversion asset. Many enterprise buyers, particularly IT decision-makers, prefer watching a quick demo over reading a long description.

- **Duration:** Keep it short, ideally 60 to 90 seconds.
- **Focus:** The video should follow the same narrative: Problem ➤ Solution ➤ Result. It must be a slick, professionally produced screen recording that highlights the speed and accuracy of the AI solution.
- **Hosting:** The video should be hosted on YouTube or Vimeo and you provide the link in Partner Center. Ensure the video is high-resolution (1080p).

Marketplace SEO: Optimizing for Discoverability

Unlike traditional web search, Marketplace Search Engine Optimization (SEO) is a closed system governed by the metadata you submit. You must strategically use the available fields to ensure your listing appears prominently when customers search within the Azure Portal or AppSource.

Categories and Industry Tags

You can select multiple primary and secondary categories. This is a critical factor for placement in category browses.

- **AI/ML ISVs:** Always select "AI + Machine Learning" as a primary category.
- **Vertical fit:** Select the relevant business categories for your solution (e.g., Security, Identity, Compliance).
- **Product integration:** If you are an AppSource SaaS offer, select the relevant M365 or Dynamics category (e.g., "Dynamics 365" if your agent integrates with customer records).

Search Keywords (The Customer's Language)

Partner Center provides a field for search keywords. This is where you must intentionally think like your customer, using both technical and non-technical language.

- **The problem keywords:** What is the customer searching for when they don't know your solution exists?
  - *Examples:* "document search," "data compliance," "support bot," "hallucination free AI," "knowledge management."

- **The technical keywords (Azure Marketplace):** What specific tools or technologies are IT Architects looking for?
    - *Examples:* "Generative AI," "RAG," "Azure OpenAI," "Vector Search," "Managed Application," "Kubernetes container."
- **The competitor keywords:** While you cannot use competitor brand names, you can use generic phrases associated with competitor products (e.g., "AI knowledge base tool").

Strategic Keyword Tip: Do not just list your product's internal features. Focus on the value delivered and the pain relieved.

Call to Action: Pricing, Trials, and Test Drives

The final section of your listing, often displayed prominently near the "Get It Now" button, is the commercial call to action. This is the last point of friction before conversion, and it must be frictionless.

Clear Pricing Structure (The Plan Schema)

The customer must be able to understand what they are buying and for how much without needing a sales call.

- **Plan naming:** Use clear, value-oriented names like "Basic Agent Plan," "Pro," and "Enterprise (MACC Eligible)." Avoid abstract names.
- **Clarity on metered vs. flat:** If using metered billing, clearly state the base fee (if any) and the consumption rate.
    - *Example:* "Includes 5 user seats. $200/month flat fee + $0.02 per 1,000 tokens processed."
- **Feature gating:** Clearly list which key AI features are included in which plan. (e.g., Basic = Chat only; Enterprise = Chat + Function Calling/Tool Use).

Free Trial: Reducing Transactional Risk

The Free Trial (for SaaS and Managed Apps) is essential for high-velocity GTM. It allows the user to experience the core value of your AI solution before the billing relationship begins.

- **Duration:** 14 or 30 days are the standard. The trial must offer full access to the core features.
- **Conversion path:** Ensure your trial is a direct path to the paid plan. The user should not have to reinstall or reconfigure the application when they convert. The billing simply commences at the end of the trial period via the Marketplace.

Test Drive: The Sandbox Experience

The Test Drive is a powerful option for Azure Marketplace offers, particularly Managed Applications or complex AI tools. It is a pre-configured, self-contained demonstration environment hosted by the ISV that a customer can access for a defined period (e.g., 2 hours) without having to deploy anything to their own Azure subscription.

- **Best use case:** A Test Drive allows an ISV to set up a dummy, locked-down environment with mock data (e.g., mock SEC filings) and let the customer run compliance queries against the AI model live. This proves the technology works and demonstrates the value proposition in a highly interactive, risk-free manner.
- **Technical implementation:** You host the environment in your Azure subscription, and the Marketplace manages the access credentials and time limit. A Test Drive dramatically increases conversion rates for high-priced or technically complex offers.

Legal and Support Requirements

The final section of your listing addresses necessary legal compliance and post-sales support. Certification checks ensure all links are functional and policies are adequate.

Legal Documents

You must provide links to

1. **Privacy policy:** Details how your AI solution handles customer data, especially sensitive data used for RAG or fine-tuning. This is critical for data-sensitive AI offerings.

2. **Terms of use/EULA:** While Microsoft provides the Standard Contract for the Marketplace, you still need your own EULA if you choose not to use the Standard Contract, or supplemental terms if you do.

3. **Support policy:** Must clearly state your Service Level Agreement (SLA), guaranteed response times, and method of contact (email, phone, support portal).

By optimizing the listing's narrative to sell outcomes, leveraging visuals to tell a compelling story, focusing keywords on the customer's pain points, and reducing friction through a clear commercial strategy, you transform your Marketplace entry from a simple catalog listing into a high-powered, autonomous sales funnel.

GTM-in-a-Box: Co-sell, Marketplace Rewards, and Private Offers

Publishing a Marketplace offer is a necessary act of creation, but your primary goal is to make that offer transactable. A transactable offer, one where Microsoft acts as the Merchant of Record, is the universal key that unlocks the entire Microsoft Go-to-Market (GTM) ecosystem. Without this key, your solution remains a static listing; with it, your solution becomes a dynamic, incentivized, and globally scaled revenue engine.

This engine comprises three highly complementary programs that Microsoft collectively calls "GTM-in-a-Box": Marketplace Rewards, the Co-sell Program, and Private Offers. These programs are designed not just to market your solution but to embed it directly into the compensation and workflow of Microsoft's global sales team and their vast network of partners, dramatically accelerating your sales velocity.

The Transactable Gate: Why Commerce Is GTM

Before diving into the GTM programs, it is crucial to understand that your transactable status is the prerequisite for nearly all benefits. By taking on the role of Merchant of Record, Microsoft validates your solution as commercially ready and aligns your revenue with its own.

The Transactional Precondition

Microsoft does not incentivize its sellers, or invest marketing funds, to promote non-transactable offers (known as "List" offers, which are essentially referrals). The reasons are pragmatic:

1. **Revenue recognition:** Microsoft must recognize revenue through its commerce engine to track the effectiveness of its programs.

2. **MACC retirement:** Only transactable offers can draw down a customer's Microsoft Azure Consumption Commitment (MACC), which is the single most powerful incentive in the entire ecosystem.

3. **Process consistency:** Transactable offers ensure a standardized, predictable purchasing experience for the customer, minimizing friction.

The investment required to integrate the SaaS Fulfillment API and Metering API or to package the solution as a Managed Application is not simply a technical hurdle, it is a strategic GTM investment that unlocks access to millions of dollars in marketing and sales support.

Marketplace Rewards: The Marketing Engine

The Marketplace Rewards program is a tiered system of co-marketing and technical benefits that begins the moment you publish a compliant, transactable offer. This program provides you with professional, Microsoft-backed collateral and consultation to enhance your listing and generate demand.

The program's philosophy is simple: **Microsoft invests marketing resources based on your commercial commitment to the Marketplace.** Your benefits grow as your billed revenue through the Marketplace increases.

Tier 1: The List Tier (Activation)

Simply having a live, compliant listing, even a non-transactable one, grants you the initial *List* tier benefits.

- **Listing optimization consultation:** This is a high-value, guided session with a Microsoft expert who reviews your Marketplace listing (title, description, keywords, visuals). For an AI solution, this consultation is invaluable for ensuring your narrative shifts away from technical jargon and focuses on business value, maximizing the effectiveness of your Marketplace SEO.
- **Self-service GTM assets:** You gain access to standardized logos, co-branded badges (e.g., "Available on AppSource"), and templates for press releases and marketing emails. Using official Microsoft branding instantly adds a layer of professional credibility to your external marketing.

Tier 2: The Transact Tier (Acceleration)

This tier is unlocked when you have a transactable offer live on the Marketplace. This is the first major commercial commitment you make, and Microsoft responds with accelerated GTM resources.

- **Co-branded marketing collateral:** Microsoft will create co-branded sales and marketing decks, often in the format used by their internal sellers. This ensures that when your sales team presents, your materials have the polished, enterprise-ready look of a Microsoft presentation.
- **"Featured in Marketplace" promotion:** Your solution becomes eligible for placement in rotating carousels, category spotlights, or dedicated emails to customers based on their Azure consumption patterns or industry.
- **Internal visibility:** Your solution begins to appear in internal Microsoft GTM systems beyond just the Co-sell Solution Finder, increasing visibility among non-seller teams like Partner Marketing and Technical Specialists.
- **Technical consultation funds:** You become eligible for limited-scope technical consultations (e.g., help optimizing your SaaS webhook or refining your ARM template for a Managed App) to improve the reliability of your transactable engine.

Tier 3: The Co-sell Tier (The Revenue Multiplier)

This is the highest tier of the Marketplace Rewards program, unlocked when your solution achieves specific revenue or Co-sell success metrics (often around $25,000 in Marketplace, billed sales or a formal Co-sell commitment). This is where the marketing engine shifts from *awareness* to direct lead generation and funding.

- **Joint demand generation:** You become eligible for co-funded campaigns. Microsoft may contribute marketing funds, resources, or dedicated internal staff to run a joint webinar, a customer case study video, or a targeted email campaign that directly highlights your AI solution. This is a critical investment that can generate highly qualified, enterprise-grade leads.
- **Dedicated Partner Success Manager (PSM):** You may be assigned a PSM who acts as your single point of contact within Microsoft for GTM strategy. The PSM helps you navigate the internal organization, connects with the right field sellers, and strategically positions your solution for major sales cycles.
- **Executive sponsorship:** For solutions with high MACC-retirement potential, Microsoft may provide executive-level sponsorship, featuring your solution in keynotes or internal executive briefings, which can dramatically influence adoption by major customers.

Strategic Takeaway: Treat Marketplace Rewards like a checklist of free services. Actively engaging with the offered consultations and co-marketing opportunities accelerates your time-to-market and builds crucial internal relationships within Microsoft.

The Co-sell Program: Your Sales Multiplier

The Co-sell Program is the single most powerful sales channel available to an ISV in the Microsoft ecosystem. Its entire design is centered on making it financially advantageous for a Microsoft seller to prioritize selling your AI solution.

The Philosophy of Co-sell: Aligned Incentives

A Microsoft field seller (Account Executive or Technical Specialist) is primarily compensated for two things, hitting their overall revenue quota and driving Azure Consumption Commitment (MACC) retirement.

The Co-sell program is the bridge that connects your product to both of these incentives. When you achieve "Co-sell Incentivized" status, your solution actively helps the Microsoft seller meet their quota, transforming them from a neutral observer into an active, incentivized advocate.

Phase 1: Co-sell Ready (Internal Visibility)

The first hurdle is achieving Co-sell Ready status. This is the baseline required for your solution to appear in Microsoft's internal sales catalog, the Co-sell Solution Finder (or similar internal tool).

Requirements for Co-sell Ready:

1. **Marketplace offer:** Must have a live, preferably transactable, offer on the Marketplace.

2. **Microsoft AI Cloud Partner Program (MACPP) status:** Must be an active member.

3. **Customer success track:** The product must meet the requirements of a specific Solution Area, such as Digital & App Innovation or Data & AI and have demonstrated technical competencies or customer success.

4. **Sales assets package:** You must provide a set of standardized sales materials to the Microsoft Partner team:

    - **The one-pager:** A concise, single-page document (often called the Solution Brief) that outlines the customer pain point, your unique AI solution, and the core benefits. This must be brief enough for a busy seller to read in 60 seconds.

    - **Customer presentation:** A professional, co-branded presentation that explains the solution in detail, focusing heavily on business outcomes and ROI.

- **Customer success stories:** One or two brief case studies demonstrating successful deployments, particularly those involving Azure services.

Once certified Co-sell Ready, your solution is discoverable by over 35,000 Microsoft sellers globally. When a seller identifies a customer need that your AI solution solves, they can formally register a Referral in Partner Center, initiating a joint sales effort.

Phase 2: IP Co-sell Incentivized (The Financial Multiplier)

This is the ultimate prize, often referred to as the "Gold Standard" of GTM alignment. IP Co-sell Incentivized status means your solution is recognized as driving significant Azure Intellectual Property (IP) consumption.

Requirements for IP Co-sell Incentivized:

1. **Transactable status:** Must be a transactable offer (SaaS, Managed App, or PAYGO VM/Container).

2. **IP consumption threshold:** Your solution must demonstrate that it is built on and drives substantial consumption of Azure services (e.g., Azure OpenAI Service, Azure AI Search, Azure Kubernetes Service). Microsoft uses specific criteria to measure the percentage of your solution's code base and run-time that is "Azure IP."

3. **High-value MACC potential:** The architecture must be designed to generate substantial Azure consumption, which is directly tied to a customer's MACC.

The Financial Incentive Mechanism:

When a Microsoft seller closes a deal for an IP Co-sell Incentivized solution:

- **Seller quota credit:** The seller receives direct quota retirement credit for the value of your software sale. In many cases, the credit the seller receives outweighs the commission they would get for a non-incentivized sale.
- **The bonus commission:** Microsoft often provides a specific, high-percentage commission bonus (e.g., 10% to 20% of the deal value) directly to the seller for every closed deal involving an incentivized ISV solution.
- **MACC retirement:** Most powerfully, the deal helps the seller achieve their most difficult objective: retiring the customer's MACC.

For the Microsoft seller, this is a triple win that is structurally irresistible. It's the most compelling reason for them to proactively bring your solution to their customers.

Tactical Co-sell Execution: Engaging the Field

Achieving Co-sell status is only the technical start. The real work is engaging the Microsoft field sales team to ensure they know when and how to position your AI solution.

1. **Targeting the Right Seller Persona**

   Do not market your solution to the generic "Microsoft seller." Target the specific roles who will be incentivized by your product:

   - **Cloud Solution Architects (CSAs):** These technical specialists need to know your Managed App's ARM template is secure and scales flawlessly. Your assets should focus on Azure consumption, reliability, and security compliance.

- **AppSource and Business Development Specialists (BDSs):** These sellers focus on Line-of-Business applications. They need to know your SaaS solution integrates seamlessly with Microsoft Teams or Dynamics 365 and is easy to demo.
- **Account Executives (AEs):** They focus on overall revenue and MACC. They need the one-pager that summarizes the ROI and the MACC retirement value.

2. **The Referral Management Process in Partner Center**

   Co-sell success is measured by the number of sales leads, or Referrals, generated through Partner Center.

   - **Inbound referrals:** A Microsoft seller initiates a referral when they identify a lead who needs your solution. You receive a notification in Partner Center and are required to accept or reject the lead within a strict time limit (usually 2 days). Always accept leads promptly, even if you quickly qualify them out, as slow response times hurt your internal reputation.
   - **Outbound referrals:** You can initiate a referral when *your* sales team identifies a deal where the customer is looking for a Microsoft product or service that you don't offer. You send the lead to the Microsoft seller, generating goodwill and reciprocal action.

- **Updating deal status:** You are required to update the status of the deal (e.g., from "Engaged" to "Proposal Sent" to "Won/Lost") in Partner Center. This data is critical for Microsoft to track the success of their incentives and is factored into your eligibility for future funding.

3. **Building Internal Champions**

   Co-sell is often a relationship-driven game. To scale your reach, focus on building internal champions within Microsoft:

   - **Regional focus:** Identify the Account Executives and CSAs in a specific region (e.g., "Pacific Northwest Enterprise Team") and run a targeted joint enablement session for them.

   - **Demonstrate wins:** When you close a deal through Co-sell, immediately ensure the Microsoft seller responsible for the Referral receives the appropriate quota credit, and send an internal communication celebrating the joint win. Success breeds further collaboration.

Private Offers: Mastering Enterprise Deal Closure

While Co-sell and Rewards drive the pipeline, Private Offers are the essential tools for closing large, customized enterprise deals. In B2B sales, the list price on the public Marketplace is often the starting point, not the final price. Enterprises require specific terms, multi-year discounts, and consolidated billing.

1. **Microsoft Private Offer (MPO): Direct Customer Customization**

   The MPO allows ISVs to create a bespoke version of your existing Marketplace offer for a single-named customer. This process provides the flexibility of a direct sale with the financial benefits of the Marketplace.

   MPO Mechanics and Use Cases:

   1. **Creation:** The ISV logs into Partner Center, selects a live transactable offer and enters the target customer's Azure Tenant ID or Subscription ID.
   2. **Customization:** The ISV defines the custom terms:
      - **Custom price/discount:** Offer a 15% discount off the list price or customize a bundle (e.g., "2-year commitment for 1,000 seats at a fixed $X price").
      - **Custom metered rates:** Define a lower price per metered unit (e.g., $0.015 instead of $0.02 per conversation) as part of a high-volume commitment.
      - **Custom legal terms:** If the customer requires specific legal riders, the MPO allows the ISV to upload custom terms that supersede the standard Marketplace contract.
   3. **Acceptance:** The customer receives a notification in their Azure Portal. They review the custom terms and accept the MPO with a single click. The purchase is immediately added to their Azure bill.

Strategic impact: The MPO is the decisive tool for competitive enterprise deals. It allows you to

- **Preserve MACC eligibility:** Since it's still a Marketplace transaction, the entire value of the MPO ($200,000, for example) still counts 100% toward the customer's MACC retirement.
- **Maintain public price integrity:** You can offer aggressive discounts to a single customer without devaluing your public list price for the general market.
- **Accelerate contracting:** Bypassing months of internal legal review at the customer's end, as the purchase is handled through their established Azure payment process.

2. **CSP Private Offer (CPPO): Unlocking the Reseller Channel**

   The CSP Private Offer (CPPO) extends the customization of the MPO to Microsoft's massive network of Cloud Solution Provider (CSP) partners. These partners are resellers, Managed Service Providers (MSPs), and systems integrators who often have deep, trusted relationships with the end customer.

   CPPO Mechanics and Strategic Value:

   1. **Channel enablement:** A CSP partner often acts as the customer's primary technology advisor, managing their entire Azure environment and often pre-billing them for all cloud services. The customer prefers to buy *everything* from the CSP.

2. **Custom pricing and bundling:** The ISV creates a CPPO for a specific CSP (e.g., "Global MSP Inc.") at a discounted partner price. Global MSP Inc. then marks up the price to the end customer, bundling the AI solution with their own managed services (e.g., AI model monitoring, user training, data integration).

3. **Consolidated billing:** The customer receives a single, consolidated bill from their trusted CSP partner, which includes the Azure cloud costs, the CSP's management fees, and the cost of the AI solution.

   The multi-channel strategy: By enabling CPPO, you transform thousands of CSP partners into potential sales multipliers. They become motivated to sell your solution because it is now easy for them to buy, mark up, and bundle into their profitable service contracts. This is essential for scaling beyond your direct sales team and accessing the vast mid-market that buys its IT through a trusted local reseller.

GTM-in-a-Box: The AI ISV's Scaling Roadmap

The GTM programs are not optional; they are the required infrastructure for scaling an AI solution in the Microsoft ecosystem. The roadmap for maximum velocity is

1. **Launch readiness:** Achieve Transactable Status (SaaS Fulfillment or Managed App deployment) to unlock all GTM doors.

2. **Marketing lift:** Leverage Marketplace Rewards for free, professional co-marketing assets and listing optimization to drive inbound traffic.

3. **Sales acceleration:** Achieve IP Co-sell Incentivized status by architecting for high Azure consumption (RAG, AKS, Azure OpenAI). This turns the entire Microsoft sales force into a commission-based extension of your own sales team.

4. **Deal closure:** Use Microsoft Private Offers (MPO) for large, customized enterprise deals and CSP Private Offers (CPPO) to scale via the partner reseller channel.

By meticulously executing this GTM-in-a-Box strategy, your innovative AI solution moves from a promising technology to a rapidly scaling, revenue-generating product that is prioritized by Microsoft's internal sales and partner ecosystem.

Advanced Strategies: Scaling and Optimization

You have successfully achieved the fundamental milestones, your AI solution is live, it is transactable, and it is Co-Sell Ready. These achievements transition your ISV from a partner to a commerce-enabled entity within the Microsoft ecosystem. The final stage is not a destination but a continuous, data-driven loop of optimization and scaling.

This advanced phase is characterized by a reliance on Marketplace Insights for decision-making, systematic testing to maximize conversion rates, and the strategic expansion of your offering's commercial footprint beyond the initial launch. The goal shifts from *getting listed* to *maximizing lifetime customer value (LTV)* and *scaling the sales channel.*

Leveraging Marketplace Insights: The Data-Driven GTM

The Partner Center's Marketplace Insights dashboard is your ISV's single source of truth for GTM performance. It tracks every stage of the customer journey, from initial view to final revenue, providing the quantitative data necessary to diagnose friction and validate improvements. Treat this dashboard like the analytics panel for a high-traffic e-commerce store.

The Four Critical Data Pillars

Marketplace Insights organizes data into four critical areas that drive specific optimization actions:

1. **Audience and acquisition metrics:** These metrics tell you *who* is looking and *where* they come from.

    - **Page views and conversion:** This is the most crucial health check. It shows how many unique visitors are viewing your listing and the percentage who click the "Get it Now" or "Contact Me" button. A high-view, low-conversion rate (e.g., 10,000 views, 10 conversions) instantly signals a problem with your listing's compelling narrative, pricing, or visual assets.

    - **Traffic sources:** Identifies whether traffic is coming from the public storefront (AppSource/Azure Marketplace), a Microsoft marketing campaign, or a direct link from your own website. This helps you prioritize which marketing channels are working best.

    - **Geographic breakdown:** Highlights which countries and regions are generating the most interest, helping you focus your targeted advertising or regional Co-sell efforts.

2. **Revenue and order metrics:** These metrics confirm the commercial success of your different product plans.

    - **Revenue by plan:** Provides a clear breakdown of sales by your defined plans (e.g., Basic, Pro, Enterprise). If the "Basic" plan sells 80% of the volume but generates 20% of the revenue, you may need to re-price or limit the features in the Basic plan to push users toward the more profitable Pro tier.

- **Recurring revenue trends:** Shows subscription renewals, churn rates, and growth over time, allowing you to project cash flow and measure the stickiness of your AI solution.
- **Custom metering reports:** Insights will show which custom units (e.g., "customer conversations" or "token usage") are generating the most consumption revenue. This data is critical for validating your consumption model and setting future pricing strategy.

3. **Customer data and usage:** This is the bridge between marketing analytics and your internal sales motion.

   - **Customer ID and company name:** You can see which specific customers (by company name) have purchased your solution and for what plan. This is invaluable for your sales team, providing a high-quality list for upselling and expansion motions.
   - **Active subscriptions:** Helps track customer health. A sudden drop in a customer's usage signals a churn risk, allowing your Customer Success team to proactively intervene before cancellation.

4. **Funnel analytics:** This pinpoints friction in the technical transaction process itself.
    - **Drop-off points:** Shows exactly where users abandon the purchase process (e.g., "70% abandoned on the landing page," "15% abandoned when selecting the plan").
    - *If customers drop off at the Plan Selection stage,* your plans are too complicated, or the value distinction is unclear.
    - *If customers drop off at the Fulfillment Landing Page,* your Azure AD authentication flow or the initial setup required on your side is too complex or broken.

Optimizing Your Listing: The A/B Testing Imperative

In the high-stakes world of the Marketplace, relying on intuition is a mistake. The key to continuously improving conversion rates is systematic A/B testing, even without a dedicated built-in tool.

Executing the 30-Day Manual A/B Test Cycle

Since Partner Center does not offer simultaneous variant testing, you must run a sequential, controlled experiment using your own data tracking.

1. **Define the baseline (A):** Run your existing, optimized listing for 30 days. Record key metrics: Views, Conversions and the Conversion Rate (CVR). This CVR is your target to beat.
2. **Isolate the variable (B):** Select only one element to change. Changing two elements (e.g., title and pricing) simultaneously will make it impossible to attribute any change in CVR to a specific cause.

3. **Run the test (B):** Publish the modified listing (B) and run it for another 30 days (or until you hit statistical significance, often 1,000 views or 100 conversions, whichever comes first). Consistency in duration is key to negate weekly seasonal variations.

4. **Analyze and iterate:** Compare the CVR of A and B.

   - *If CVR(B) > CVR(A):* The change was positive. Implement the change permanently (this becomes your new A) and select a new variable to test.
   - *If CVR(B) $\approx$ CVR(A):* The change was neutral. Discard the variable and revert to the original (A).
   - *If CVR(B) < CVR(A):* The change was negative. Immediately revert to the original (A).

High-Impact Elements to Test

For an AI solution, the following elements have the highest leverage in influencing conversion:

Element tested	Hypothesis/rationale	Example test
Offer name/ title	Does the customer care more about the *tool* or the *outcome*?	**A:** "AcmusAI Financial Agent" vs. **B:** "Instant SEC Filing Analysis & Reporting Tool"
Pricing model	Does friction decrease with a lower entry price?	**A:** "$99/month Flat Fee" vs. **B:** "Free 30-Day Trial, then Metered Billing"

(continued)

Element tested	Hypothesis/rationale	Example test
Lead visual (screenshot 1)	Is a technical diagram or a simple UI screenshot more effective?	**A:** A screenshot of a complicated RAG data flow diagram vs. **B:** A clean screenshot of the Q&A box showing a cited answer
Call to Action (CTA)	Does the customer prefer a demo or immediate access?	**A:** "Contact Us for a Demo" vs. **B:** "Start Free Trial Now" (Requires a live trial offer)
Short summary	Which keyword combination drives the most initial clicks from search results?	**A:** Focus on "Generative AI and RAG" vs. **B:** Focus on "Document Search and Time Saving"

Advanced Monetization and Footprint Scaling

Optimization gets you the most out of your current traffic. Scaling strategies focus on expanding your market reach, increasing deal size and maximizing the Customer Lifetime Value (CLV).

Strategy 1: The Consulting Service Upsell Loop

Once a customer is on your platform, your goal shifts from initial license revenue to high-margin service revenue. The Consulting Service Offer which we established is typically a lead-generating (non-transactable) offer and is perfectly positioned for this upselling.

The AI Upsell Motion:

1. **The initial sale (low friction):** Customer purchases a SaaS Basic Plan ($99/mo).
2. **The data-driven trigger:** Customer Success notes that the customer has indexed a high volume of data (via Metered Billing data) but has low agent utilization because their internal data governance is complex.

3. **The high-margin offer:** Your sales team approaches the customer with an existing, published Consulting Service Offer on AppSource: "Premium Onboarding and AI Model-Tuning Package (5-Day Engagement)" for $25,000.
    - The service packages your team's expertise (data mapping, security hardening, custom prompt engineering, and fine-tuning your AI model).
    - The purchase of this service is handled directly with you, providing high-margin revenue and dramatically increasing the likelihood of long-term retention of the core software.

Strategic Advantage: By listing this service on the Marketplace, you professionalize the upselling. It is a Microsoft-vetted, defined, and packaged service that your customer's procurement department can easily approve, leveraging the credibility of the platform.

Strategy 2: Multi-channel Distribution and Buyer Persona Expansion

A key scaling strategy is ensuring your core AI intellectual property (IP) is accessible to every relevant buyer persona, often requiring listing on both storefronts.

- **Azure Marketplace to AppSource (the LOB expansion):** If your core product is an Azure Marketplace Managed Application, the buyer is the CIO/IT Architect.
    - **Scaling step:** Create a parallel SaaS Offer on AppSource that is a lightweight, pre-configured version of the compliance agent.

- **Target:** The Line-of-Business (LOB) Manager (e.g., Chief Compliance Officer). They don't care about ARM templates; they care about compliance reports integrated into their Dynamics 365 or Teams workflow. This expansion effectively doubles your GTM surface area and taps into new budget owners.

- **Co-sell incentives across channels:** By having transactable offers on both platforms, you empower different parts of the Microsoft sales organization (the Azure sellers and the Business Applications sellers) to sell your product and retire their respective quotas.

Strategy 3: Private Plans (The Beta and Partner Enablement Tool)

Within a single public offer (SaaS or Managed App), Partner Center allows you to create "Private Plans" that are invisible to the public and accessible only to specific-named customers or partners via their Azure Tenant ID.

Advanced Uses of Private Plans for AI ISVs:

1. **"Friends and Family" beta:** Use a Private Plan to run a closed beta program for an unreleased AI feature (e.g., a new "function calling" capability in your agent) with a small group of trusted customers. This allows you to collect real-world usage data and feedback before a broad release without cluttering your main listing.

2. **Strategic partner pricing:** Create a Private Plan named "Premier Reseller Tier" with a special discount rate. Only your key CSP partners (who you trust to add value with managed services) can see and purchase this plan. This is a crucial step for managing channel conflict and protecting the margins of your most valuable resellers before deploying a full CPPO.

3. **Pilot program gating:** Create a highly discounted plan named "Q4 Enterprise Pilot - $1,000." You only offer this to customers your sales team is actively engaged with. This avoids the public exposure of a deeply discounted price while ensuring the MACC-retiring benefits of the Marketplace transaction remain intact for the pilot.

The Scaling Pillar: Continuous Architecture for Consumption

For ISVs with IP Co-sell Incentivized status, scaling is not just about sales; it is about scaling Azure consumption. Every architectural decision must reinforce the MACC retirement loop.

1. **Architecting for Azure Native Services**
   To maximize Azure IP consumption, your solution must be deeply integrated with Microsoft's proprietary and high-consumption services:

   - **Data and search:** Use Azure AI Search (formerly Azure Cognitive Search) for your RAG retrieval pipelines and vector indexing, not open-source alternatives. Use Azure Cosmos DB or Azure SQL Database, not self-hosted PostgreSQL instances.

   - **Compute and inference:** The largest consumption driver is often the LLM inference.

     - For dedicated customer models, ensure your model is deployed on a dedicated Azure Machine Learning Compute Instance or Azure Kubernetes Service (AKS) running with specific, dedicated node pools. This consumption is easily measured and heavily contributes to MACC retirement.

- For multi-tenant SaaS, ensure your API calls are routed through the Azure OpenAI Service, consuming tokens that count toward MACC.

2. **The Cloud Cost Management Dialogue**
   Scaling usage means scaling cloud costs, both yours and the customer's. A key advanced strategy is integrating a Cloud Cost Management Dashboard into your AI solution's administrative panel.

   - **Transparency:** If your solution is metered (SaaS) or deployed as a Managed App, customers need visibility into their consumption. Provide a clean graph showing
     - Your Software Fee (the Marketplace charge)
     - The estimated underlying Azure Consumption (the customer's Azure bill)
   - **Trust building:** ISVs can show their customers a dashboard that transparently tracks TB_of_Scanned_Data (the metered unit) and the corresponding Azure Storage and Compute consumed. This level of transparency builds trust with the CIO/CISO, reinforcing the narrative that the solution is a well-governed, cost-optimized asset within their environment.

3. **Proactive Updates and Certification**
   The pace of AI innovation requires constant product updates (new foundation models, new features like function calling). Scaling requires a robust process for updating your Marketplace listing itself:

- **Update discipline:** When you release a major product update, you must update your Marketplace listing's description and screenshots immediately. A stale listing suggests a product that is not keeping pace with the rapid advancement of the AI market.
- **Recertification:** Major changes to your offer's technical configuration (e.g., moving your SaaS Fulfillment API endpoint, or modifying the resources in a Managed App's ARM template) require a new submission and a full recertification process in Partner Center. Treat recertification as a critical path item in your product release cycle, not as an afterthought.

By adopting these advanced, data-driven strategies, from micro-optimization using Marketplace Insights to macro-scaling using multi-channel distribution and Private Plans, you transform your live offer into a mature, resilient, and continuously growing business unit within the Microsoft ecosystem.

Chapter Summary: The Commercial Marketplace As a Commerce and Sales Engine

The journey of an Independent Software Vendor (ISV) within the Microsoft ecosystem is marked by a critical transition, moving from building a brilliant AI solution to achieving significant commercial scale. Chapter 7, "Publishing on Azure Marketplace," defines the strategic and technical roadmap for this transition. We've established that the Microsoft Commercial Marketplace is not simply a static digital catalog; it is a sophisticated commerce engine, with a global distribution system and a powerful sales incentive mechanism designed to connect your AI solution directly to Microsoft's vast enterprise customer base and its field sales team.

The chapter's core thesis is simple, transactable status is the prerequisite for scale**.** Every key program, from Co-sell to Marketplace Rewards, is predicated on the ISV using Microsoft as the Merchant of Record. By adhering to the principles outlined in this chapter, an AI ISV can transform its product into a favored solution that helps Microsoft sellers meet their own quotas, creating a highly efficient, symbiotic sales partnership.

The Foundational Decision: Offer Type and Transactability

The initial steps in the GTM journey are deeply technical yet fundamentally commercial. The choice of Offer Type dictates your eligibility for the most valuable programs.

Distinguishing the Storefronts

We began by clarifying the two critical storefronts:

- **Azure Marketplace:** The destination for IT professionals, cloud administrators, and technical architects. This is the natural home for infrastructure-focused AI solutions, such as Azure Managed Applications and Virtual Machine/Container Offers.
- **Microsoft AppSource:** The domain of Line-of-Business (LOB) users and decision-makers. This is the essential platform for user-facing AI solutions, such as SaaS Offers that integrate with Microsoft 365 or Dynamics 365.

The crucial finding is that the most successful ISVs employ Multi-Channel Distribution, listing their solutions across both storefronts (or creating dual-listed SaaS offers) to capture the attention of both technical and business buyers.

The Power of Transactability

The single most important technical step is making your offer transactable. This requires integrating your solution with the Marketplace's commerce engine via the SaaS Fulfillment API and, for advanced pricing, the Metering API. Transactability yields two immediate, game-changing benefits:

1. **Global billing and back-office management:** Microsoft handles all complex global invoicing, tax, payment, and currency conversion, allowing the ISV to focus entirely on product development and sales.

2. **MACC eligibility:** Transactable offers are the *only* way to count your software sale value toward a customer's Microsoft Azure Consumption Commitment (MACC). This financial mechanism is the ultimate competitive advantage, making your solution effectively "free" to customers who have already committed spend to Azure, instantly elevating your product from a discretionary purchase to a strategic spend priority.

Go-to-Market in a Box: The Incentive Stack

Once transacted, your solution gains access to a potent, layered set of GTM programs collectively termed "GTM-in-a-Box." These programs use financial incentives and marketing support to scale your business.

Marketplace Rewards: The Marketing Foundation

This program provides a tiered set of benefits that grow as your sales increase, acting as a continuous marketing accelerator:

- **List tier:** Provides basic listing optimization consultations and self-service branding assets.

- **Transact tier:** Unlocks co-branded sales materials and eligibility for "Featured in Marketplace" promotions, focusing on driving awareness and confidence.
- **Co-sell tier:** Grants access to high-impact benefits, including funds for Joint Demand Generation Campaigns, allowing the ISV to run Microsoft-subsidized marketing activities.

The Co-sell Program: The Sales Force Multiplier

This is the chapter's centerpiece, transforming the relationship between the ISV and the Microsoft field sales team.

- **Co-Sell ready:** The foundational status achieved by providing mandatory sales assets (the one-pager, customer-ready deck) and securing a transactable listing. This ensures your solution is discoverable in Microsoft's internal Co-sell Solution Finder catalog, enabling sellers to initiate referrals.
- **IP Co-sell incentivized:** The ultimate goal, achieved by demonstrating that your solution is architected to drive significant consumption of Azure Intellectual Property (IP) (e.g., Azure OpenAI Service, AKS, Azure AI Search). This status is the Financial Multiplier because it provides the Microsoft seller with

    1. Direct Quota Retirement Credit for your software sale
    2. An actual Commission Bonus (typically 10%–20%) on the deal value
    3. A direct path to retiring their customers' MACC

- In short, IP Co-sell Incentivization makes the sale of your AI solution one of the most financially rewarding activities a Microsoft seller can pursue, guaranteeing prioritization within the sales cycle.

Private Offers: Mastering Enterprise Deal Closure

For large, complex enterprise deals, the Marketplace supports negotiation flexibility:

- **Microsoft Private Offer (MPO):** Allows the ISV to create a custom, discounted price, customized metered rates, and unique legal terms for a single, named customer. This enables complex deal closure while retaining MACC retirement benefits and avoiding public price erosion.
- **CSP Private Offer (CPPO):** Extends the MPO model to Microsoft's vast Cloud Solution Provider (CSP) partner channel. This enables resellers to purchase your AI solution at a pre-negotiated partner rate, bundle it with their own managed services and deliver a single, consolidated bill to the end customer, unlocking the crucial reseller distribution path.

The Loop of Optimization and Scaling

The final phase involves transitioning to a continuous improvement model driven by data.

Data-Driven Optimization

The Marketplace Insights dashboard is central to this phase, providing granular data on

- **Conversion rate:** Analyzing the ratio of Page Views to "Get It Now" clicks to diagnose problems with the listing's visual appeal or messaging.

- **Funnel analytics:** Pinpointing drop-off points in the technical purchase flow to eliminate customer friction.
- **Customer and revenue data:** Providing your sales team with an immediate list of purchasing companies for high margin upsell motions.

This data supports a disciplined A/B testing methodology, where ISVs systematically test and optimize elements like the Offer Name, Pricing Structure, and Media Assets to maximize conversion efficiency.

Scaling the Commercial Footprint

Scaling strategies move beyond the initial license sale to maximize customer lifetime value and market reach:

- **Consulting service offers:** Creating non-transactable listings to formalize and market high-margin professional services (e.g., "AI Model-Tuning Package") that can be upsold to existing software customers.
- **Private plans:** Utilizing non-public plans for managed beta programs, strategic partner pricing, or controlled enterprise pilots.

Conclusion

Chapter 7 serves as the culminating guide, merging the technical innovation of AI development with a strategic commercial roadmap. The Commercial Marketplace is your launchpad, by selecting the right offer type (like a transactable SaaS offer with metered billing), you secure MACC eligibility and create a highly defensible commercial position. By crafting a compelling, value-driven listing, you convert visitors into customers. And most powerfully, by achieving IP Co-sell Incentivized status, you transform Microsoft's global sales team into a committed, compensated force multiplier into your own. The journey from developer to ISV partner culminates here, where your technical innovation meets unstoppable commercial scale.

CHAPTER 8

Integration with Microsoft Copilot

Introduction

This chapter provides ISVs with step-by-step guidance for integrating AI agents into the Microsoft Copilot ecosystem. By publishing your agents to Microsoft 365 Copilot, Teams, and other Microsoft channels, you expand your product's reach, simplify customer acquisition, and embed your solution directly into enterprise workflows where users spend their time.

Microsoft offers multiple approaches for building agents that integrate with Copilot. Declarative agents use Microsoftvs orchestrator and foundation models, requiring no additional hosting. Custom engine agents use your own models and orchestration, providing greater control over complex scenarios. Both approaches can be published across Microsoft 365 Copilot, Teams, and other channels through the Agent Store.

Microsoft 365 Copilot reaches over 350 million users across Teams, Outlook, Word, Excel, PowerPoint, and the Microsoft 365 Copilot app. When you build an agent, it can reach all the applications that support Copilot extensibility across Microsoft 365. This chapter covers the tools and pathways available to ISVs, from low-code Copilot Studio to pro-code development with the Microsoft 365 Agents SDK and Microsoft Foundry.

J. Soh et al., *Building and Distributing Agentic AI Solutions*,
https://doi.org/10.1007/979-8-8688-2586-6_8

Understanding the Integration Options

Before building your integration, understand the tools and pathways available. Microsoft provides multiple entry points depending on your technical requirements and target audience.

Agent Core Components

All agents consist of two core components. Knowledge tailors the agent's responses by providing specialized instructions and data sources. Actions develop triggers and workflows that automate business processes.

Beyond these core components, additional layers enhance an agent's functionality. The orchestrator acts as the central engine that manages how the agent interacts with knowledge, actions, and autonomy. Foundation models power the agent's reasoning, language understanding, and response generation. The user experience layer integrates agents into Microsoft 365 applications or external platforms.

Declarative Agents

Declarative agents customize Microsoft 365 Copilot through instructions, knowledge sources, and actions. They run on Copilot's orchestrator and foundation models, so you do not need to host or manage AI infrastructure. Declarative agents are suitable for scenarios where you want to ground Copilot in your organization's data, automate specific workflows, or provide specialized assistance for business domains.

Because declarative agents use Copilot's AI infrastructure, model, and orchestrator, they adhere to Microsoft's security, compliance, and Responsible AI requirements. This inheritance simplifies governance and reduces compliance burden for ISVs building solutions for enterprise customers.

To configure a declarative agent, you provide three elements. Custom instructions shape Copilot's responses to your organization's specific needs or workflow. Custom knowledge connects Microsoft 365 data sources, such as Teams messages, SharePoint, and OneDrive, as well as external data via Microsoft Graph connectors/Microsoft 365 Copilot connectors. Custom actions integrate with APIs to interact with external systems in real time.

Key Characteristics of Declarative Agents

- **Hosting**: Use Copilot's orchestrator and foundation model. No additional hosting is required.
- **Tooling**: Build agents using low-code tools in Microsoft 365 Copilot or Copilot Studio, or pro-code tools like Visual Studio, Visual Studio Code, and the Microsoft 365 Agents Toolkit.
- **Channels**: Run in Microsoft 365 Copilot and Microsoft 365 apps, including Teams, Word, Excel, PowerPoint, and Outlook.
- **Compliance**: Adhere to Microsoft's security, compliance, and Responsible AI requirements automatically.

Custom Engine Agents

Custom engine agents are fully customizable AI assistants that let you bring your own models, orchestration, and hosting. They are appropriate for scenarios requiring complex workflows, specific language models, or integration patterns that declarative agents cannot support. Building a custom engine agent requires you to provide hosting infrastructure and ensure compliance with security and governance requirements.

Unlike declarative agents, custom engine agents give developers full control over orchestration, AI models, and data integrations. You can create these agents using Copilot Studio, the Microsoft 365 Agents SDK, the Teams SDK, or Microsoft Foundry, depending on your preferred development approach and hosting environment.

To develop a custom engine agent, you need three elements. Custom orchestration takes full control of workflows and integrates additional knowledge and external API calls. Custom models let you choose the most suitable model for your use case, whether foundation large language models, small language models, fine-tuned models, or industry-specific models. Autonomy and proactive agentic support programmatically initiate workflows and actions, enabling agents to operate independently, make decisions, and escalate tasks as needed.

Key Characteristics of Custom Engine Agents

- **Hosting**: Requires additional hosting outside of Microsoft 365, typically with cloud services such as Azure. Copilot Studio provides a managed SaaS option.
- **Tooling**: Orchestration can be built using low-code Copilot Studio or pro-code tools. Supported languages include C#, Python, and JavaScript. Compatible frameworks include Semantic Kernel and LangChain.
- **Channels**: Can run in Microsoft 365 Copilot and Microsoft 365 apps, as well as external apps and websites such as customer service portals or internal dashboards.
- **Collaboration**: Support agent-to-agent communication, allowing agents to delegate tasks and coordinate workflows.
- **Compliance**: You must ensure your own compliance, Responsible AI practices, and security measures.

Choosing Your Approach

Choose declarative agents when you want Copilot's orchestration and models to ensure consistency with Microsoft's security and compliance framework. Choose custom engine agents when you need specific AI services, complex orchestration logic, or deployment to platforms beyond Microsoft 365.

For ISVs, the decision often depends on where your customers expect to find your solution. If your target customers primarily use Microsoft 365 applications, declarative agents offer a faster time-to-market. If you need to differentiate through proprietary AI capabilities or serve customers across multiple platforms, custom engine agents provide the flexibility you need.

Feature Comparison

The following table summarizes the key differences between declarative agents and custom engine agents.

Feature	Declarative agents	Custom engine agents
Use case	Use Microsoft 365 Copilot for focused scenarios	Use complex workflows or advanced integrations
Customization	Limited to Copilot's orchestrator and models	Fully customizable, including choice of AI models
Proactive interactions	Limited; typically user-invoked in chat/UI	Enable agents to trigger actions automatically
Channels	Integrated into Microsoft 365 apps	Microsoft 365 and external apps
Engine hosting	Hosted in Microsoft 365	Copilot Studio or externally with Azure
Compliance	Inherits Microsoft 365 compliance and security	Must ensure your own compliance and security

Cost Considerations

Consider the cost implications of your agent solution design from both user and hosting perspectives. Your Microsoft 365 Copilot license type determines access to extensibility features and whether additional usage charges apply.

Microsoft 365 Copilot is available with two license options. Microsoft 365 Copilot Chat is included with eligible Microsoft 365 subscriptions at no additional charge. It provides access to web-based Copilot Chat and optional pay-as-you-go access to work-based chat. The Microsoft 365 Copilot add-on license is available with an eligible Microsoft 365 subscription and includes both web-based and work-based Copilot Chat, plus embedded Copilot features in Word, Excel, Outlook, and Teams.

Note Licensing options evolve, so make sure to check the latest licensing documentation.

Declarative agents that access shared tenant data, such as SharePoint or Copilot connectors, generate metered-consumption charges via Copilot Studio. Declarative agents are hosted by Microsoft 365 Copilot at no additional cost. Custom engine agents are hosted outside of Microsoft 365 Copilot using your own orchestrator and models. Hosting these agents incurs additional costs based on your cloud provider and model inference charges.

Building with Copilot Studio

Microsoft Copilot Studio is a SaaS-based environment for creating agents without writing code. Business users and makers can build agents using natural language descriptions, then configure knowledge sources, tools, and publishing channels. Developers can integrate Copilot Studio agents into custom applications using the Microsoft 365 Agents SDK.

Copilot Studio empowers teams to quickly create powerful agents through a guided, no-code graphical experience, without requiring data scientists or developers. You can describe the agent you want in plain language, specify instructions, triggers, knowledge sources, and tools, then test your agent before deployment. When ready, publish your agent across multiple channels, including Microsoft Teams, Microsoft 365 Copilot, websites, and mobile applications.

Understanding Orchestration Modes

Copilot Studio supports two orchestration methods that determine how your agent responds to users.

Classic orchestration relies on predefined workflows and rule-based systems. The agent selects topics by matching user queries with predefined trigger phrases. Actions can only be called explicitly from within a topic. Knowledge serves as a fallback when no topics match a user's query. Use classic orchestration for straightforward interactions where user queries can be easily matched to specific topics.

Generative orchestration uses AI to dynamically select the best actions, knowledge, and topics to answer user queries or respond to event triggers. The agent can chain multiple actions or topics to provide comprehensive responses. For example, if a user says "I need to get store hours and find my nearest store," the agent handles both requests in a single interaction. To enable generative orchestration, go to your agent's Overview page and turn on "Use generative AI to determine how best to respond to users and events."

Creating Your First Agent

When you create an agent, you can describe everything you want your agent to be and do in your own words or configure those details as separate pieces of information.

1. Sign in to Copilot Studio (`www.copilotstudio.microsoft.com`) or sign up for a trial.
2. Enter a brief description of what you want your agent to do. The description can have up to 1,000 characters.
3. A page appears with two panes where you set up your agent on the left and test it on the right.
4. Chat with Copilot in the left pane to define your agent. Copilot asks questions to guide you and uses your responses to fill in details such as name, description, instructions, and knowledge.
5. Specify the agent name (maximum 30 characters) and refine the instructions (up to 8,000 characters).
6. Specify the conversation style and tone your agent should use.
7. Add knowledge sources such as public websites, SharePoint sites, or uploaded documents.
8. Test your agent in the test pane and refine as needed.
9. Select Create. The Overview page for your agent appears.

You cannot change an agent's primary language after it is created. However, you can change the agent's primary language region if available and add secondary languages.

Writing Effective Instructions

Instructions determine the goals, tone, and limitations of your agent. The agent uses instructions to decide which tool or knowledge to invoke for tool inputs and when to generate responses to users.

When writing instructions, use conversational language with a full description of how you want your agent to behave. Provide details about the specific goal you want your agent to help users achieve. Describe the tone as you would want a person to respond in a conversation. Reference tools, knowledge, and variables in the instructions so the agent can use them to generate context-aware responses. Use simple and direct language, avoiding jargon, slang, or technical terms. Use the active voice and present tense.

Agents cannot act on instructions to use tools or knowledge if those tools or knowledge sources are not configured. You must first add the appropriate tools and knowledge sources before referencing them in instructions.

Adding Knowledge Sources

Knowledge sources ground your agent's responses in specific content. Copilot Studio supports several types of knowledge sources.

Public websites: Enter URLs for public documentation or websites your agent should reference. Public website URLs must be no more than two levels deep. You can add up to four public website URLs per agent.

SharePoint: Connect to SharePoint sites for organizational knowledge. By default, Copilot Studio preconfigures agents to authenticate users using Microsoft authentication when connecting to SharePoint sources via Microsoft Teams, Power

Apps, or Microsoft 365 Copilot. SharePoint lists provide quick access to tabular data with real-time connections. For agents grounded in SharePoint knowledge sources, enabling Tenant graph grounding with semantic search yields significantly better knowledge retrieval and response quality.

Copilot connectors: Use Power Platform connectors to access data from external systems such as customer accounts, incident tickets, code repositories, and knowledge articles. Administrators must enable and configure Copilot connectors in the Microsoft 365 admin center.

Dataverse: Query business data stored in Microsoft Dataverse. Dataverse knowledge enables agents to respond in natural language to user queries about CRM data or Dataverse tables.

File upload: Upload individual files from your device or add files from SharePoint sites. Uploaded files count against the OneDrive and SharePoint capacity in your tenant.

Azure AI search: Connect to Azure AI Search indexes for enterprise search scenarios requiring custom indexing and retrieval.

When adding knowledge sources, be selective. Focus on content that directly helps the agent answer users' questions. Relevance matters more than volume. The description for each knowledge source should be as detailed as possible, especially when generative AI is enabled, as it aids generative orchestration.

Adding Tools and Actions

Tools extend your agent's capabilities beyond answering questions. Through tools, agents can perform actions such as creating records, sending notifications, or querying external APIs. When you define a tool in Copilot Studio, you provide information that describes its purpose. This information helps the agent identify when to use the tool and enables the orchestrator to use generative AI to generate questions to collect inputs.

Copilot Studio Supports Several Tool Types

Power Platform connectors: Over 1,400 prebuilt connectors provide access to enterprise systems. Standard connectors such as SharePoint are included with all Copilot Studio plans. Premium connectors are available with premium plans.

Custom connectors: Build connectors to your own APIs for systems that lack prebuilt connectors. Custom connectors integrate REST or SOAP APIs with Copilot Studio, Power Automate, Power Apps, and Logic Apps.

Agent flows: Streamline business processes and automate repetitive tasks using Power Automate flows. Agent flows are preconfigured to start with an agent trigger and end with a response back to your agent.

Prompts: Define AI prompts as reusable tools using the embedded prompt builder. Prompts let you create custom AI behaviors your agent can invoke during conversations.

REST APIs: Copilot Studio provides a guided experience for uploading Swagger files to create REST API tools. These tools connect agents with external data sources or services not covered by prebuilt connectors.

Model Context Protocol (MCP): Connect to the MCP servers to access external tools. Each tool or resource published by a connected MCP server is automatically made available for use. Name, description, inputs, and outputs are inherited from the server. As tools and resources are updated or removed on the MCP server, Copilot Studio dynamically reflects these changes

Computer use: Enable agents to automate tasks across apps and websites by clicking, typing, and navigating interfaces. Computer use is ideal for scenarios like data entry, updating records in a web portal, or retrieving information from systems without APIs.

Working with Topics

Topics are portions of conversational threads between users and your agent. Topics allow you to define specific conversation flows for different scenarios. For agents using generative orchestration, the default topic trigger is "The agent chooses," which activates when the agent determines that the topic's name and description match the incoming message. For agents using classic orchestration, the default trigger is "User says a phrase," which activates when the trigger phrase closely matches the user's query.

When creating topics for generative orchestration, focus on providing clear names and descriptions. If multiple topics have similar descriptions, your agent might invoke all of them to answer a question. Topics can include question nodes to collect user input, message nodes to send responses, action nodes to invoke tools, and condition nodes to branch the conversation based on variables.

Testing Your Agent

Test your agent throughout development using the built-in test panel. The best way to improve your agent is to test it, make changes, test again, and repeat. Test your conversation starters to verify they work as expected. Test edge cases, long questions, and irrelevant questions to understand how your agent handles unexpected input.

When testing agents that use generative orchestration, you can open the activity map to follow how your agent responds. The activity map shows which topics, tools, and knowledge sources the agent selected and why. Enter "-developer on" in the chat to see detailed information about why the generative AI selected or did not select specific tools.

Testing Recommendations

- Use the built-in test chat frequently while building your agent.
- Test in multiple apps, including Word, Excel, Teams, and Outlook, to catch discrepancies early.
- Check confirmation flows if your agent uses actions requiring confirmations.
- Conduct peer testing to find gaps in instructions or knowledge.

Using the Microsoft 365 Agents SDK

The Microsoft 365 Agents SDK enables developers to build custom engine agents using code. The SDK supports C# with .NET 8.0, JavaScript with Node.js 18 and above, and Python 3.9 to 3.11. Agents built with the SDK can deploy to Microsoft 365 Copilot, Teams, web applications, and other channels.

Key Features

- Build an agent container with state, storage, and activity management.
- Deploy across multiple channels, including Microsoft 365 Copilot and Teams.
- Use any AI service of your choice without being restricted to a specific technology stack.
- Customize agent behavior to align with specific client requirements.

Getting Started with the Agents SDK

1. Install prerequisites: .NET 8.0 SDK for C#, Node.js 18+ for JavaScript, or Python 3.9-3.11.
2. Clone the Agents SDK repository from GitHub (github.com/microsoft/Agents).
3. Navigate to the samples folder and select QuickStart/Empty Agent.
4. Follow the README instructions to build and run the sample.
5. Test locally using the Microsoft 365 Agents Playground.

Using the Microsoft 365 Agents Toolkit

The Microsoft 365 Agents Toolkit for Visual Studio and Visual Studio Code provides project scaffolding, built-in templates, and testing capabilities. The toolkit includes templates for creating empty agents and weather agents with pre-configured AI services.

1. Install the Microsoft 365 Agents Toolkit extension.
2. Select Create a New Agent/App.
3. Choose your template (Empty Agent or Weather Agent).
4. Configure your AI service (Azure OpenAI or OpenAI).
5. Provide connection details for your AI service.
6. Run the agent locally using the Agents Playground.

Integrating with Copilot Studio from Code

The Microsoft 365 Agents SDK provides interoperability with Copilot Studio in two directions. You can reference Copilot Studio agents from your SDK-built agents, or you can integrate Copilot Studio directly into your web or native applications.

When building multi-agent systems, you can reference agents built-in Copilot Studio from your custom SDK agent. This allows makers to build and maintain agents in Copilot Studio while developers bring the functionality together in code. Copilot Studio provides access to over 1,000 connectors through the Power Platform ecosystem.

The Agents SDK includes a client library for integrating Copilot Studio agents into your applications. Samples are available in .NET, JavaScript, and Python. To integrate, clone the Copilot Studio client sample from the

Agents SDK repository, configure authentication settings in your Copilot Studio agent, obtain the connection string from the Channels page in Copilot Studio, and implement the client methods to send messages and receive responses.

Building Declarative Agents with the SDK

Declarative agents can be built using the Agent Builder feature in Microsoft 365 Copilot, Copilot Studio, or the Microsoft 365 Agents Toolkit. Choose your tool based on the complexity of your requirements and your target audience.

For simple agents, use Agent Builder directly in Microsoft 365 Copilot. This provides an immediate, interactive experience for building agents using natural language. For agents requiring advanced capabilities such as multi-step workflows, custom integrations, or complex governance controls, use Copilot Studio. Developers who prefer working in Visual Studio or Visual Studio Code can use the Agents Toolkit to build declarative agents with TypeSpec to define agent configurations and to integrate directly with source control and CI/CD pipelines.

Microsoft Foundry

Microsoft Foundry, formerly Azure AI Studio, is an interoperable AI platform that enables developers to build faster and smarter, while organizations gain fleetwide security and governance in a unified portal. It provides everything needed to build, deploy, and scale AI apps and agents that understand business context and deliver business impact.

The platform combines models, agents, tools, and observability behind a single portal, SDK, and REST endpoint. Developers can ship to cloud or edge with governance and cost controls in place from day one. More than 80,000 enterprises use Foundry, including 80% of Fortune 500 companies. The platform powers more than 3 billion search queries daily.

Core Components

Microsoft Foundry integrates several key services into a unified AI development platform.

Foundry Models provide access to more than 11,000 foundational, open, reasoning, multimodal, and industry-specific models. The platform supports model fine-tuning, distillation, and automatic upgrades with minimal coding. Model router enables automatic request routing to the most suitable model for high-quality results while minimizing costs. Azure is the only cloud offering both OpenAI and Anthropic models, with Claude Sonnet 4.5, Opus 4.1, and Haiku 4.5 available alongside the full GPT model family.

Foundry Agent Service is a fully managed cloud service with SDKs for Python, C#, and TypeScript that simplifies AI agent development. The service provides ready-to-use templates, actions, and connectors to more than 1,400 enterprise data sources. More than 10,000 organizations have used Foundry Agent Service to automate complex business processes.

Foundry IQ, powered by Azure AI Search, reimagines retrieval-augmented generation as a dynamic reasoning process rather than a one-time lookup. It centralizes RAG workflows into a single grounding API, simplifying orchestration and improving response quality while respecting user permissions and data classifications.

Foundry Tools provides pre-built and customizable tools for tasks such as OCR, translation, speech, and object detection. Developers can bring their own APIs using the Model Context Protocol (MCP). Azure Logic Apps integration enables automation of business processes through more than 1,400 connections to enterprise systems, including SAP, Salesforce, and Dynamics 365.

Foundry Control Plane centralizes identity, policy, observability, and security signals for AI developers in one portal. It integrates with Microsoft Defender and Entra ID for comprehensive security and governance.

Foundry Local is a runtime for Windows, macOS, and Android that supports AI models and agents. Developers can build cross-platform AI apps that work offline, keep sensitive data locally, and reduce bandwidth costs.

Building Agents with Foundry Agent Service

Foundry Agent Service connects models, tools, and frameworks into a single runtime. It manages conversations, orchestrates tool calls, enforces content safety, and integrates with identity, networking, and observability systems.

Agents created through Foundry are composable units. Each agent has a specific role, is powered by the right model, and is equipped with the right tools. You deploy each agent within a secure, observable, and governable runtime. Agent components include a model (LLM) for reasoning, instructions for goals and behavior, tools for knowledge and actions, and knowledge sources such as Bing, SharePoint, Microsoft Fabric, and Azure AI Search.

Foundry Agent Service supports multiple agent types. Prompt-based agents are declaratively defined single agents that combine model configuration, instructions, tools, and natural language prompts to drive behavior. Workflow agents are defined in YAML or code to orchestrate multiple agents. Hosted agents are containerized agents created and deployed in code, hosted by Foundry with built-in scaling, observability, and governance.

Multi-agent Orchestration

Real-world workflows often require multiple agents working together. Multi-agent workflows in Foundry Agent Service provide a stateful layer for managing context, handling errors, and maintaining long-running processes. This is particularly useful for scenarios like financial approvals or supply chain operations.

Instead of building a single monolithic agent, developers can coordinate a network of agents, each focused on a specific task, into a structured workflow. Features include persistent state management with error recovery and context sharing, fine-grained control through visual design or code, human-in-the-loop controls for approval workflows, role-based access control with auditability and life cycle management, and built-in observability for debugging and scaling.

The platform implements open interoperability standards, including Agent-to-Agent (A2A) communication and Model Context Protocol (MCP). These standards ensure agents can collaborate seamlessly across Azure, AWS, Google Cloud, and on-premises environments.

Microsoft Agent Framework

Microsoft Agent Framework is an open-source SDK and runtime for building, deploying, and managing sophisticated multi-agent systems. It unifies the enterprise-ready foundations of Semantic Kernel with the innovative orchestration patterns from AutoGen, creating a unified foundation for both experimentation and production.

The framework supports Agent Orchestration for LLM-driven creative reasoning and decision-making, Workflow Orchestration for business-logic driven deterministic multi-agent workflows, open standards, including MCP, A2A, and OpenAPI, and local development with cloud deployment. The framework provides deep integrations with Foundry Agent Service, the Microsoft 365 Agents SDK, and Copilot Studio's low-code connectors.

Deploying to Microsoft 365 from Foundry

Foundry Agent Service connects natively with Microsoft 365 and Agent 365, bridging agent development and enterprise deployment. With one-click publishing, developers can instantly deploy agents from Foundry to Microsoft 365 Copilot and Teams Chat without manual setup or manifest editing.

A single build can now reach multiple Microsoft 365 channels, bringing agents directly into the flow of work. Every deployment routes through the Microsoft Admin Center for approval, giving IT administrators unified governance, compliance, and visibility. When you publish a hosted agent, Microsoft Foundry automatically creates an agent application resource with a dedicated invocation URL, provisions a distinct agent identity, registers the agent in the Microsoft Entra agent registry, and enables stable endpoint access that remains consistent across new agent versions.

Comparing Foundry Agent Service and Copilot Studio

Copilot Studio is a streamlined, low-code platform that emphasizes ease of use and native Microsoft 365 integration for rapid AI agent creation. Foundry Agent Service is a flexible, pro-code solution with extensive developer tooling and CI/CD integration designed for complex enterprise scenarios.

Foundry Agent Service uniquely supports multi-agent orchestration, enabling dynamic collaboration among specialized agents. It offers advanced security, compliance features, flexible model support, and a wide array of connectivity options, making it better suited for large-scale, regulated environments. Because Azure AI Foundry powers Microsoft Copilot Studio, developers maintain a continuous loop from model selection and fine-tuning through deployment of pre-built agents.

Getting Started with Foundry

Developers can begin exploring Foundry at ai.azure.com without an Azure account. However, an Azure subscription is required before building agents.

1. Ensure the account creating the project has the Azure AI Account Owner role at the subscription scope, or the Contributor or Owner role at the subscription level.
2. Create a Foundry project in your Azure subscription.
3. Deploy a compatible model such as GPT-4o from Models + Endpoints.
4. Find your project endpoint in the overview under Libraries > Foundry.
5. Begin making API calls using the Python, C#, or TypeScript SDKs.

Publishing to Microsoft 365 Copilot and Teams

After testing, publish your agent so it's available to users. Publishing applies your agent to all connected channels. When you update and republish, changes propagate to all channels. You must publish your agent at least once before users can interact with it in Teams and Microsoft 365 Copilot.

Prerequisites for Publishing

Before publishing to Teams and Microsoft 365 Copilot, verify the following requirements:

- All agent users in your organization can use Microsoft 365 Copilot.
- Agent makers have permissions to create and access a Copilot Studio environment.
- You have shared your agent with other users so they can install and chat with it.
- Your organization allows Microsoft Power Platform apps to be added to Teams.
- You have published the agent at least once before installing it for yourself or sharing it with others.

Publishing from Copilot Studio

1. Open your agent in Copilot Studio.
2. Select Publish from the top navigation menu.

3. Confirm you want to publish in the confirmation dialog.
4. Wait for the publication process to complete. A green banner appears when successful.

New content in a freshly published agent does not appear in ongoing conversations. Users can enter "Start over" in an existing conversation to start a new conversation and see the latest updates.

Connecting to Teams and Microsoft 365 Copilot Channels

After publishing, connect your agent to the Teams and Microsoft 365 Copilot channels so users can interact with it.

1. Open your agent in Copilot Studio.
2. On the top menu bar, select Channels.
3. Select the Teams and Microsoft 365 Copilot tile.
4. Under Turn on Microsoft 365, ensure "Make agent available in Microsoft 365 Copilot" is selected.
5. Select Add channel.

If you do not select "Make agent available in Microsoft 365 Copilot," your agent is only available in Teams. To prevent individuals outside your organization from using these agents, turn on security settings for agents built for Teams, Microsoft 365 Copilot, or internal employee use.

Customizing Agent Appearance

Before sharing your agent, customize its appearance to help users understand its purpose and branding. This information is visible in the Teams app store and on the app's About tab after installation.

Open the configuration panel for the Teams and Microsoft 365 Copilot channels. Select Edit details to change the agent's icon, color, and descriptions. The icon must be in PNG format, less than 30 KB in size, with a maximum resolution of 192 × 192 pixels. Select More to add the developer name, website, privacy statement, and terms of use.

Users who already installed the agent from a shared link or from the Built with Power Platform section do not see changes to agent details. Users must reinstall the agent to get updates. For agents already approved by an admin, you must submit the agent again for approval.

Sharing Your Agent

You can share your agent through several methods, depending on your target audience and organizational policies.

Installation Link

Share a direct installation link with users. Only users who have access to the agent can use the link to install it. Open the configuration panel, select Availability options, and select Copy link. Share the link with users so they can install the agent in Teams. The installation link cannot be used in the Teams mobile app.

Built with Power Platform Section

Show your agent in the Teams app store's Built with Power Platform section. Only shared users can find the agent there. This option has user count limits based on your tenant's Teams app store discovery policy.

Open the configuration panel, select Availability options, select "Show to my teammates and shared users," confirm the "Show in Built By Your Colleagues" checkbox is selected, and select Update. Your agent becomes available in the Built with Power Platform section.

Built for Your Org Section

Submit your agent for admin approval to appear in the Built for your Org section of the Teams app store. If you also publish your agent to Microsoft 365, submitting for admin approval applies to the Microsoft 365 Agent Store as well. This is the recommended approach for broad distribution across the organization.

Submitting for Admin Approval

Before submitting an agent to your organization, verify that your agent is ready for release and complies with company standards. Coordinate with other agent managers, as only one submission can be pending at a time. Remove the agent from the Built with Power Platform section if previously added to avoid duplicate listings.

1. Open the configuration panel for the Teams and Microsoft 365 Copilot channels.

2. Select Availability options.

3. Confirm the agent is not shown to teammates or shared users.

4. Select "Show to everyone in my org."
5. Review the requirements for submission.
6. Select "Submit for admin approval."
7. Select Yes in the confirmation prompt.
8. Wait for your admin to approve the agent.

After submitting the agent for admin approval, do not change the agent's access setting to be less than that of everyone in your organization. Content updates do not require resubmission. You can make content updates and publish as often as desired without submitting for approval again. Only changes to agent details, such as icons and descriptions, require a new approval request.

Admin Approval Process

When a maker submits an agent, admins can review and approve it in the Microsoft Teams Admin Center or Microsoft 365 Admin Center. During review, admins inspect metadata, including the agent's name, description, icon, and connectors, to support compliance with organizational policies.

Agents submitted for admin approval appear in the Copilot Control System in the Microsoft 365 admin center. The admin can view pending submissions in the Requests tab. When ready, admins select Start publishing to open the publishing wizard, choose the users or groups for the agent, and optionally pre-install or deploy the agent for the selected audience.

Once approved, the agent publishes to the Agent Store. Approved agents appear in the Agent Store with internal agents labeled and easy to find in the Built for your org section. Admins can assign access, push deployments to specific users or groups, or remove agents if needed.

Adding an Agent to Team Channels and Group Chats

In Teams, users can add an agent to a specific team. Once an agent is available for a team, team members can @mention it in any team channels, and all teammates see the responses. This feature is useful when your agent supports collaboration or when you want to allow all team members to engage with the agent without having to manually install it.

To allow users to add an agent to a team, open the configuration panel for the Teams and Microsoft 365 Copilot channels, select Edit details, select "Allow your users to add this agent to a team," and select Save. The agent should be configured to allow everyone in the organization to chat with it.

Teams caches information, so it can take a while before users see the option to add the agent to a team or group chat. If you previously submitted the agent for admin approval, you must submit it again after enabling this option. Group chats and meeting chats do not support agents configured for manual authentication with Teams single sign-on (SSO).

The Agent Store

The Agent Store is a centralized, curated marketplace that features agents built by Microsoft, trusted partners, and customers. Whether you are a developer looking to reach millions of users or an employee seeking AI tools to boost productivity, the Agent Store provides a single destination for discovering, installing, and using the next generation of AI assistants.

Microsoft 365 Copilot serves as the user interface for AI in the workplace. Agents extend this capability as purpose-built assistants designed to automate specific business processes. The Agent Store makes it easier to discover agents that solve real business problems, share and deploy agents across teams and organizations, and build and publish agents using both low-code and pro-code tools.

What the Agent Store Offers

The Agent Store provides an immersive experience within Microsoft 365 Copilot, enabling users to browse, install, and try agents tailored to their needs. Key capabilities include agents from Microsoft, trusted partners, and customers, personalized discovery based on user activities and profiles, seamless integration across Microsoft 365 products, including Teams and m365copilot.com, support for both Microsoft 365 Copilot licensed customers and unlicensed Copilot Chat users, curated collections, agent detail pages with descriptions and capabilities, search with zero-query suggestions, merchandising to highlight top agents, and URL-based sharing to drive adoption.

Types of Agents in the Store

The Agent Store includes several categories of agents organized by their source and purpose.

Microsoft agents are built and maintained by Microsoft. These include Researcher, which synthesizes information and creates in-depth content by reasoning across public and organizational data, and Analyst, which transforms complex data into clear insights and visualizations. Other Microsoft agents include Facilitator for managing Teams meetings, Interpreter for real-time speech-to-speech translation, and People Agent for finding colleagues.

Partner-built agents are developed by trusted external developers and integrate with enterprise systems. Examples include SAP Joule for navigating the SAP ecosystem, ServiceNow Now Assist for finding answers and completing ServiceNow tasks within Copilot and Teams, Jira for project management integration, Monday.com for work management, Miro for collaboration, and Snowflake Cortex Agents for AI-powered data interactions.

Organization-published agents are custom agents approved and published by your organization for broader internal use. These agents combine instructions, knowledge, and skills to perform specific tasks tailored to organizational needs.

Shared agents are created and shared by individual users or developers within your organization. Creators can build and share these agents through multiple channels, including Copilot Studio and Agent Builder.

Accessing the Agent Store

1. Open the Microsoft 365 Copilot app.
2. In the navigation panel, find Agents and select the dropdown to see pre-installed agents.
3. Select all agents to view everything available in the Agent Store.
4. Select an agent and choose Add or Open.
5. Select a prompt or type a question into the Message Copilot box.

Once added, agents greet users with an introductory message and offer suggested prompts to help them get started. Users can pin favorite agents for quick access and share agent links with colleagues.

Microsoft Marketplace Integration

The Agent Store works in conjunction with the Microsoft Marketplace, providing a unified catalog powered by the same publishing process and infrastructure. This ensures consistent listings, pricing, and management across both platforms.

Customers can research and transact on the Microsoft Marketplace, then deploy and manage agents through the Agent Store. The Microsoft Marketplace serves as a single web destination for finding, trying, and buying cloud solutions, AI apps, and agents. Both experiences share the same catalog, allowing organizations to choose their preferred entry point while maintaining consistency.

Publishing to the Agent Store

The Agent Store provides a platform for developers and partners to showcase solutions and drive user adoption. Publishing to the Agent Store provides access to Microsoft 365 Copilot users across Microsoft 365 hubs, including Teams and m365copilot.com, as well as co-marketing and partner support opportunities, and insights into usage and feedback.

Agents built with Copilot Studio can be published to multiple channels, including Microsoft 365 Copilot and Teams. When a maker submits an agent, it appears in the Copilot Control System in the Microsoft 365 admin center for admin review and approval. Once approved, the agent publishes to the Agent Store, where internal agents are labeled and appear in the Built for your org section.

IT Administration and Governance

IT teams maintain full governance and control over agents that employees can install from the Agent Store through the Microsoft 365 admin center. The Agent Registry page provides a centralized view of all agents available in the organization.

Administrators can perform the following actions on agents:

- **Activate:** Allow only selected users or groups to install the agent and create instances.
- **Deploy:** Automatically install an agent for users so it is ready to use without manual setup.
- **Pin:** Surface key agents prominently in the Copilot interface for selected users or all users.
- **Block:** Restrict access to an agent across the organization.
- **Remove:** Remove an agent from the tenant's inventory; it can be re-added later.
- **Delete:** Delete agents directly from the admin center, removing the agent and all associated files.
- **Approve updates:** Review and approve new versions or changes before deployment.

Agent 365 Control Plane

Microsoft Agent 365 is the control plane for AI agents, empowering organizations to confidently deploy, govern, and manage all agents at scale. Whether agents are created using Copilot Studio, Microsoft Foundry, open-source frameworks, or by partners such as Adobe, SAP, ServiceNow, and Workday, Agent 365 helps deploy, organize, and govern them securely.

Agent 365 includes five key capabilities. Registry provides a single source of truth for all agents in your organization, including agents with Microsoft Entra agent ID, agents you register yourself, and shadow agents. Access Control manages agents and limits their access to only the resources required. Visualization provides a unified dashboard and advanced analytics to see connections between agents, people, and data, and monitor agent behavior in real time. Interoperability equips agents with apps and data to simplify human-agent workflows. Security helps protect agents from threats and vulnerabilities using Microsoft Defender, Entra, and Purview.

Licensing and Costs

Microsoft 365 Copilot Chat offers agents available at no additional cost, as well as metered-consumption billing.

Declarative agents grounded in instructions and public websites are available at no additional cost. These agents appear by default in the store based on existing store settings for Teams and Microsoft 365 apps.

Agents that access shared tenant data, such as SharePoint or Graph Connector content, are billed based on metered consumption. These agents are off by default for users in Copilot Chat. To enable agents utilizing metered consumption, admins need to set up or use an existing Copilot Studio subscription. Admins can configure pay-as-you-go billing through either the Microsoft 365 admin center or the Power Platform admin center.

Conclusion

Integrating your AI agent with Microsoft Copilot positions your solution directly within the productivity tools used by hundreds of millions of enterprise users. This chapter has outlined the complete pathway from understanding your integration options to publishing your agent in the Agent Store.

The decision between declarative and custom engine agents depends on your specific requirements. Declarative agents offer rapid development with Microsoft's hosted orchestrator and models, automatic compliance with Microsoft's security framework, and straightforward publishing to Microsoft 365 Copilot and Teams. Custom engine agents provide complete control over AI models, orchestration logic, and hosting, enabling complex multi-agent workflows and deployment across Microsoft 365 and external platforms.

Microsoft provides multiple development paths to match your team's capabilities. Copilot Studio enables business users to build agents without writing code using natural-language descriptions and guided configuration. The Microsoft 365 Agents SDK gives developers full control with support for C#, JavaScript, and Python across multiple channels. Microsoft Foundry offers an enterprise platform for building, deploying, and scaling AI apps and agents with comprehensive governance and observability.

The publishing workflow ensures agents reach users through appropriate channels. Testing locally, publishing from Copilot Studio, connecting to Teams and Microsoft 365 Copilot channels, and submitting for admin approval establishes a governed distribution path. The Agent Store then provides discovery, installation, and management across the organization.

For ISVs, the Agent Store represents an opportunity to reach Microsoft 365 Copilot users at scale. The unified catalog with Microsoft Marketplace ensures consistent listings and transactions. IT governance through Agent 365 gives enterprise customers confidence in deploying your agents while providing you with usage insights and feedback.

As you build your Copilot integration, consider your target customers, their licensing situation, and their IT governance requirements. Start with a clear use case, choose the appropriate agent type and development tool, test thoroughly, and work with administrators to achieve broad organizational distribution. The Microsoft Copilot ecosystem provides the infrastructure, the Agent Store provides the marketplace, and your agent provides the value.

CHAPTER 9

Go-to-Market Execution

Introduction: From Published to Profitable

You have completed the hardest part. Your AI agent is built, tested, priced, enrolled in the Microsoft AI Cloud Partner Program, and published on the Microsoft Marketplace. The technical work is done. Now begins the disciplined execution that transforms a Marketplace listing into a revenue-generating, scalable business.

This transition from builder to seller can be where an ISV struggles. The skills that made you successful in product development are different from the skills required for commercial success. Technical founders can underestimate the effort required to generate pipeline, close enterprise deals, and build sustainable revenue. It is easy to assume that a superior product will sell itself. It rarely does.

The data tells a clear story. According to research from First Page Sage, analyzing over 50 B2B SaaS companies, the average visitor-to-lead conversion rate is just 1.7%, and the lead-to-closed-customer rate hovers around 2–5%. These numbers mean that for every thousand qualified visitors to your Marketplace listing traffic, you might convert 17 to leads and close fewer than one as a paying customer through a traditional sales motion.

J. Soh et al., *Building and Distributing Agentic AI Solutions*,
https://doi.org/10.1007/979-8-8688-2586-6_9

Without systematic execution across every stage of the funnel, even the best AI solution will languish in obscurity. The development of sophisticated AI agents and generative solutions, detailed in previous chapters, represents the technical foundation of a successful Independent Software Vendor (ISV) offering. You have completed the hardest part, building a robust, secure, and intelligent product on the Microsoft AI Cloud. However, technical excellence alone does not guarantee commercial success.

Key Insight The difference between ISVs that achieve modest traction and those that scale to significant revenue is not technical superiority – it is execution velocity and commercial discipline.

This chapter is your execution playbook. We move beyond program enrollment and platform mechanics into the specific actions that an ISV must take to generate pipeline, close deals, expand through partners, and build sustainable growth. Every recommendation is grounded in the realities of the Microsoft programs available, the incentives at play, and the behaviors that drive results.

The Marketplace Advantage: Why Execution Here Matters More

Before diving into tactics, it is worth understanding why the Microsoft Marketplace creates unique leverage for ISVs who execute well. A 2023 Forrester Total Economic Impact study performed by interviewing 10 customers that actively use Microsoft commercial marketplace found that organizations using the commercial marketplace experience

- **587%** ROI over three years for ISVs actively engaging the platform
- **50%** reduction in employee effort required for each procurement engagement
- **33–40%** shorter sales cycles compared to traditional enterprise software procurement
- **30%** time savings for finance and payments teams processing invoices
- **75%** reduction in vendor onboarding effort

These are the economics you are now positioned to capture. The Marketplace eliminates friction that typically kills deals, such as procurement complexity, legal redlining, vendor onboarding, and invoice management. When your solution is transactable through the Marketplace, customers can purchase using existing Microsoft agreements, draw from pre-committed Azure budgets (MACC), and consolidate billing through a vendor relationship they already trust. But these benefits only materialize when you actively work the system. A passive listing generates passive results. This chapter shows you how to be aggressive.

The Go-to-market (GTM) Execution Framework

GTM execution for AI ISVs in the Microsoft ecosystem operates across five interconnected domains. Success requires simultaneous progress in each:

1. **Demand generation:** Creating awareness and driving qualified traffic to your Marketplace listing and sales conversations.

2. **Sales acceleration:** Converting pipeline to revenue through structured sales processes that leverage Marketplace mechanics.
3. **Co-sell execution:** Engaging Microsoft's sales organization to amplify your reach and credibility.
4. **Channel expansion:** Scaling through Cloud Solution Providers, System Integrators, and resellers who extend your distribution.
5. **Customer success:** Driving expansion revenue through adoption, satisfaction, and advocacy.

Each domain has its own metrics, tactics, and cadence. The remainder of this chapter addresses each in turn, providing the specific actions you should take in your first 90 days post-publication and the ongoing practices that sustain growth.

Building Your Demand Generation Engine

Pipeline is the lifeblood of any software business. For AI ISVs operating in the Microsoft ecosystem, demand generation requires a multi-channel approach that leverages both your own marketing efforts and Microsoft's considerable reach.

The goal is to create a predictable, scalable system that converts market awareness into qualified opportunities. The execution is complex, requiring coordination across content, campaigns, events, digital presence, and partner relationships. This section provides the tactical playbook.

Leveraging Campaign-in-a-Box for Rapid Deployment

Microsoft's Partner Marketing Center provides Campaign-in-a-Box (CiaB) resources - pre-built, co-branded marketing campaigns that you can customize and deploy immediately. These are professionally designed assets aligned with Microsoft's solution priorities and validated messaging frameworks.

Instead of spending weeks developing creative campaigns, messaging, and assets from scratch, you can deploy professional-quality campaigns within days. Each CiaB includes email nurture sequences, social media content, landing page templates, sales enablement materials, and measurement guidance.

Priority Campaigns for AI Solution Providers

Not all Campaign-in-a-Box resources are equally relevant for AI ISVs. Prioritize these campaigns based on your solution positioning and target buyer:

Era of AI

Use a "Top-of-funnel" awareness campaign to demonstrate how AI delivers business value. Use this to educate prospects who are curious about AI, but not yet committed to specific initiatives. The messaging focuses on transformation potential rather than technical implementation, making it ideal for reaching business decision-makers who influence but do not directly control technology purchases.

- **Target audience:** C-suite executives, line-of-business leaders, digital transformation officers
- **Funnel stage:** Awareness/education
- **Best for:** ISVs with horizontal AI solutions applicable across industries

Build and Modernize AI Apps

Technical buyer campaign positioning your solution within the Azure AI platform ecosystem. This campaign targets IT architects, development leads, and technical decision-makers who evaluate solutions based on integration capabilities, scalability, and architectural fit. Messaging emphasizes Azure-native development, cloud-native architecture, and enterprise readiness.

- **Target audience:** CTO/CIO, enterprise architects, development managers, platform engineers
- **Funnel stage:** Consideration/evaluation
- **Best for:** ISVs with deep Azure integration and technical differentiation

Innovate with Azure AI Platform

Generative AI-focused campaign for organizations exploring Azure OpenAI Service and related technologies. This campaign capitalizes on the current surge of enterprise interest in large language models, copilots, and intelligent automation. Messaging emphasizes responsible AI, enterprise security, and Azure OpenAI's unique positioning.

- **Target audience:** AI/ML leads, data science teams, innovation groups, R&D leadership
- **Funnel stage:** Awareness/consideration
- **Best for:** ISVs leveraging Azure OpenAI, Cognitive Services, or custom ML models

AI-Powered Customer Service

Line-of-business campaign for Dynamics 365 integrations, targeting customer experience leaders. This vertical-specific campaign speaks directly to the pain points of customer service organizations: rising support volumes, agent burnout, inconsistent customer experiences, and pressure to do more with less.

- **Target audience:** VP/Director of Customer Service, Customer Experience leaders, Contact Center managers
- **Funnel stage:** Consideration/decision
- **Best for:** ISVs with customer service AI solutions integrating with Dynamics 365

Campaign Execution Workflow

Deploying a Campaign-in-a-Box requires more than downloading assets and sending emails. Follow this structured workflow to maximize campaign performance:

1. **Select your campaign strategically:** Choose the CiaB best aligned with your target buyer persona and solution positioning. Access the Partner Marketing Center via partner.microsoft.com/marketing-center. Review all available campaigns before committing. New campaigns are added quarterly aligned with Microsoft's fiscal priorities.

2. **Download and audit all assets:** Each CiaB includes multiple asset types. Download and inventory all materials, including email templates, social media posts, landing page copy, display ad creative, sales playbooks, and objection handling guides.

3. **Customize with your value proposition:** Replace placeholder content with your brand, solution name, and specific value propositions. The key is maintaining Microsoft's approved messaging framework while differentiating your specific solution. The Microsoft co-brand provides credibility you should leverage.

4. **Build your campaign infrastructure:** Before launching, confirm that your infrastructure includes landing pages with form capture, configured email automation, and UTM parameters for tracking. You must also verify CRM integration for lead routing and website conversion tracking because launching without these systems creates unattributed leads.

5. **Deploy across channels simultaneously:** Execute the email nurture sequences, social media assets, and landing page content at the same time. Multi-touch, multi-channel exposure drives higher conversion than single-channel campaigns. Coordinate timing so prospects encounter consistent messaging across touchpoints.

Measure, analyze, and iterate: Track click-through rates, form completions, and downstream pipeline. Review performance weekly for the first month, then monthly thereafter. A/B test subject lines, calls-to-action, and landing page variants. Adjust messaging based on performance data.

Creating Original Demand Generation Content

Campaign-in-a-Box provides a foundation, but sustainable demand generation requires original content that establishes your thought leadership and addresses the specific questions your buyers ask. AI buyers require substance, not marketing fluff. Different content types serve different purposes in the buyer journey. Build a content portfolio that addresses needs at each stage (see Table 9-1 for all stages):

Technical Architecture Guides

Show how your AI agent integrates with Azure services. Developers and architects influence buying decisions even when they do not control budgets. Technical content that demonstrates your solution's architecture, integration patterns, and operational characteristics builds credibility with this critical audience. Include reference architectures, API documentation, and deployment guides.

ROI Calculators and Business Cases

Quantify the business impact of your solution. Every enterprise purchase requires internal justification. Make this easy by providing calculators that help prospects estimate ROI based on their specific parameters. By providing these models, you help your internal champion build a data-driven justification that translates agent performance into measurable financial outcomes.

Customer Proof Points and Case Studies

Document specific results from existing deployments. Nothing builds credibility like evidence of success. Structure case studies around the challenge, solution, and results. Include specific metrics: time saved, costs reduced, outcomes improved. Secure customer permission to use logos and quotes because named references carry more weight than anonymous testimonials.

Comparison and Evaluation Content

Help buyers understand how your AI agent compares to alternatives. Highlight differentiation on capabilities, integration depth, and total cost of ownership. Create evaluation guides that help prospects assess their options systematically. Position yourself as a trusted advisor, not just a vendor.

Industry-Specific Solution Briefs

If your AI solution serves specific verticals, create content tailored to each. Healthcare AI buyers have different concerns than financial services AI buyers. Speak their language, address their regulatory requirements, and reference relevant use cases. Industry-specific content converts at higher rates than generic content because it demonstrates domain expertise.

Table 9-1. Content types and their strategic purpose in the buyer journey

Content type	Funnel stage	Target audience	Primary goal
Architecture guides	Consideration	Technical buyers	Technical credibility
ROI calculators	Decision	Business buyers	Business case support
Case studies	Decision	All stakeholders	Social proof
Comparison guides	Evaluation	Evaluators	Differentiation
Industry briefs	Awareness	Vertical buyers	Domain expertise

Optimizing Your Marketplace Listing for Conversion

Your Marketplace listing is your most important demand generation asset. It is where prospects land after hearing about your solution, where Microsoft sellers send referrals, and where channel partners direct customers. Treat your listing like a high stakes landing page. Every element should be optimized for conversion.

Listing Elements That Drive Conversion

Solution Title and Tagline

Your title should be clear, searchable, and descriptive. Include keywords that your target buyers search for. The tagline should communicate your core value proposition in one sentence. Avoid jargon and buzzwords and focus on clarity.

Solution Description

Lead with the problem you solve, not the features you offer. The first paragraph should answer: What pain does this eliminate? What outcome does it enable? Who is this for? Only after establishing relevance describe capabilities. Include specific metrics where possible. For instance, "reduces processing time by 60%" is more compelling than "improves efficiency."

Screenshots and Media

Visual assets drive conversion rates by providing evidence of your solution's capabilities. High-performing listings feature product screenshots of the user interface, architecture diagrams for Azure integration, and demo videos under 90 seconds. You should also include authorized customer logo grids to build credibility. Every image must have a clear purpose and should not be used as stock photography filler.

Compliance Note: Customer logos require written permissions; hence always verify Marketplace media requirements.

Pricing Transparency

Unclear pricing creates friction and kills conversions. Display your pricing model prominently. If you offer multiple tiers, explain what each includes and who it is best for. If pricing is complex or usage-based, provide examples: "A typical mid-size deployment costs $X-Y per month." Make it easy for prospects to understand what they will pay.

Social Proof

Include customer testimonials, case study summaries, industry awards, certifications, and review ratings. Every trust signal reduces buyer hesitation. If you have Microsoft designations (Co-sell Ready, IP Co-sell Incentivized, Certified Software), display these badges prominently as they signal Microsoft's endorsement.

A/B Testing Your Listing

Do not assume your first listing version is optimal. Use data to drive improvements:

1. **Establish baseline metrics:** Track page views, unique visitors, "Get It Now" clicks, and conversion to contact or trial. Partner Center provides analytics, which you should supplement with your own tracking.
2. **Test one element at a time:** Change your title for two weeks, measure impact. Then test a new description. Then new screenshots. Changing everything simultaneously makes attribution impossible.
3. **Document learnings:** Create a testing log that records what you changed, when, and the resulting metrics. Over time, this builds institutional knowledge about what resonates with your audience.
4. **Refresh quarterly:** Markets evolve, competitors launch, and messaging gets stale. Schedule quarterly reviews of your listing to ensure it remains current and competitive.

Demand Generation Metrics Dashboard

Effective demand generation requires disciplined measurement. Build a metrics dashboard that you review weekly and share with your leadership team. The following metrics shown in Table 9-2 provide visibility (mostly natively available) into funnel health:

Table 9-2. *Demand generation metrics dashboard with benchmarks and action triggers*

Metric	Benchmark	Frequency	Action trigger
Listing page views	500+/month	Weekly	<200: increase promotion
Conversion rate	2–5%	Weekly	<1%: optimize listing
MQLs generated	20+/month	Weekly	<10: expand campaigns
Campaign CTR	2–3%	Per campaign	<1%: revise messaging
Cost per lead	$50–$200	Monthly	>$300: audit spend

Accelerating Sales Cycles

Enterprise software sales cycles are notoriously long. According to industry research, the average B2B SaaS deal takes 84 days from first contact to close. For enterprise deals exceeding $100,000, that timeline extends to 170 days or more - nearly six months of sustained effort before revenue recognition. Mid-market deals targeting companies with 100–999 employees typically run 60–120 days, while small business transactions can close in weeks (see Table 9-3).

These timelines represent enormous capital consumption. Every day a deal remains open, you are investing sales resources, engineering time for demonstrations and POCs, and executive attention for relationship building. The cost of a protracted sales cycle is cash flow constraint, forecasting uncertainty, and opportunity cost from deals your team could have pursued instead.

Marketplace transactions, however, compress this timeline dramatically. The Forrester Total Economic Impact study found that organizations using the Microsoft commercial marketplace experience 33–40% shorter sales cycles compared to traditional procurement. The

Marketplace provides established commercial and legal infrastructure, including standard terms, pre-negotiated agreements, streamlined procurement, and consolidated billing. You must exploit this advantage systematically to reduce sales friction and accelerate your time-to-market.

Table 9-3. *Sales cycle benchmarks by deal size – traditional vs. marketplace-enabled*

Deal size/segment	Traditional cycle	Marketplace cycle	Key accelerators
SMB (<$10K ACV)	2–6 weeks	1–3 weeks	Self-serve, instant provisioning
Mid-market ($10K-$100K)	60–120 days	40–80 days	Standard terms, MACC eligibility
Enterprise ($100K+)	170–270+ days	100–180 days	Private Offers, co-sell support

The MACC Advantage in Every Conversation

Customers with Microsoft Azure Consumption Commitments (MACC) have already allocated budget to Azure spending. These are committed funds that the customer must spend or forfeit. When your transactable AI solution qualifies for MACC drawdown, you transform from a discretionary purchase requiring new budget approval into a strategic expenditure that helps the customer fulfill existing commitments.

This fundamentally changes the procurement conversation. Consider the typical enterprise software purchase: a business leader identifies a need, builds a business case, requests budget approval, navigates procurement review, negotiates terms, and finally executes a contract. Each step introduces delay and the possibility of deal death. With MACC-eligible purchases, you bypass the budget approval step entirely. The money is already allocated.

The MACC Message: *"Your investment in our AI solution counts toward your Azure commitment. We're helping you optimize spend you've already committed—not asking for new budget."*

Qualifying for MACC Drawdown

Not every Marketplace transaction counts toward MACC. To qualify, your offer must meet specific criteria:

- **Transactable offer:** Your solution must be listed as a transactable offer (SaaS or Azure Application), not just a listing or contact-me offer.
- **Azure IP Co-sell eligible:** You must have achieved Azure IP Co-sell status, which requires demonstrating that your solution runs on or extends Azure services.
- **Customer MACC agreement:** The customer must have an active MACC with Microsoft. Larger enterprises typically have MACC agreements, while smaller organizations may not.

Identifying MACC Customers

Train your sales team to identify MACC customers early in the qualification process. Discovery questions should include

- "Do you have an enterprise agreement with Microsoft?"
- "Have you committed to Azure consumption targets?"
- "How are you currently tracking against your cloud spend commitments?"
- "Would it be helpful if this purchase counted toward your existing Azure commitments?"

When you confirm a customer has MACC, immediately reframe the procurement conversation. You are no longer competing for discretionary budget, you are helping them optimize committed spend. This positioning often moves your solution from "nice to have" to "strategic priority."

Structuring Effective Proof-of-Concept Engagements

AI solutions require proof. Unlike traditional software, where buyers can evaluate features through demonstrations, AI buyers need to see your solution working with their data, in their environment, addressing their specific use case. The proof-of-concept (POC) is where deals are won or lost.

The Forrester study found that Marketplace access to free trial versions eliminated POC fees that customers would otherwise pay, savings that averaged $20,000 per engagement. The value extends beyond cost. Structured POCs accelerate deal cycles by replacing theoretical evaluation with concrete evidence.

The POC Framework

1. **Define success criteria up front:** Before the POC begins, agree on specific, measurable outcomes that constitute success. Vague POCs create vague decisions. Document: What specific business problem will we address? What metrics will we measure? What threshold constitutes success? Who will evaluate results?

2. **Time-box:** Two weeks maximum for most AI solutions. Longer POCs indicate either unclear requirements or insufficient urgency. The longer a POC drags beyond four weeks, the less likely it is to convert.

3. **Use Azure Sponsorship strategically:** Marketplace Rewards provides Azure credits specifically for POCs and customer trials. These credits offset the customer's infrastructure costs during evaluation, reducing friction. Allocate sponsorship to high-potential opportunities where cost is a barrier to POC initiation.

4. **Assign dedicated resources:** A POC should not be a purely self-serve evaluation. Assign a solutions engineer or customer success manager to guide the customer through setup, configuration, and evaluation. Proactive engagement dramatically increases POC success rates.

5. **Document everything:** The POC should produce performance benchmarks, integration documentation, user feedback, screenshots of results that feed directly into the business case, and procurement justification. These artifacts accelerate the approval process.

Private Offers for Enterprise Deals

When standard pricing does not fit a large enterprise opportunity, use Private Offers to create custom terms without eroding your public pricing. Private Offers are negotiated deals between you and a specific customer, executed through the Marketplace infrastructure. They allow you to offer volume discounts, extended payment terms, or custom metered rates while maintaining MACC eligibility and transaction simplicity.

When to Use Private Offers

- **Large deal negotiation:** When a customer requests pricing concessions for significant volume commitments.
- **Multi-year commitments:** When customers want to lock in pricing for 2–3 year terms in exchange for up-front commitment.
- **Custom configurations:** When the standard SKUs do not match the customer's specific deployment requirements.

- **Competitive situations:** When you need pricing flexibility to win against a specific competitor without changing your public price list.

Private Offer Best Practices

- **Establish a minimum deal size threshold:** Private Offers require administrative effort. Set a floor, typically $50,000 annual value or higher, below which you use standard pricing.
- **Build internal approval workflows in advance:** When a large deal emerges, you cannot afford delays waiting for discount approvals. Define authority levels and escalation paths before you need them.
- **Document the business rationale:** For every discount offered, record why. This data informs future pricing strategy and prevents ad hoc discounting that erodes margins over time.
- **Set expiration dates:** Private Offers should include reasonable expiration windows (typically 30–60 days) to create urgency and prevent indefinite negotiation cycles.

Executing Co-Sell with Microsoft

Co-sell is the mechanism through which Microsoft sellers actively engage with partners to pursue joint customer opportunities. When executed well, co-sell transforms your go-to-market from a solo effort into a collaborative motion backed by Microsoft's global sales organization. Microsoft reports that partners see 5x higher close rates on co-sell deals compared to deals pursued independently.

But co-sell is not passive. Achieving Co-sell Ready or IP Co-sell Incentivized status makes your solution visible to Microsoft sellers, but visibility alone does not generate revenue. You must actively work the co-sell motion by preparing materials, responding to referrals, building relationships, and creating value for the Microsoft sellers who engage with you.

Preparing Sales-Ready Materials

Microsoft sellers are busy. They manage dozens of accounts across multiple product lines and partner solutions. They will not invest time understanding your solution unless you make it effortless. The quality of your sales materials directly determines whether sellers engage with you or move on to better-prepared partners.

The Co-Sell Collateral Stack

Solution One-Pager

A single page problem statement, solution overview, key differentiators, target customer profile, and clear call to action. A Microsoft seller should understand your value proposition in 60 seconds. No jargon, no technical deep-dives, only a clear articulation of what you solve and for whom. Include the business problem you address, your unique approach, three key differentiators, ideal customer profile (industry, size, use case), and how to engage (contact information, next steps).

Customer-Ready Pitch Deck

A presentation of 10–15 slides maximum, business outcomes first, technical architecture second, pricing last. Lead with customer pain points and the value you deliver, not features. Include customer logos and quantified results from existing deployments. Microsoft sellers may use this deck directly with customers or adapt it for their own presentations.

Battle Card

A competitive positioning guide. How do you win against alternatives? What objections arise? What questions should sellers ask to qualify opportunities? Structure by competitor, including key differentiators, objection handling, and proof points.

Reference Architecture Diagram

Required for IP Co-sell eligibility, shows how your solution consumes Azure services and drives Azure consumption. This technical diagram demonstrates integration depth and helps Microsoft sellers understand why your success benefits their Azure revenue goals. Include Azure services consumed, data flows, deployment topology, and consumption estimates.

Working the Referral Pipeline

When a Microsoft seller identifies a customer need that your solution addresses, they initiate a referral through Partner Center. This referral represents a warm introduction to a customer with an active need. Your response to these referrals determines if you build credibility with the Microsoft seller network.

The Referral Response Framework (see Table 9-4)

1. **Respond within 24 business hours:** This is non-negotiable. Acknowledge the referral immediately. Confirm receipt, express appreciation, and outline your next specific step. Microsoft tracks partner responsiveness, and slow partners stop receiving referrals. A simple response is all that is needed "Thank you for the referral. I will reach out to [Customer Contact] within 24 hours and update you on our conversation."

2. **Provide status updates proactively:** Remember that the referring seller has skin in the game; if you are IP Co-sell Incentivized, they receive quota credit and potentially commission on the deal. They need to know what is happening. Update them after the initial call is completed, POC scheduled, proposal delivered, or contract negotiated. Weekly updates at minimum for active opportunities.

3. **Close the loop on outcomes:** Whether you win or lose the deal, report back. If you win, the seller celebrates the joint success and will send more referrals. If you lose, explain why so that the seller learns and may be able to provide better-qualified referrals in the future. Sellers remember partners who follow through.
4. **Initiate outbound referrals:** Do not wait for Microsoft to send you leads. Register your opportunities in Partner Center and request Microsoft seller engagement on deals where their involvement adds value. When you bring value to the relationship, such as customer access, market intelligence, a joint pipeline, Microsoft sellers prioritize your requests.

Table 9-4. *Referral response SLAs – meet these or lose the relationship*

Action	Target SLA	Impact of missing SLA
Referral acknowledgment	< 24 hours	Seller loses confidence, fewer referrals
Customer first contact	< 48 hours	Customer interest cools, competition enters
Status update to seller	Weekly minimum	Seller cannot forecast, relationship weakens
Outcome reporting	Within 5 days of close	Seller cannot claim credit, stops referring

Building Field Relationships

Systems enable co-sell. Relationships accelerate it. The Microsoft sellers and Partner Development Managers (PDMs) who prioritize your solution are those who know you, trust you, and have seen you deliver value. Invest in these relationships systematically.

Relationship-Building Tactics

- **Attend Microsoft field events and partner days:** These events exist specifically for relationship building. Arrive prepared with your one-pager and clear articulation of your ideal customer profile. Meet as many sellers as possible, collect contact information, and follow-up within 48 hours.
- **Request joint customer calls on strategic opportunities:** When you have a significant opportunity where Microsoft involvement would add value, invite the relevant Microsoft seller to join the customer conversation. Let them see you execute, how you position, how you handle objections, and how you build rapport. Successful joint engagements build seller confidence in recommending your solution.
- **Share market intelligence:** If you learn about a customer's cloud strategy, competitive dynamics, or upcoming initiatives through your engagement, share that insight with your Microsoft contacts. Information flows both ways. When you bring value, you receive value. Reciprocity builds trust.
- **Celebrate joint wins publicly:** When you close a deal with Microsoft's help, acknowledge that help publicly by posting on LinkedIn, in press releases, at partner events. Sellers appreciate recognition and remember partners who share credit.

- **Invest in your PDM relationship:** Your assigned Partner Development Manager is your advocate within Microsoft. Build a genuine relationship. Meet regularly. Share your pipeline and goals. Ask for their advice. Make their job easier by being a responsive, professional partner.

Scaling Through the Partner Ecosystem

Direct sales create revenue. Channel partnerships create scale. Microsoft's partner ecosystem includes over 500,000 organizations, including Cloud Solution Providers (CSPs), System Integrators (SIs), Managed Service Providers (MSPs), and Value-Added Resellers (VARs). Each represents potential distribution leverage for your AI solution. The most successful ISVs in the Microsoft ecosystem treat channel development as seriously as direct sales.

Industry data confirms the leverage potential. Microsoft reports that 95% of its commercial revenue flows through partners. Research from Forrester shows that mature channel programs can account for 28% or more of total ISV revenue while requiring 15–20% lower customer acquisition costs than direct sales. Partners extend your sales capacity without proportional headcount increases.

CSP Private Offers (CPPO)

Cloud Solution Providers resell Microsoft cloud services to their customer bases. These are typically regional or vertical-focused IT services firms with established customer relationships. Through CSP Private Offers (CPPO), you can authorize these partners to resell your solution at negotiated partner pricing, enabling them to bundle your AI agent with their managed services and deliver a single, consolidated bill to end customers.

CPPO Execution Steps

1. **Identify target CSPs:** Focus on CSPs serving your target verticals with existing Azure practices. A CSP specializing in healthcare IT is a natural partner for a healthcare AI solution. Use Microsoft's Partner Center to discover CSPs active in your segments.
2. **Define partner economics:** What margin will you offer? Typical partner discounts range from 10–30%, depending on expected volume, services value-add, and strategic importance. Build a tiered structure with higher margins for partners who commit to volume targets or invest in enablement.
3. **Enable effectively:** Partners cannot sell what they do not understand. Provide training, demo environments, sales playbooks, and technical documentation. The investment in enablement pays dividends in partner-generated revenue.
4. **Create private offers in Partner Center:** Execute the CPPO workflow to extend your negotiated terms to each authorized partner. The partner can then transact on behalf of their customers while you retain visibility and revenue recognition.

System Integrator Partnerships

System Integrators implement complex enterprise solutions. When an SI includes your AI agent in their implementation practice, you gain access to their customer relationships, delivery capacity, and credibility with enterprise buyers. SI partnerships are particularly valuable for enterprise-focused AI solutions that require professional services to deploy successfully.

Approaching System Integrators

- **Start with specific practice leaders:** Global SIs are decentralized. Target the AI practice lead or industry vertical lead relevant to your solution. Generic partnership inquiries disappear, while specific outreach to relevant leaders gets traction.
- **Co-develop a joint solution:** SIs want differentiated offerings. Work together to create a packaged solution combining your technology with their implementation methodology. A named, joint solution gives SI sellers something concrete to position.
- **Train their consultants:** SI consultants deliver the solution to customers. Invest in certification programs that build their capability and confidence. Certified consultants become advocates for your solution within the SI.
- **Establish referral mechanisms:** Define how leads flow between organizations, how revenue is recognized, and how services revenue (theirs) and software revenue (yours) are allocated. Clear economics prevents friction.

Multiparty Private Offers

The Marketplace now supports multiparty private offers, transactions involving you (the ISV), a channel partner, and the end customer. This capability unlocks complex deal structures where a reseller or SI procures your solution on behalf of their customer through the Marketplace, maintaining MACC benefits while enabling partner-led sales.

For reference: `https://www.microsoft.com/en-us/software-development-companies/resources/articles/leveraging-ai-for-isvs`

Multiparty private offers are particularly powerful for enterprise deals where the customer has an existing relationship with a trusted partner and prefers to transact through that partner rather than directly with you. Instead of choosing between direct sales (you capture full margin) or channel sale (partner captures margin but you lose visibility), multiparty offers provide a middle path with transparent economics and Marketplace benefits for all parties.

Driving Expansion Through Customer Success

New customer acquisition is expensive. Industry research indicates that acquiring a new B2B SaaS customer costs 5–7x more than retaining and expanding an existing one. Expansion revenue from existing customers through upsells, cross-sells, and renewals is far more efficient and carries higher margins because you have already paid the acquisition cost.

For AI solutions with usage-based pricing, customer success directly translates to revenue growth. When customers use your AI agent more, you earn more. When they achieve outcomes, they expand. When they fail to achieve value, they churn. The customer success function is not a cost center, it is a growth engine.

Structured Onboarding for Time-to-Value

The first 90 days after deployment determines customer lifetime value. Customers who achieve meaningful outcomes quickly renew and expand. Customers who struggle churn. According to a 2023 ChurnRX study, simply measuring account data doubles customer lifespan and dramatically reduces churn. The best moment to begin tracking is during onboarding, when you are already calibrating expectations and success metrics with the customer.

The 90-Day Onboarding Framework (see Table 9-5)

1. **Define success milestones:** What should customers achieve in Week 1? Week 4? Week 12? Map these milestones explicitly. For example, an AI document processing solution, milestones might include: Week 1 - First document processed successfully; Week 4 - Production workflow established; Week 12 - Measurable efficiency gains documented.

2. **Assign ownership:** Every new customer needs a named success manager responsible for their outcomes. This ownership cannot be shared or ambiguous. One person owns the relationship, coordinates resources, and is accountable for customer health.

3. **Instrument for monitoring:** Track usage patterns that indicate healthy adoption versus risk signals that predict churn. Key metrics include login frequency, feature adoption rate, processing volume trends, support ticket volume, and user expansion within the account.

4. **Intervene proactively:** When usage data shows a customer is not progressing, reach out before they disengage. Do not wait for the customer to complain or request cancellation. Proactive intervention dramatically improves save rates and customer sentiment.

Table 9-5. Customer onboarding phases with health indicators and risk signals

Phase	Success milestones	Health indicators	Risk signals
Week 1–2	Technical setup complete, first successful use	Daily logins, help docs accessed	No login after Day 3, setup incomplete
Week 3–4	Production workflow active, multiple users	Usage growth, feature exploration	Single user only, no production use
Month 2–3	Measurable outcomes documented	Executive engagement, expansion interest	Flat usage, support complaints

Expansion Playbooks

Once customers achieve initial success, drive expansion systematically. Do not wait for customers to request more. Proactively identify expansion opportunities and execute them.

User Expansion

If you price per user or seat, identify opportunities to extend access to additional teams or departments. Success signals include multiple users requesting access, users sharing credentials (compliance risk you can solve), and business outcomes that benefit adjacent teams. Identify the stakeholder who owns the successful implementation, ask about other teams with similar needs, and propose an expansion with volume pricing.

Usage Expansion

For consumption-based models, help customers discover additional use cases that increase utilization. Success signals include customers approaching tier limits, high satisfaction scores, and questions about additional capabilities. Conduct quarterly business reviews that explore new use cases, share relevant case studies from similar customers, and offer professional services to accelerate new deployments.

Feature Expansion

Upsell to higher tiers or add-on modules as customer maturity increases. Success signals include customers hitting feature limits, requests for capabilities in higher tiers, and sophisticated usage patterns indicating advanced needs. Demonstrate the value of additional features through targeted training, offer time-limited trials of premium capabilities, and align upgrades to contract renewals.

Professional Services

Offer premium implementation, customization, or training services. These can be listed as Consulting Service Offers on the Marketplace. Success signals include complex deployment requirements, requests for custom integrations, and organizational change management needs. Professional services increase customer lifetime value while deepening relationship stickiness.

Key Customer Success Metrics: *Net Revenue Retention (NRR) >110% target|Customer Lifetime Value (CLV) >3x CAC|Time-to-Value <30 days|Feature Adoption Rate >60%|Net Promoter Score (NPS) >40*

Building a Customer Reference Program

Successful customers become your most powerful sales asset. A structured reference program converts customer success into sales acceleration.

1. **Identify referenceable customers systematically:** After customers achieve documented success, ask if they would be willing to serve as a reference. Build a database of references by industry, use case, company size, and geography.

2. **Produce case studies with quantified results:** Written case studies with specific metrics are sales gold. Work with marketing to produce professional case studies that you can share publicly and with prospects.

3. **Facilitate reference calls carefully:** Do not overuse your references. Match reference calls to prospects with similar profiles. Prepare the reference with context about the prospect. Follow up with a thank-you.

4. **Reward reference participation:** Recognize customers who serve as references through exclusive access, early feature previews, advisory board invitations, or marketing co-promotion. Reciprocity sustains participation.

Measuring What Matters

Execution without measurement is guessing. The ISVs that scale build a culture of data-driven decision-making, establishing dashboards of key metrics and reviewing them with discipline. Weekly reviews catch problems early. Monthly analysis reveals trends. Quarterly assessments drive strategic adjustments. The data does not lie. But only if you collect it, analyze it, and act on it.

This section provides the comprehensive metrics framework for AI ISV go-to-market execution. We organize metrics into four categories: Marketplace performance, sales efficiency, customer health, and operational benchmarks. For each metric, we provide the definition, calculation method, industry benchmark, and action triggers that indicate when intervention is needed.

Marketplace Performance Metrics (see Table 9-6)

These metrics measure how your Marketplace presence is performing, discoverability, conversion, and commercial traction through the Microsoft ecosystem.

Page Views

Definition: The number of unique visitors viewing your Marketplace listing during a given period.

Why it matters: Page views measure discoverability. How many potential customers are finding your solution through Marketplace search, Microsoft referrals, or direct navigation? Low page views indicate that your listing is not visible, your SEO is weak, or your promotional efforts are insufficient.

Target benchmark: 500+ unique views per month for actively marketed solutions. Early-stage ISVs may see 100–300; scaled ISVs with strong promotion should target 1,000+.

Action triggers: If page views fall below 200/month, audit your Marketplace listing SEO, increase promotional activity, and investigate whether Marketplace search algorithms are surfacing your listing for relevant queries.

Conversion Rate

Definition: The percentage of listing visitors who click "Get It Now," "Contact Me," or initiate a free trial.

Why it matters: Conversion rate measures the effectiveness of your listing in persuading visitors to act. A high conversion rate indicates compelling positioning, clear value proposition, and appropriate pricing. Low rates suggest messaging issues, pricing concerns, or poor listing quality.

Target benchmark: 2–5% for transactable offers is the industry standard. Contact-me listings typically see lower conversion (1–2%) because the call to action requires more commitment. Free trial offers can achieve 5–10% if the trial experience is friction-free.

Action triggers: Conversion below 1% requires immediate listing optimization, review your headline, value proposition, screenshots, pricing presentation, and call to action. A/B test different versions to identify improvements.

Marketplace Billed Sales (MBS)

Definition: Your trailing 12-month revenue transacted through the Microsoft Marketplace.

Why it matters: MBS determines your Marketplace Rewards tier and the benefits you receive, marketing funds, sales engagement, Azure credits, and technical support. Higher MBS unlocks greater benefits that further accelerate growth.

Target benchmark: Marketplace Rewards tiers: $1K-$250K MBS (Base tier), $250K-$1M (Build tier), $1M-$5M (Grow tier), $5M+ (Scale tier). Each tier unlocks additional benefits. Target progression to the next tier within 12–18 months.

Action triggers: If MBS growth stalls, analyze whether the bottleneck is top-of-funnel (not enough visitors), middle-funnel (low conversion), or bottom-funnel (deals not closing). Target interventions accordingly.

Azure Consumed Revenue (ACR)

Definition: The Azure infrastructure consumption generated by your solution when deployed in customer environments.

Why it matters: ACR is critical for IP Co-sell eligibility and Microsoft Certified Software designation. Microsoft incentivizes solutions that drive Azure consumption because it benefits their core cloud business. Higher ACR makes your solution more strategically valuable to Microsoft.

Commonly cited target: \$100K+ trailing 12-month ACR for IP Co-sell eligibility. Scaled AI solutions consuming significant Azure compute can drive \$500K-\$1M+ ACR.

Action triggers: If ACR is below the IP Co-sell threshold, optimize Azure service utilization, and consider whether additional Azure services could enhance your solution.

Table 9-6. Marketplace performance metrics summary

Metric	Benchmark	Review frequency	Action trigger
Page views	500+/month	Weekly	<200: Audit discoverability
Conversion rate	2–5%	Weekly	<1%: Optimize listing immediately
MBS (TTM)	Tier-dependent	Monthly	Stalled growth: Diagnose funnel
ACR (TTM)	$100K+ for IP Co-sell	Monthly	<$100K: Review Azure architecture

Sales Efficiency Metrics

These metrics measure how efficiently your sales organization converts pipeline into revenue.

Sales Cycle Length

> **Definition:** Average number of days from first qualified contact to closed-won deal.
>
> **Why it matters:** Shorter sales cycles accelerate cash flow, improve forecasting accuracy, and increase sales capacity. Marketplace transactions should be significantly faster than traditional procurement due to streamlined commercial and legal processes.
>
> **Target benchmark:** SMB deals (<$10K): 2–4 weeks. Mid-market ($10K–$100K): 40–80 days via Marketplace (vs. 60–120 traditional). Enterprise ($100K+): 100–180 days via Marketplace (vs. 170–270+ traditional). Aim for 30–40% reduction compared to non-Marketplace transactions.

Action triggers: If Marketplace deals are not significantly faster than traditional sales, investigate: Are you leveraging MACC positioning? Are POCs time-boxed? Is the customer using Marketplace procurement or reverting to traditional processes?

Co-sell Referral Volume

Definition: Number of customer referrals received from Microsoft sellers through Partner Center per month/quarter.

Why it matters: Referral volume indicates how actively Microsoft sellers are engaging with your solution. Low volume suggests awareness problems (sellers do not know about you), positioning problems (sellers do not understand when to refer), or relationship problems (sellers have stopped engaging).

Target benchmark: Early-stage Co-sell Ready partners: 1–3 referrals/month. Established IP Co-sell partners: 5–10+ referrals/month. Strategic partners with strong field relationships: 20+ referrals/month.

Action triggers: If referral volume is below expectations, increase field engagement activities, refresh your co-sell materials, request PDM support in promoting your solution to relevant seller teams, and ensure your solution appears in Co-sell Opportunities correctly.

Co-Sell Win Rate

Definition: Percentage of co-sell referrals that convert to closed-won deals.

Why it matters: Microsoft reports that partners see 5x higher close rates on co-sell deals compared to deals pursued independently. Your Co-sell win rate should exceed your direct sales win rate. If it does not, you are likely not fully leveraging the Microsoft relationship.

Target benchmark: 30–50% win rate on co-sell referrals (vs. 10–20% typical for direct prospecting). Top performers achieve 50%+ win rates because referrals represent pre-qualified, high-intent opportunities.

Action triggers: If Co-sell win rate is below 25%, analyze lost deals: Were referrals well-qualified? Did you respond quickly? Were joint sales activities effective? Provide feedback to Microsoft sellers on referral quality to improve future leads.

Customer Acquisition Cost (CAC)

Definition: Total sales and marketing spend divided by number of new customers acquired in the same period.

Formula: CAC = (Sales Costs + Marketing Costs) / New Customers Acquired

Why it matters: CAC measures the efficiency of your go-to-market investment. The Marketplace channel should deliver lower CAC than pure direct sales because you leverage Microsoft's infrastructure, reach, and credibility rather than building everything yourself.

Target benchmark: Average B2B SaaS CAC is approximately $200 for SMB customers, scaling to $1,000+ for mid-market and $5,000+ for enterprise. According to Benchmarkit's 2024 report, the median ratio of sales and marketing spend to acquire $1.00 of new ARR is $2.00 – meaning it costs $2,000 to acquire a customer worth $1,000 ARR.

Action triggers: If CAC exceeds industry benchmarks significantly, audit your channel mix. Are you over-investing in high-cost channels? Is the Marketplace generating sufficient organic discovery? Are co-sell referrals reducing your prospecting costs?

CAC Payback Period

Definition: Number of months required to recover the cost of acquiring a customer from their gross margin contribution.

Formula: CAC Payback = CAC / (Monthly Revenue per Customer × Gross Margin %)

Why it matters: CAC payback measures how quickly you recoup your acquisition investment. Shorter payback periods indicate efficient growth and healthier cash flow. Longer periods strain working capital and increase risk if customers churn before payback.

Target benchmark: 12 months or less is typically healthy for B2B SaaS. Top-performing companies achieve 6–9-month payback. Payback periods exceeding 18 months signal efficiency problems.

Action triggers: If CAC payback exceeds 18 months, focus on reducing acquisition costs (shift to lower-cost channels), increasing initial contract values (annual vs. monthly), or improving onboarding to accelerate time-to-value and reduce early churn.

Customer Health Metrics (see Table 9-7)

These metrics measure the health of your customer relationships and the sustainability of your revenue.

Net Revenue Retention (NRR)

Definition: Revenue from existing customers in the current period compared to the same customer cohort in the prior period, including expansion, contraction, and churn.

Formula: NRR = (Starting MRR + Expansion MRR – Contraction MRR – Churned MRR) / Starting MRR × 100%

Why it matters: NRR is widely considered the most important SaaS metric because it measures whether your business can grow from its existing customer base alone. NRR above 100% means you grow even without acquiring new customers. Research shows that companies with NRR ≥100% grow at 2x the rate of companies below 100%. Public SaaS companies with NRR above 120% trade at valuation multiples 25% higher than those below 100%.

Target benchmark: Average NRR is 85–115% across B2B SaaS. Target >110% for healthy growth. Top-performing companies achieve 120–140%. Enterprise-focused companies with expansion-driven business models can exceed 150%.

Action triggers: NRR below 100% indicates you are shrinking from your existing base and must acquire customers faster than you lose revenue - an unsustainable position. Immediately focus on churn reduction and expansion revenue programs.

Customer Lifetime Value (CLV)

Definition: Total expected revenue from a customer over the entire duration of the relationship.

Formula: CLV = Average Revenue per Account × Gross Margin % × Customer Lifespan (or: ARPA × Gross Margin / Monthly Churn Rate)

Why it matters: CLV determines how much you can afford to spend acquiring customers while maintaining profitability. The relationship between CLV and CAC is the fundamental unit economics equation for SaaS businesses.

Target benchmark: The widely accepted healthy ratio is CLV:CAC of 3:1 or higher - meaning lifetime value should be at least 3x the acquisition cost. According to Benchmarkit's 2024 data, the median CLV:CAC ratio is 3.6:1. Top-quartile companies achieve 5:1 or better.

Action triggers: CLV:CAC below 3:1 indicates unsustainable unit economics. Either reduce CAC (more efficient acquisition), increase revenue per customer (upsell, price increases), or extend customer lifespan (reduce churn). A ratio above 5:1 may indicate under-investment in growth - you could acquire customers faster.

Gross Revenue Retention (GRR)

Definition: Revenue retained from existing customers excluding expansion - measures pure retention without upsell masking churn.

Formula: GRR = (Starting MRR - Contraction MRR - Churned MRR) / Starting MRR × 100%

Why it matters: GRR isolates your ability to retain customers and revenue without the confounding effect of expansion. A company with 80% GRR and 120% NRR is growing through expansion but losing 20% of its base - a concerning pattern that NRR alone might obscure.

Target benchmark: 90%+ GRR is healthy for B2B SaaS. Below 85% indicates significant churn problems that expansion is temporarily masking.

Action triggers: GRR below 85% requires immediate attention to churn causes. Analyze churned customers by segment, tenure, and reason. Implement proactive retention programs targeting at-risk accounts.

Net Promoter Score (NPS)

Definition: Customer satisfaction and loyalty metric based on the question: "How likely are you to recommend our solution to a colleague?" Scored 0-10, calculated as % Promoters (9–10) minus % Detractors (0–6).

Why it matters: NPS predicts customer behavior. Promoters renew, expand, and refer. Detractors churn and damage your reputation. NPS serves as an early warning system for customer health before it appears in financial metrics.

Target benchmark: B2B SaaS average NPS is typically 30–40. Above 50 is excellent. Above 70 is world-class. Negative NPS indicates serious customer satisfaction problems.

Action triggers: NPS below 30 warrants customer research to understand dissatisfaction drivers. Follow up personally with Detractors to understand concerns and attempt recovery. Use Promoter feedback for testimonials and references.

Table 9-7. *Customer health metrics summary*

Metric	Target	Review frequency	Action trigger
NRR	>110%	Monthly (cohort basis)	<100%: Urgent churn intervention
CLV:CAC	>3:1	Quarterly	<3:1: Review unit economics
GRR	>90%	Monthly	<85%: Churn analysis required
NPS	>40	Quarterly survey	<30: Customer research needed

Building Your Metrics Cadence

Metrics are only valuable if reviewed consistently and acted upon. Establish a review cadence that matches the volatility and importance of each metric:

- **Daily:** Pipeline status, deal progression, referral responses. Operational awareness
- **Weekly:** Page views, conversion rate, sales cycle movement, customer health scores. Tactical adjustments
- **Monthly:** MBS, ACR, NRR, GRR, CAC, win rates. Trend analysis and emerging issues
- **Quarterly:** CLV, CLV:CAC ratio, CAC payback, NPS, strategic metrics. Strategic planning and resource allocation

Best Practice: *Create a single executive dashboard that surfaces the 8–10 most critical metrics at a glance. Review this dashboard at every leadership meeting. Drive accountability by assigning owners to each metric with explicit targets and action plans for underperformance.*

Conclusion: The Execution Imperative

Go-to-market execution is a discipline. The ISVs that scale are not necessarily those with the most sophisticated AI technology. They are the ones that execute relentlessly by generating pipeline, accelerating sales cycles, working co-sell motions, building partner leverage, driving customer success, and optimizing based on data.

This chapter has provided the tactical playbook for commercial execution in the Microsoft ecosystem. We covered the complete scope of go-to-market activities:

- **Demand generation:** Leveraging Campaign-in-a-Box, creating original content, optimizing your Marketplace listing, and building a predictable pipeline engine
- **Sales acceleration:** Exploiting the MACC advantage, structuring effective POCs, and using Private Offers for enterprise deals
- **Co-sell execution:** Preparing sales-ready materials, responding to referrals within 24 hours, and building genuine field relationships
- **Partner ecosystem:** Scaling through CSPs and System Integrators, enabling partners effectively, and leveraging multiparty private offers
- **Customer success:** Structuring onboarding for time-to-value, executing expansion playbooks, and building reference programs
- **Metrics and measurement:** Tracking the KPIs that matter across Marketplace performance, sales efficiency, and customer health

Microsoft has built a commercial infrastructure for AI ISVs. The Marketplace reduces procurement friction. MACC creates budget pathways. Co-sell connects you to a global sales force. Partner programs extend your reach. Marketplace Rewards provides investment to fuel growth. But this infrastructure only delivers value when you engage it actively and execute with discipline.

The Bottom Line: *The Forrester study documented 587% ROI, 50% procurement time reduction, and 33–40% shorter sales cycles for ISVs actively engaging the Microsoft commercial marketplace. These economics are available to you – but only if you execute.*

The journey from builder to seller is complete. You have chosen a use case, architected a solution, built an AI agent, set your pricing, enrolled in the programs, and published to the Marketplace. Now execute. Generate demand. Close deals. Expand through partners. Delight customers. Measure everything. Iterate constantly.

The AI solutions that win in the Microsoft ecosystem will be those backed by ISVs who master commercial execution. Your technology is ready. Your platform is ready. Go to market.

Index

A

J. Soh et al., *Building and Distributing Agentic AI Solutions*,
https://doi.org/10.1007/979-8-8688-2586-6

B

C

D

E

F

G

H

I

J

K

L

M

N

O

P

Q

R

S

U

V

W, X, Y, Z

GPSR Compliance
The European Union's (EU) General Product Safety Regulation (GPSR) is a set of rules that requires consumer products to be safe and our obligations to ensure this.

If you have any concerns about our products, you can contact us on

ProductSafety@springernature.com

In case Publisher is established outside the EU, the EU authorized representative is:

Springer Nature Customer Service Center GmbH
Europaplatz 3
69115 Heidelberg, Germany

www.ingramcontent.com/pod-product-compliance
Lightning Source LLC
Chambersburg PA
CBHW061424100826
49614CB00016B/346

* 9 7 9 8 8 6 8 8 2 5 8 5 9 *